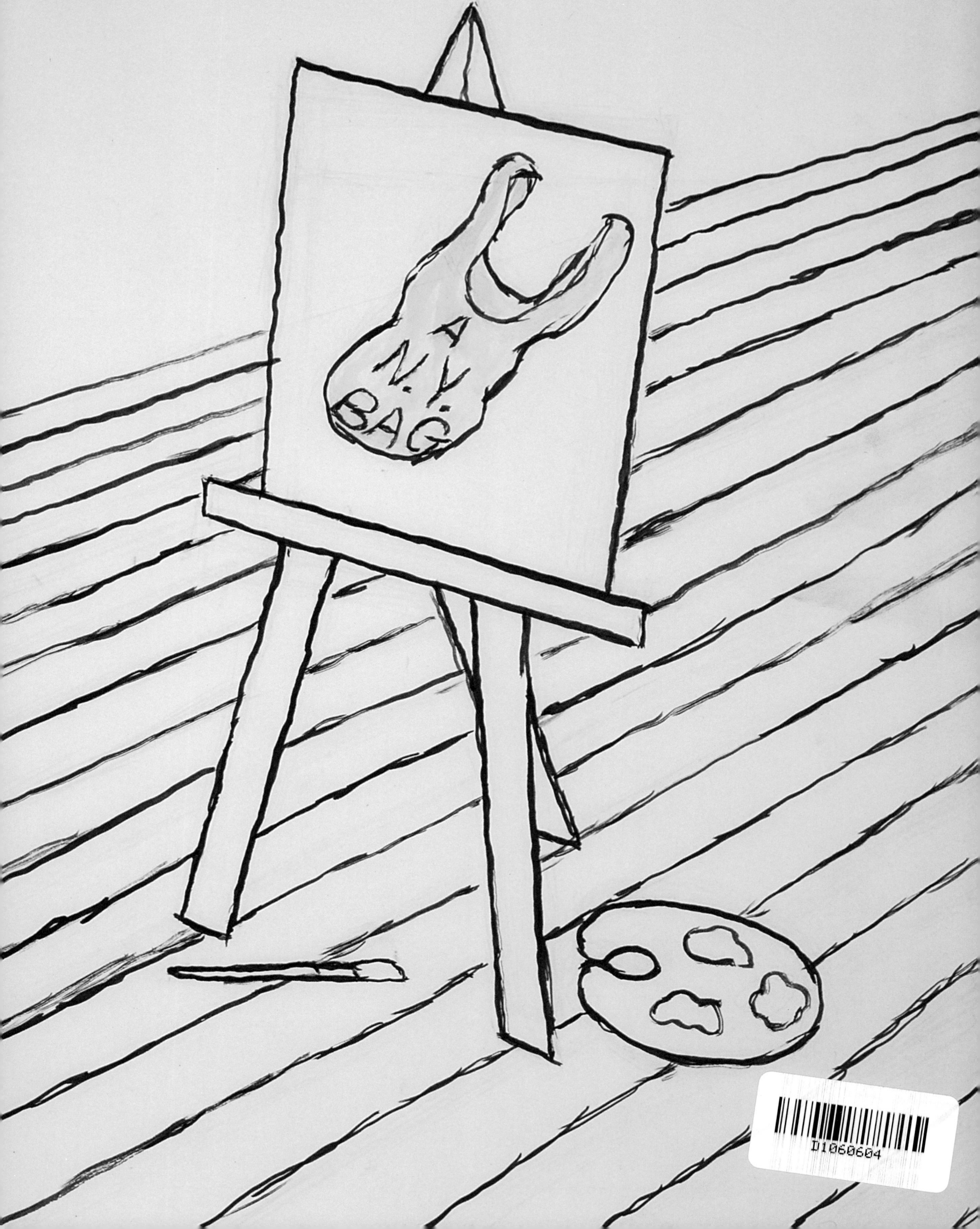
A.N.Y.
BAG

Editor: Gary Groth
Designer: Keeli McCarthy
Production: Paul Baresh
Associate Publisher: Eric Reynolds
Publisher: Gary Groth

Fantagraphics Books, Inc.
7563 Lake City Way NE
Seattle, WA 98115

www.fantagraphics.com
facebook.com/fantagraphics
@fantagraphics.com

ISBN: 978-1-68396-408-7
Library of Congress Control Number: 2020942305
First Fantagraphics Books edition: July 2021
Printed in China

VISUAL CRIME

by

JERRY
MORIARTY

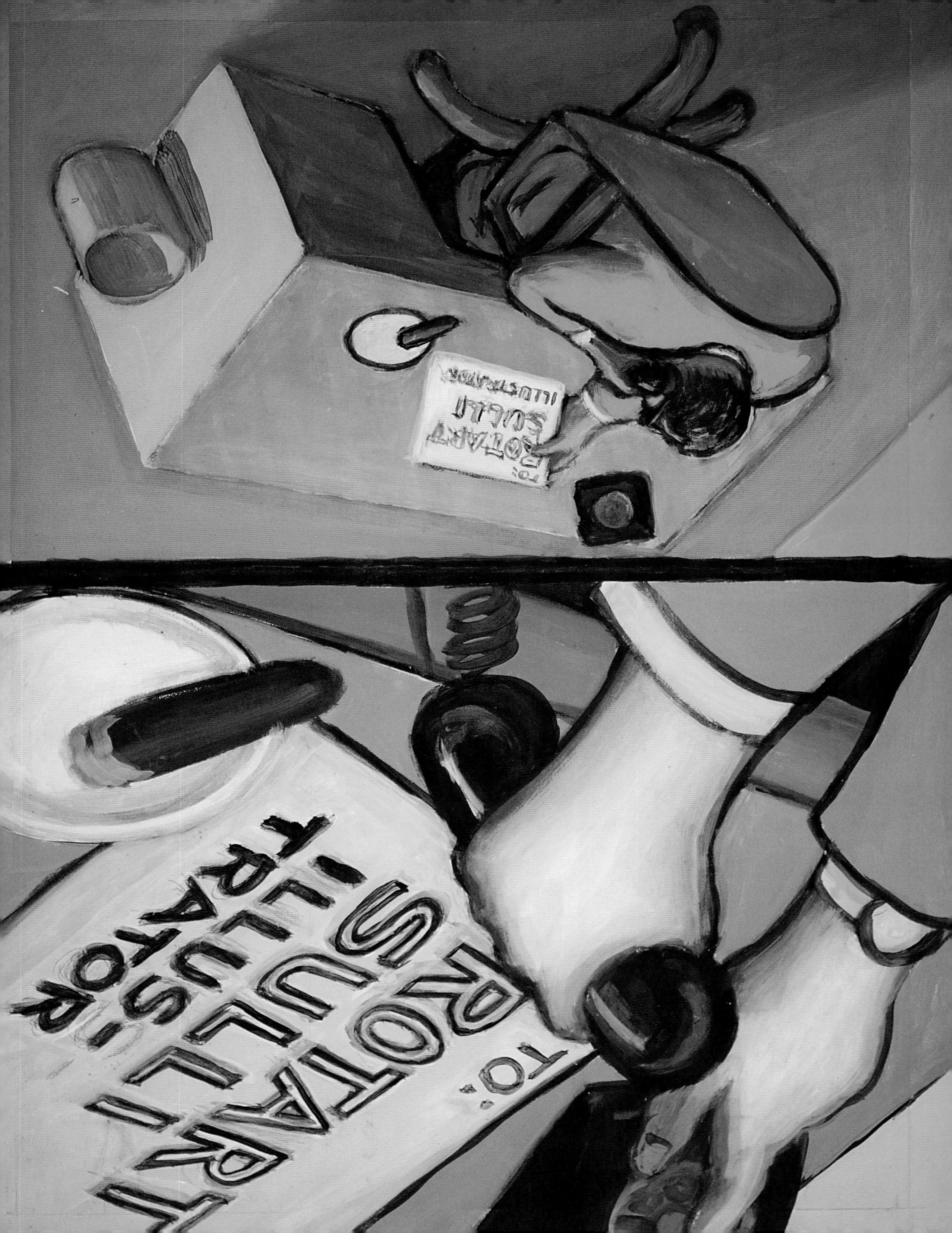
TO:
ROTART
SULLI

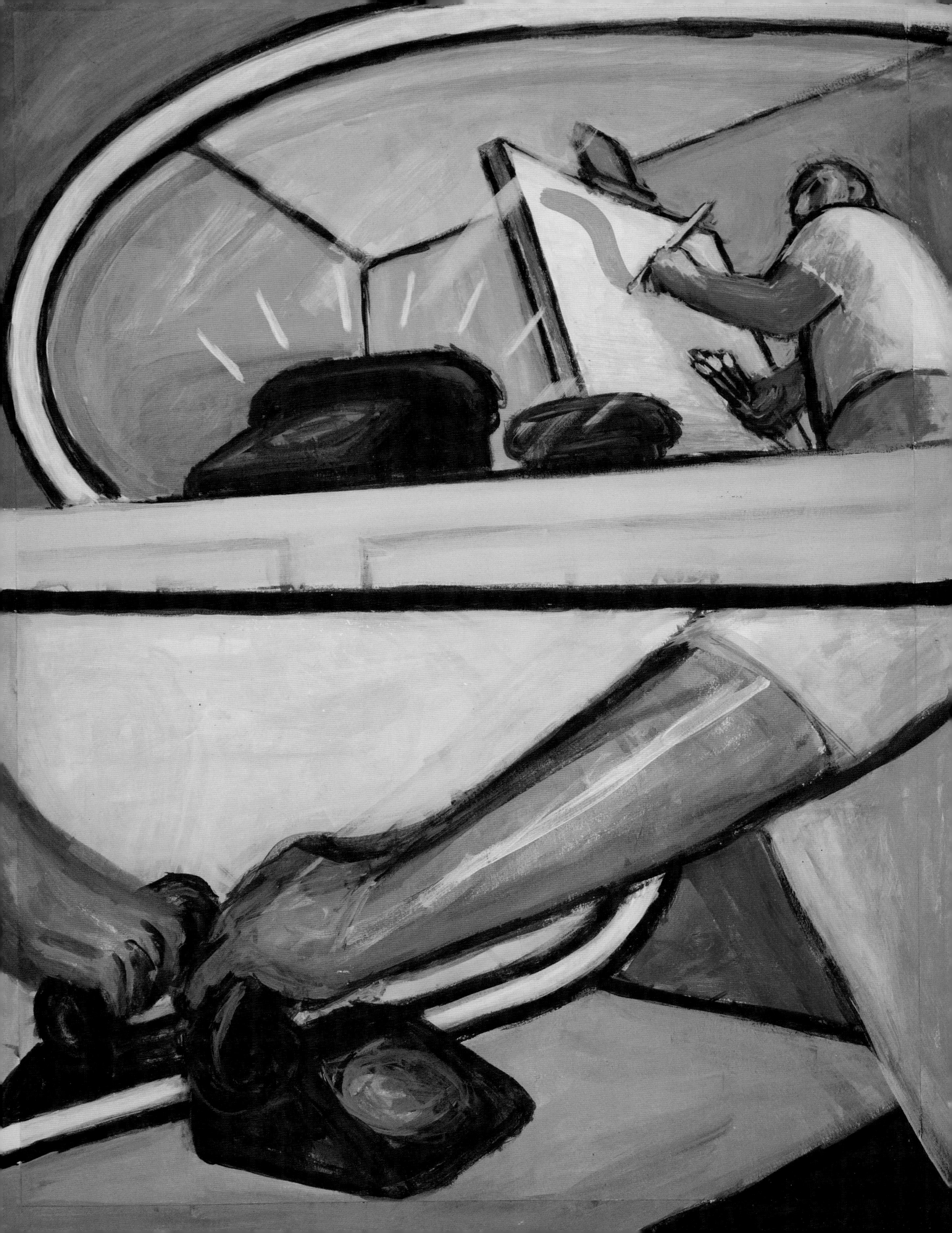

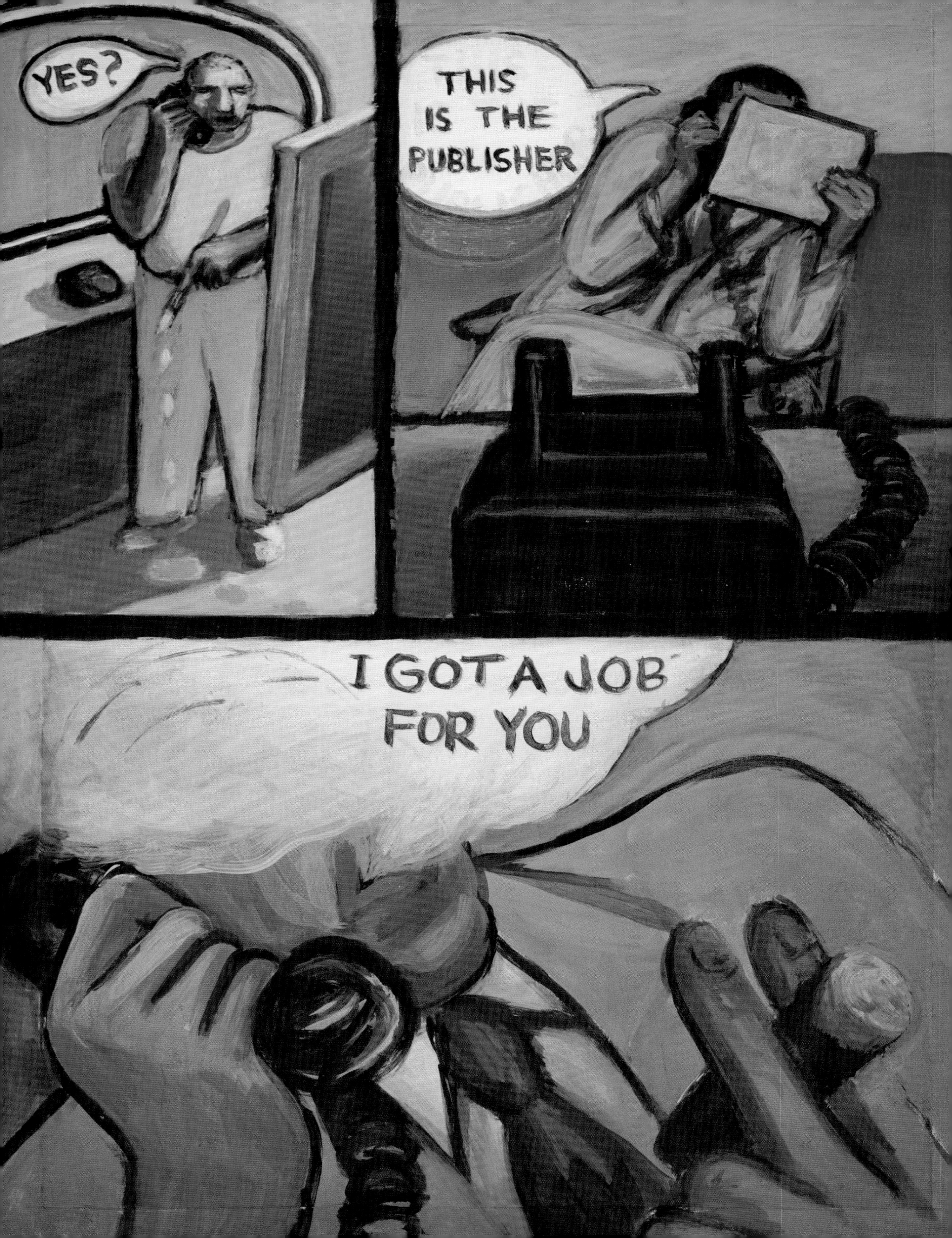
YES?
THIS IS THE PUBLISHER
I GOT A JOB FOR YOU

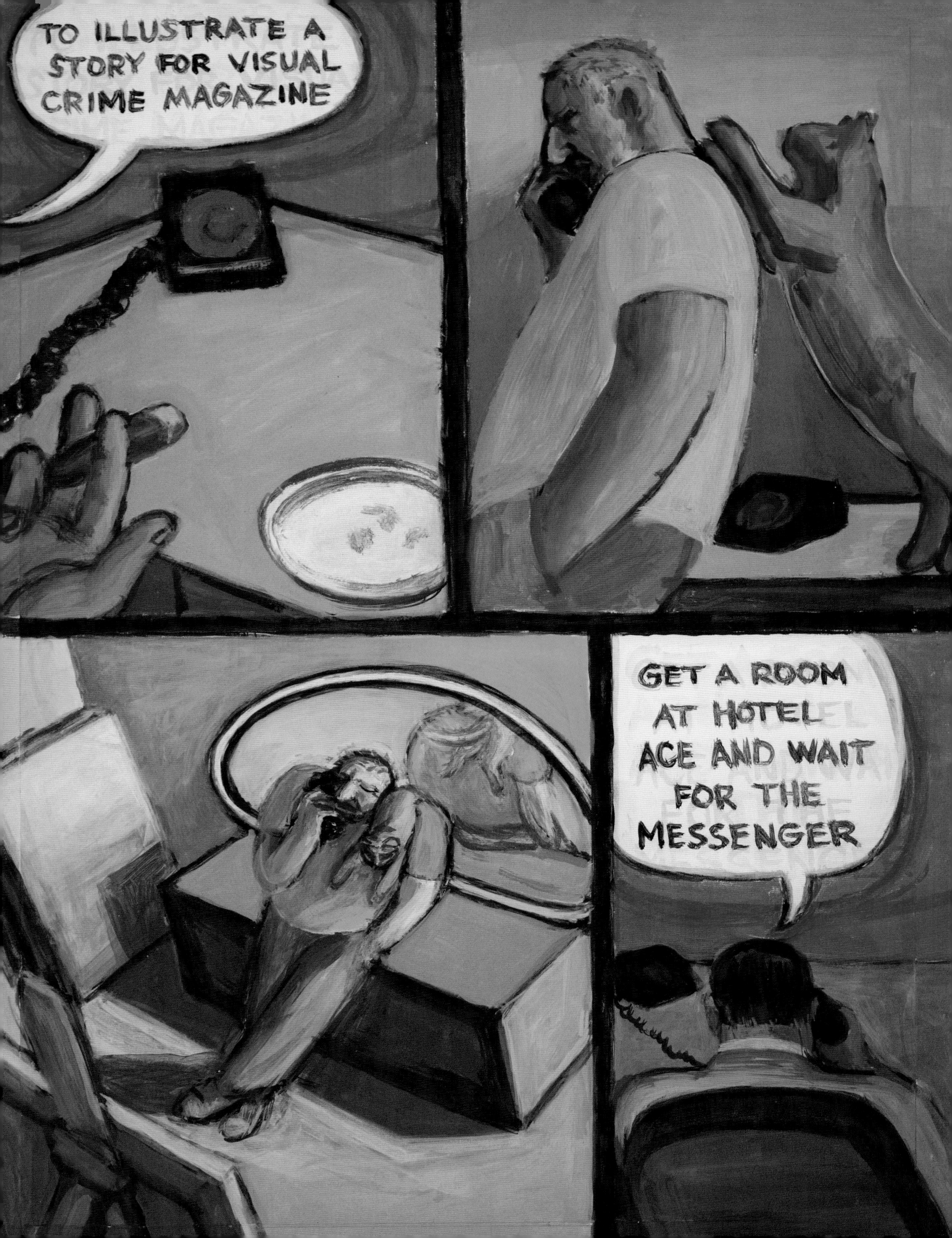
TO ILLUSTRATE A STORY FOR VISUAL CRIME MAGAZINE
GET A ROOM AT HOTEL ACE AND WAIT FOR THE MESSENGER

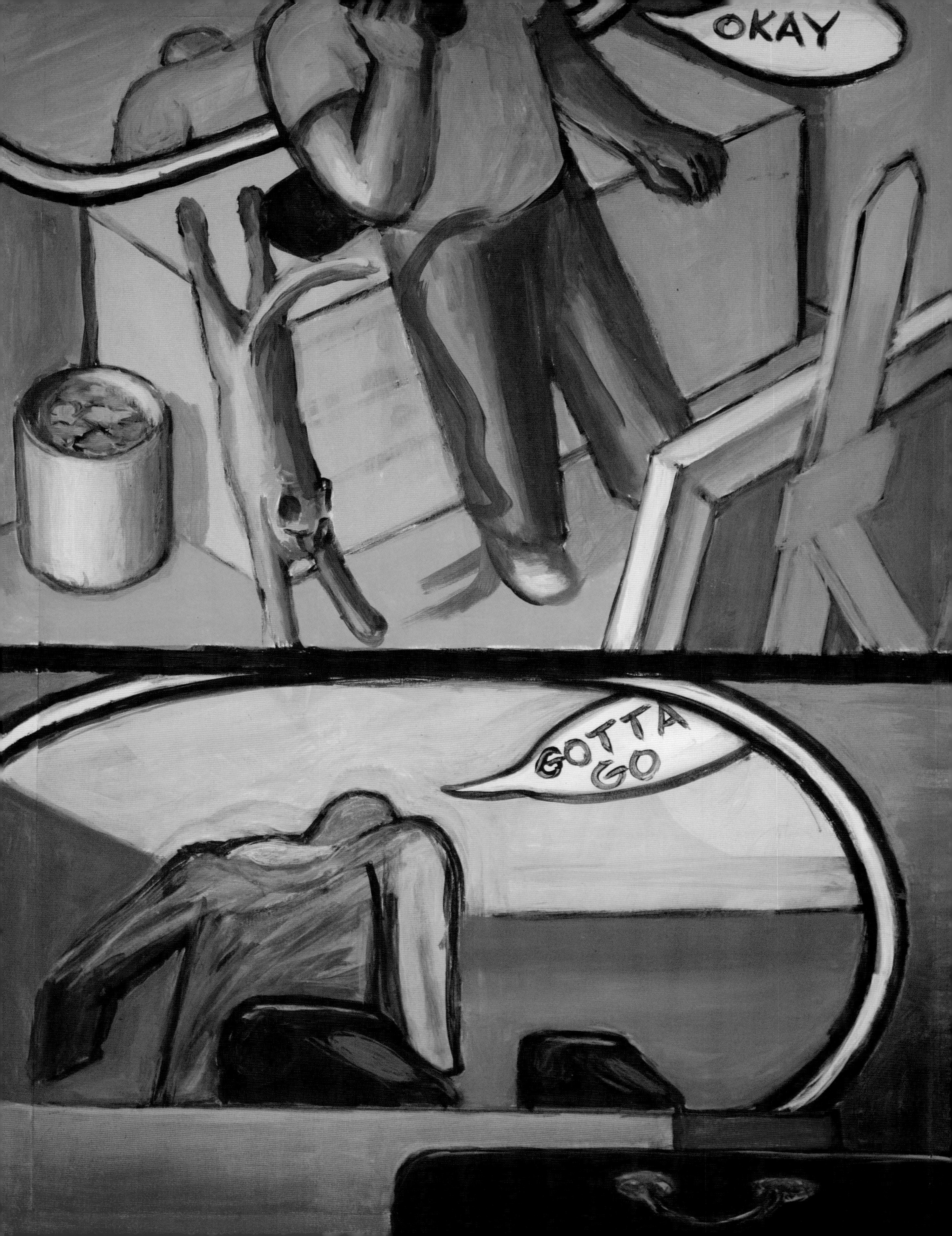
OKAY
GOTTA GO

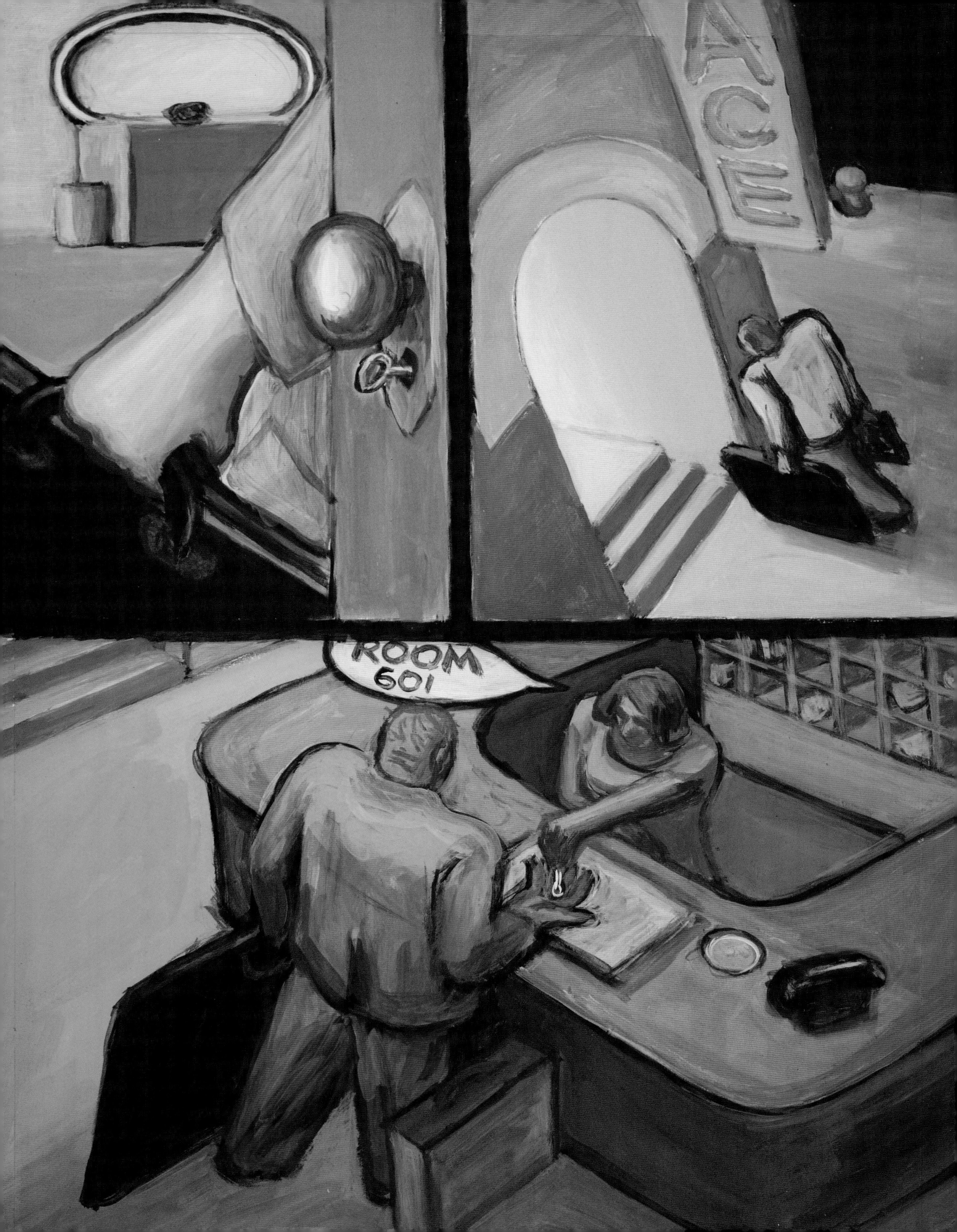
ACE
ROOM 601

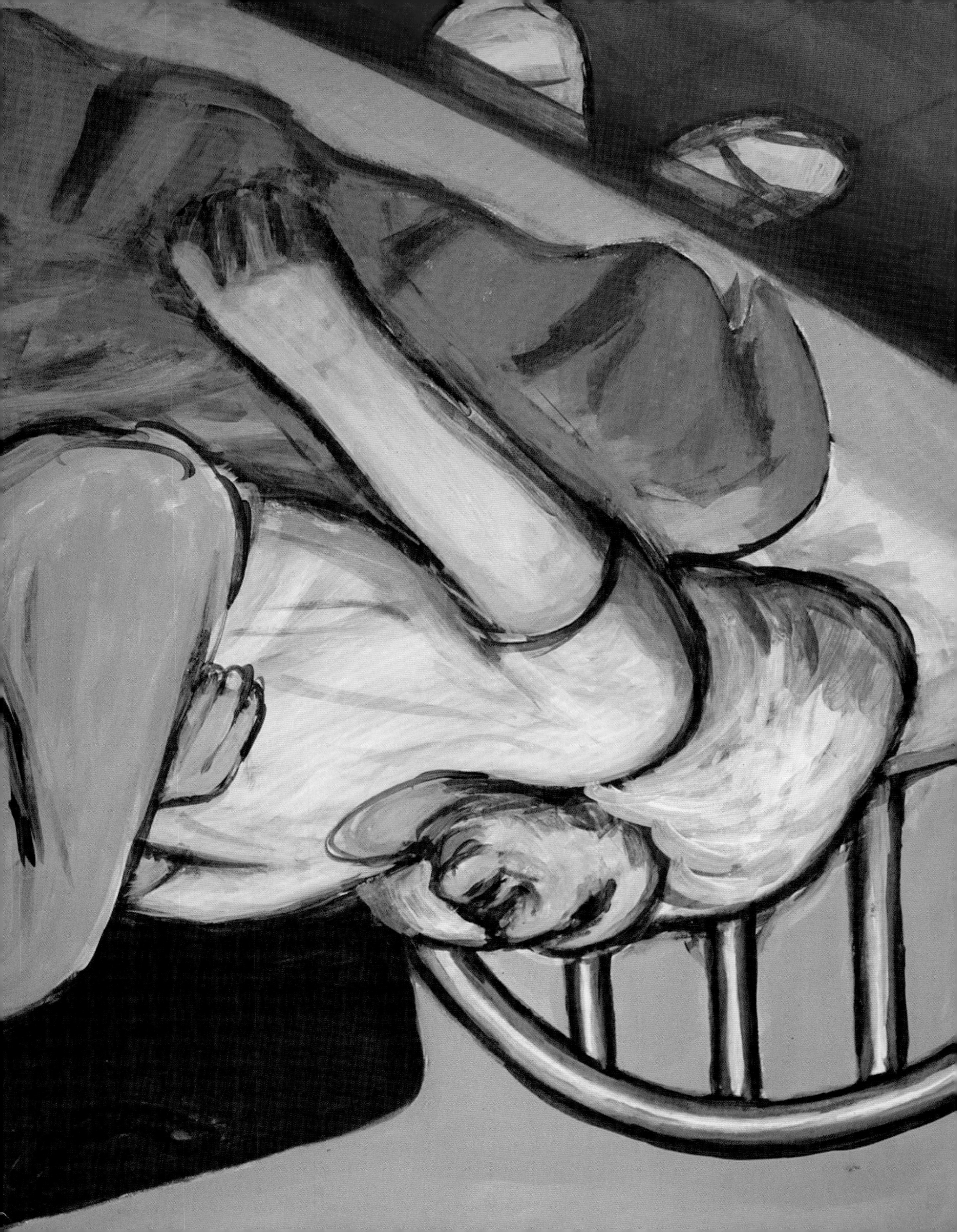

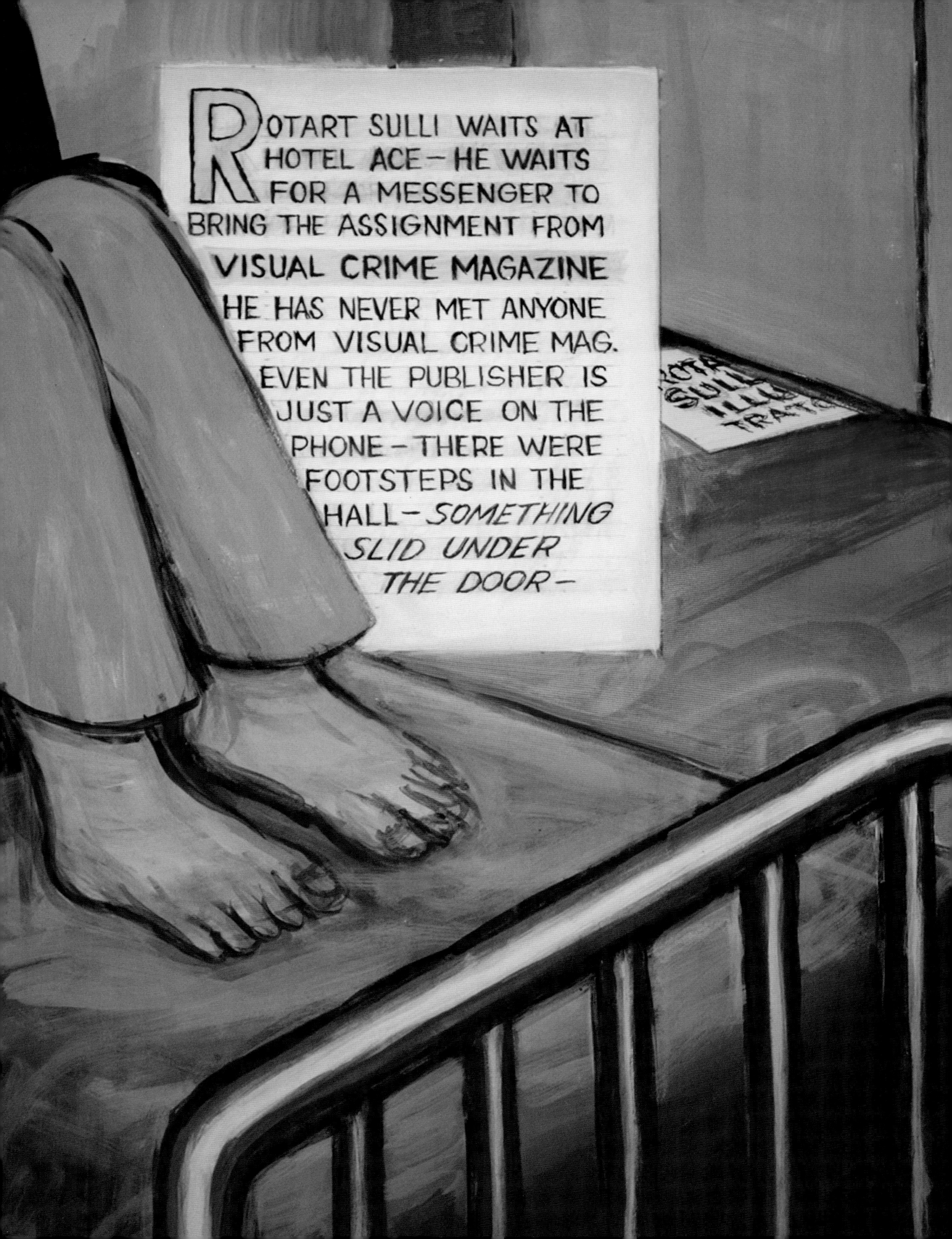
ROTART SULLI WAITS AT HOTEL ACE—HE WAITS FOR A MESSENGER TO BRING THE ASSIGNMENT FROM
VISUAL CRIME MAGAZINE
HE HAS NEVER MET ANYONE FROM VISUAL CRIME MAG. EVEN THE PUBLISHER IS JUST A VOICE ON THE PHONE—THERE WERE FOOTSTEPS IN THE HALL—*SOMETHING SLID UNDER THE DOOR—*

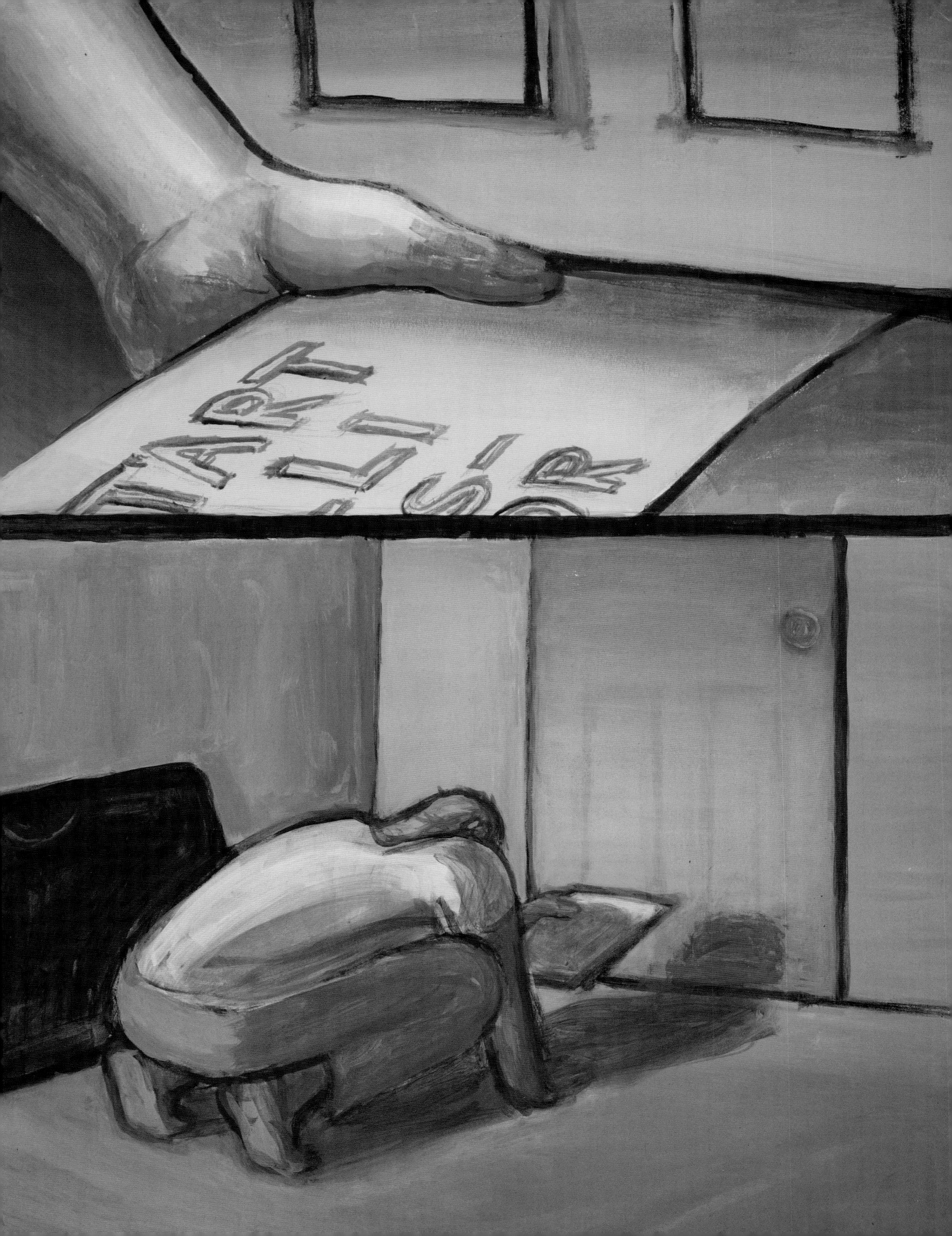

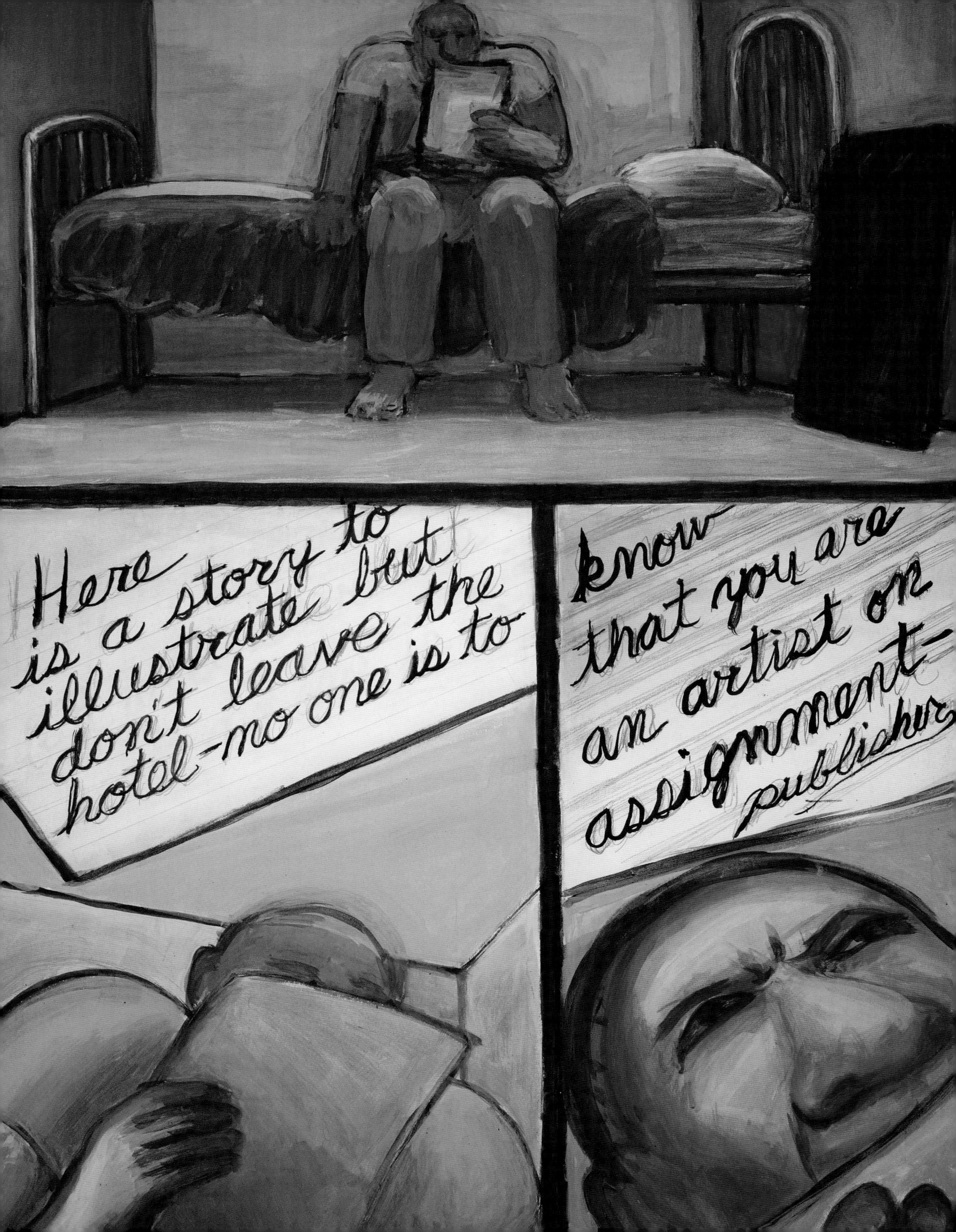
Here is a story to illustrate but don't leave the hotel—no one is to
know that you are an artist on assignment—
publisher

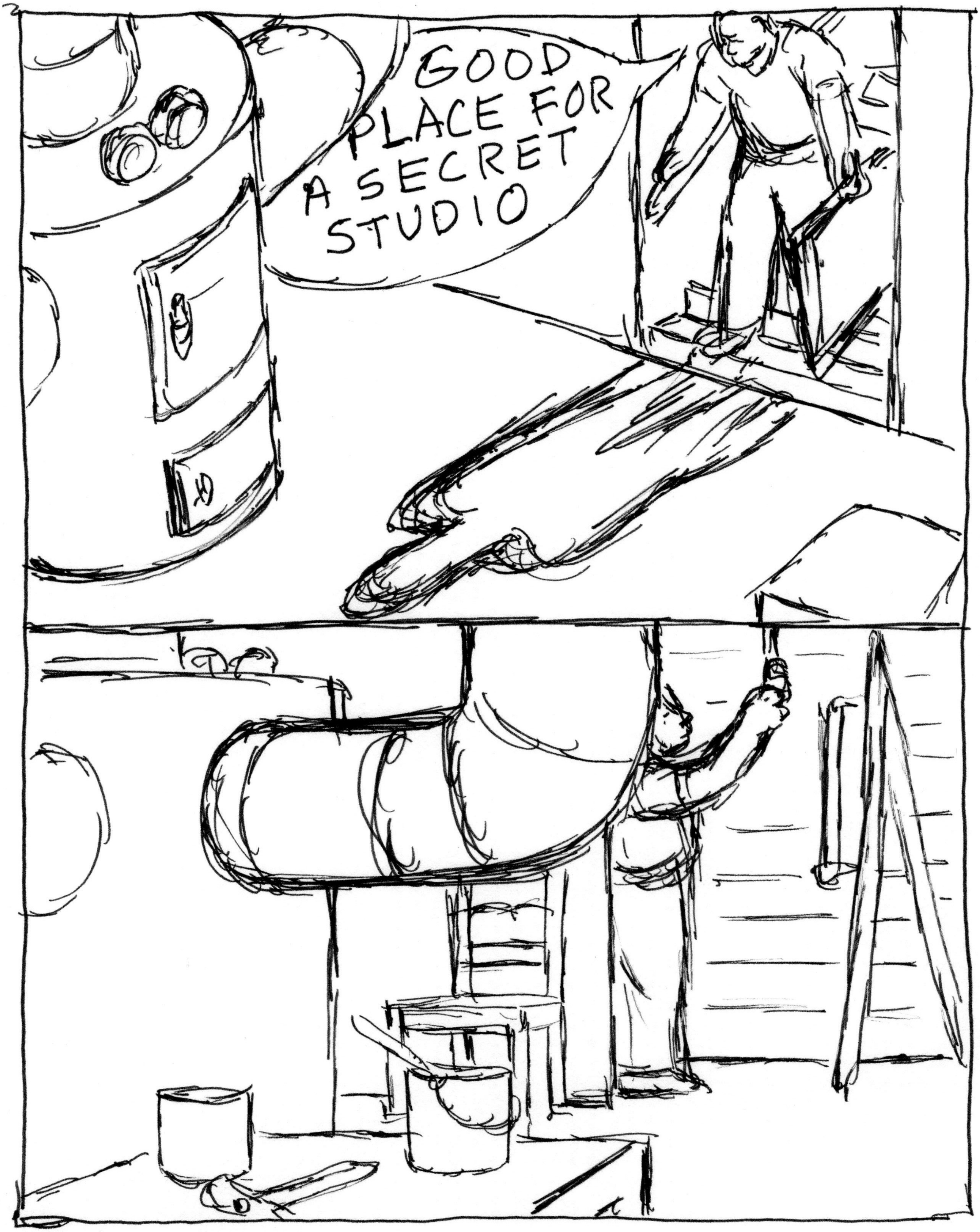
GOOD PLACE FOR A SECRET STUDIO

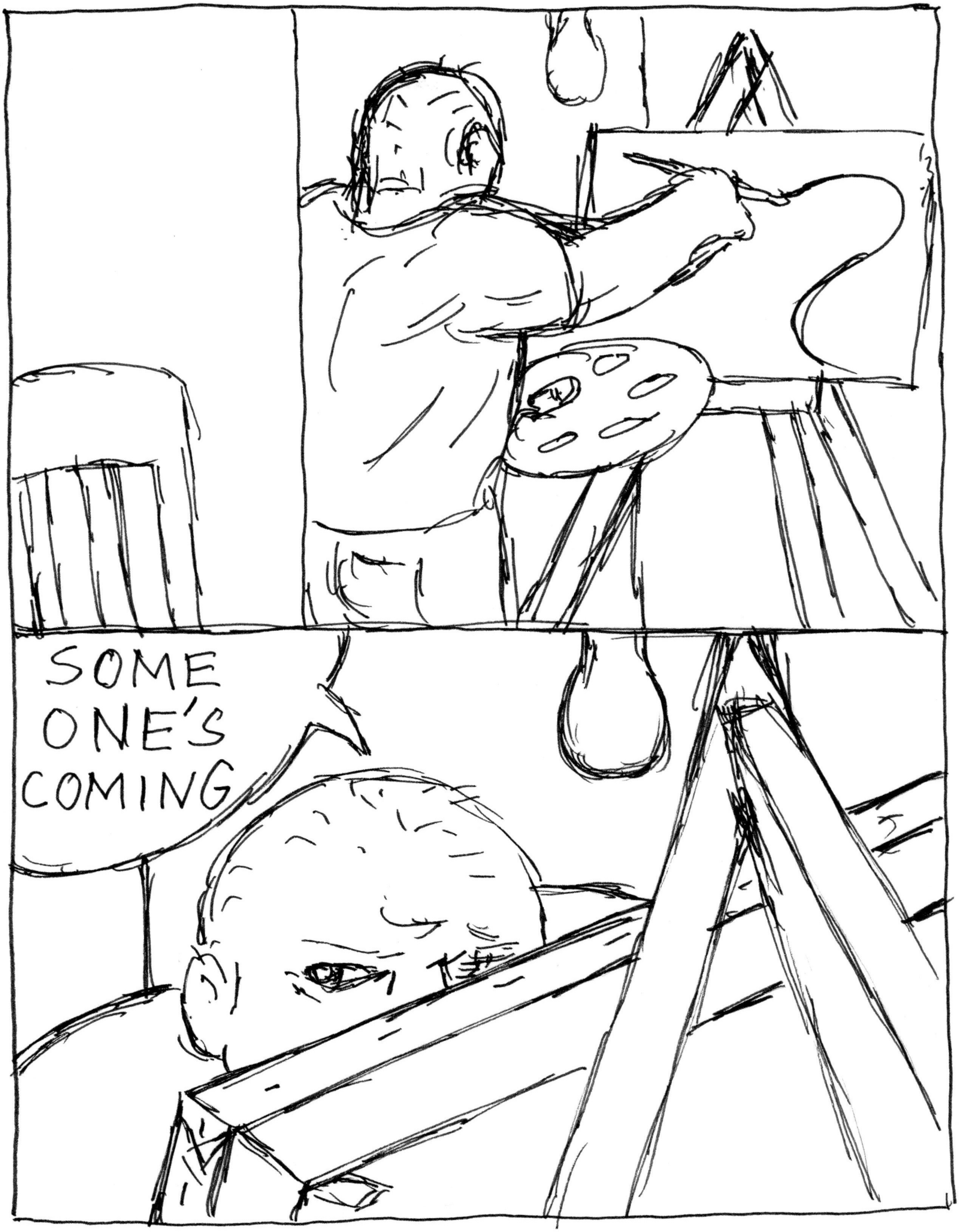
SOME ONE'S COMING

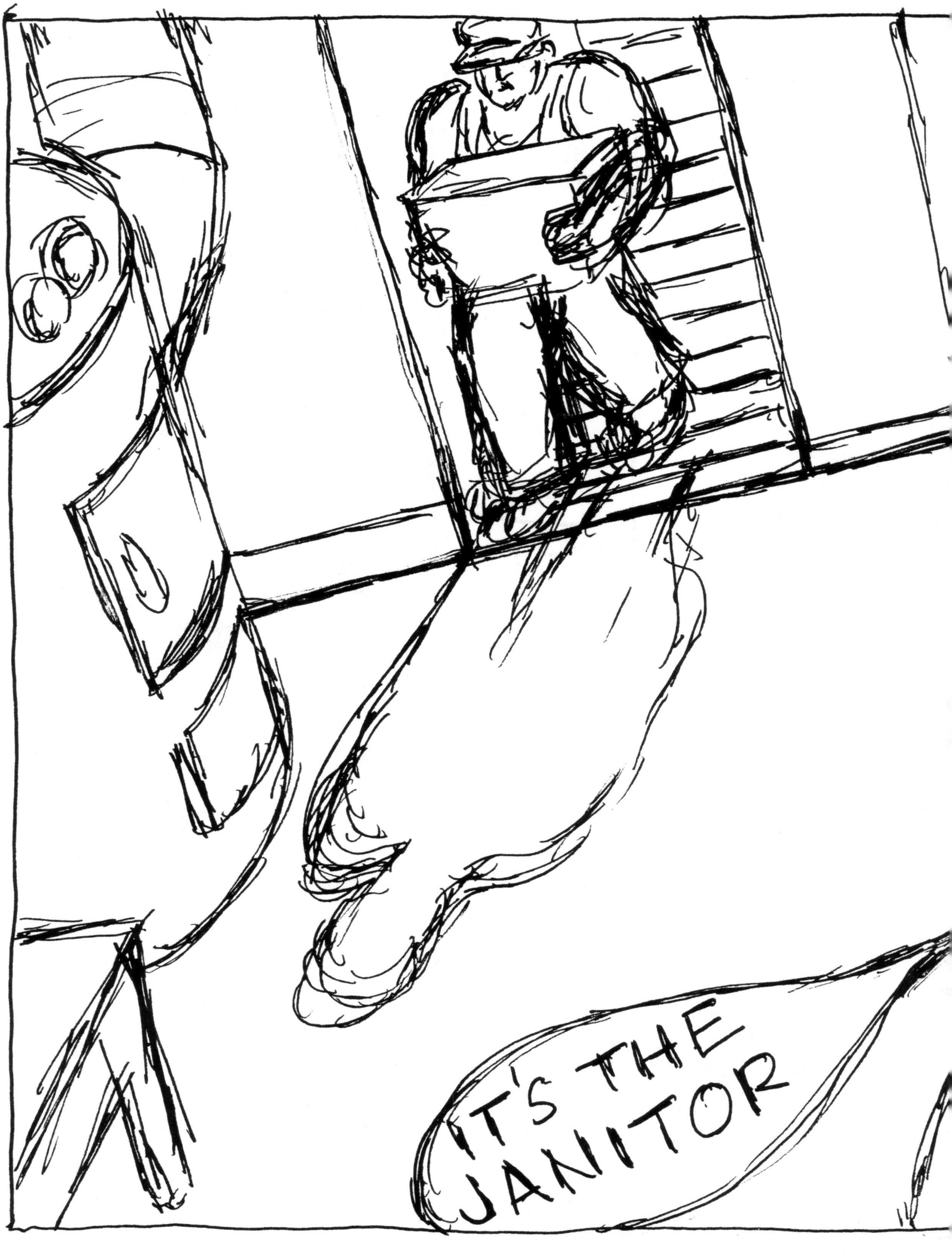
IT'S THE JANITOR

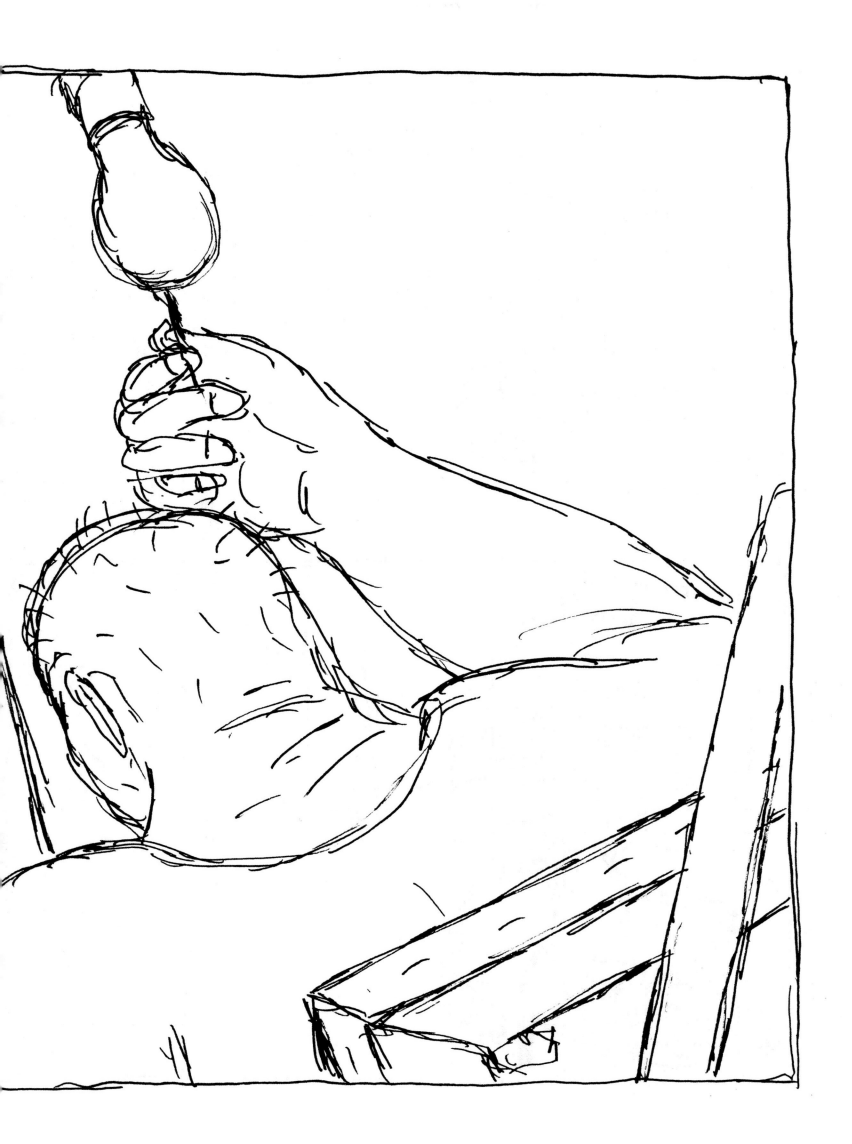

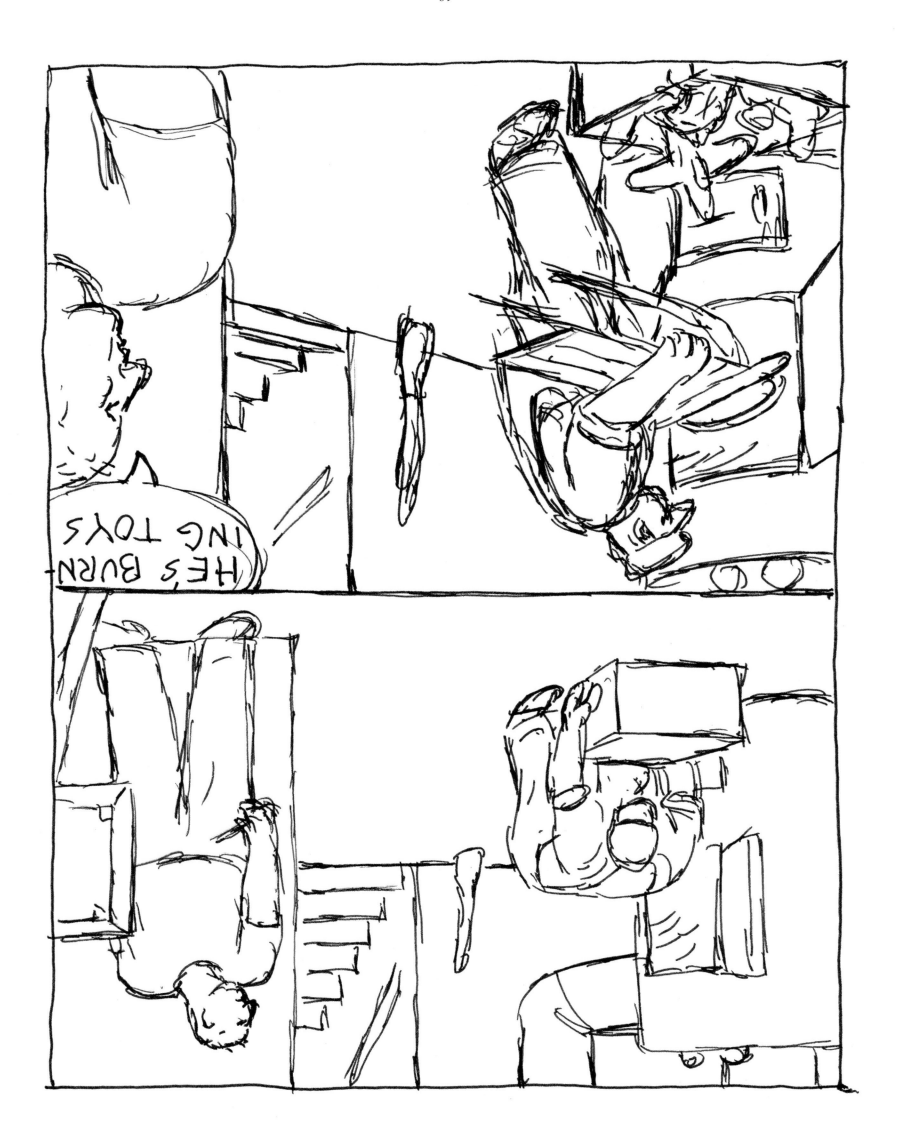

HE'S BURN-
ING TOYS

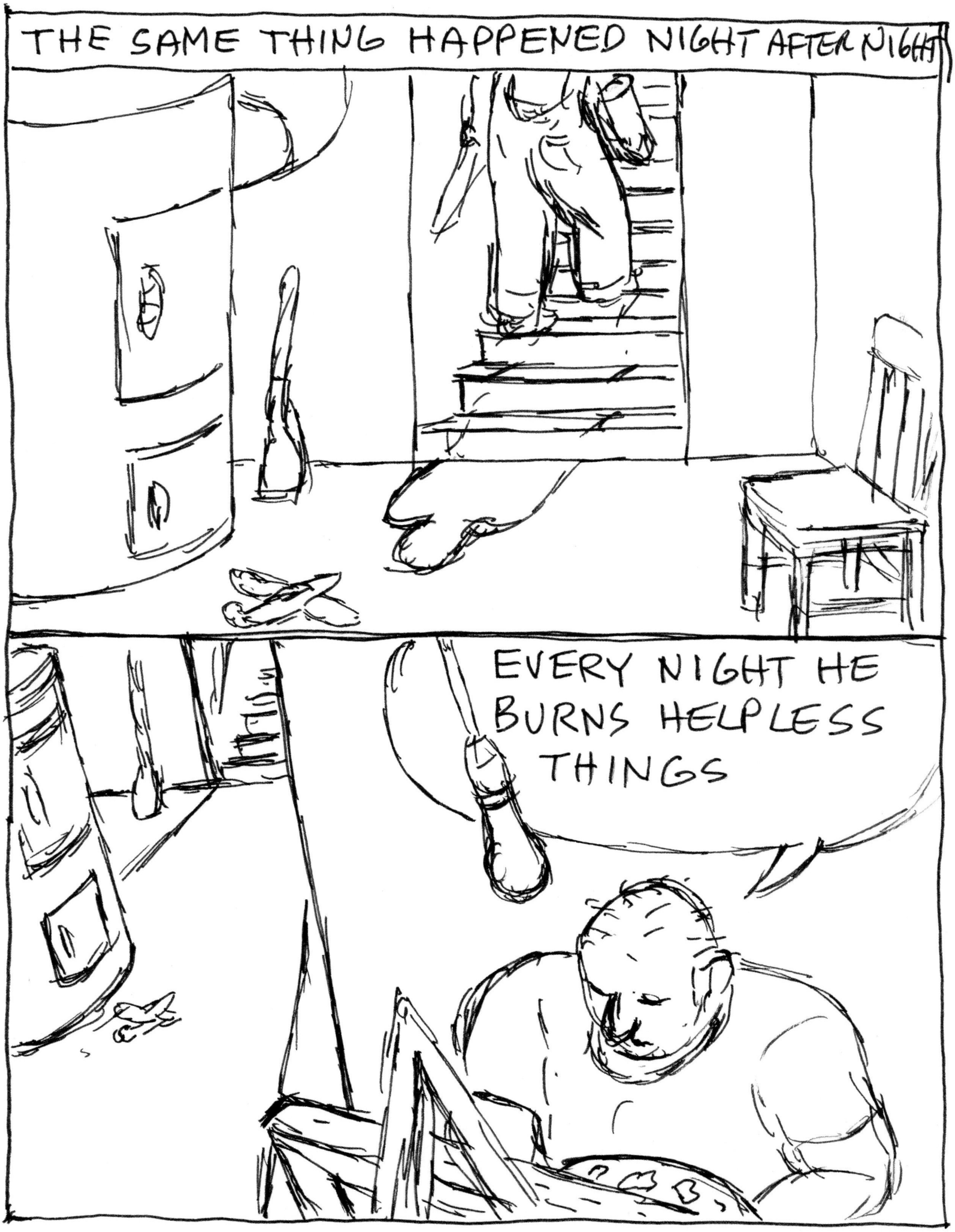
THE SAME THING HAPPENED NIGHT AFTER NIGHT
EVERY NIGHT HE BURNS HELPLESS THINGS

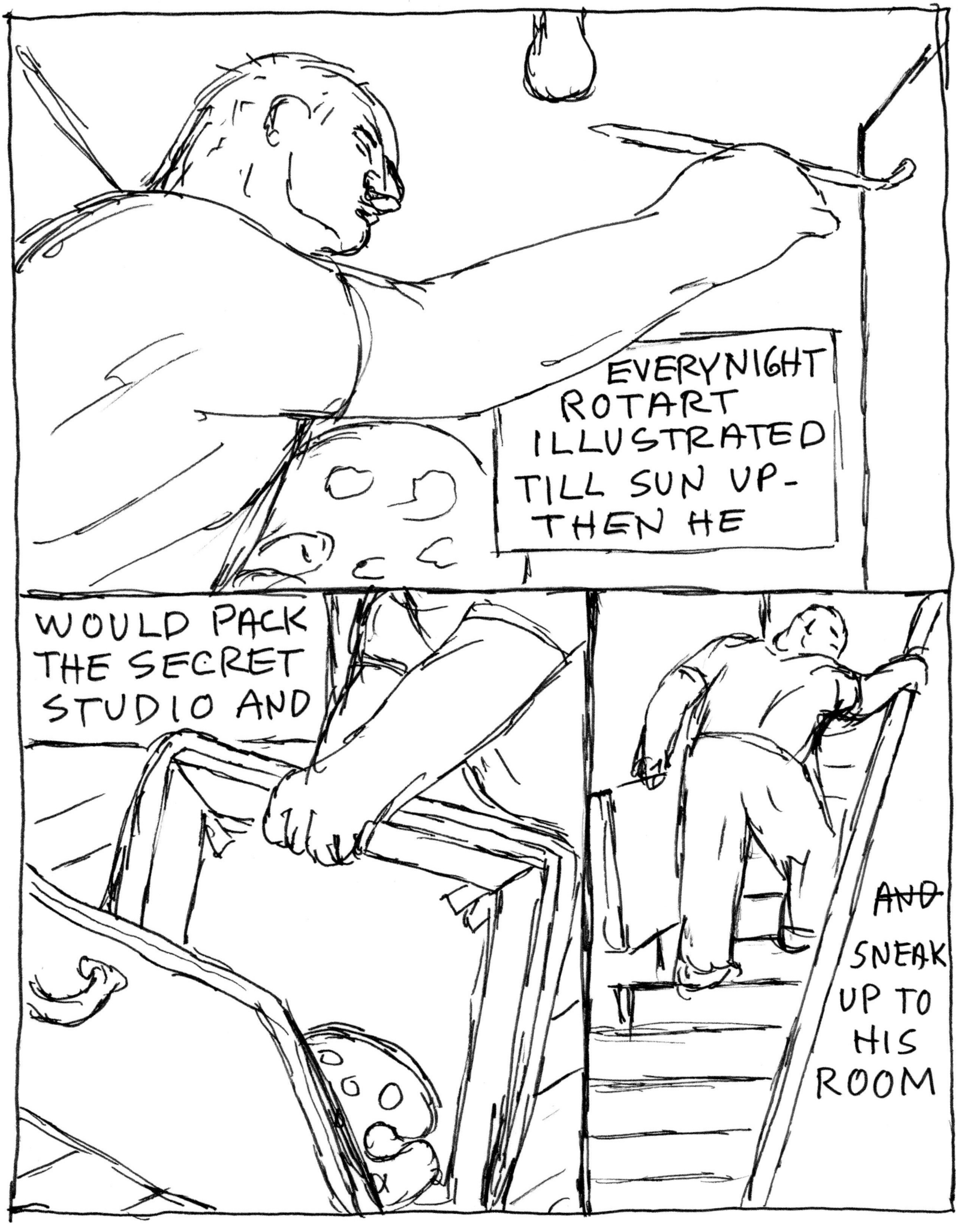
EVERYNIGHT ROTART ILLUSTRATED TILL SUN UP- THEN HE
WOULD PACK THE SECRET STUDIO AND
~~AND~~ SNEAK UP TO HIS ROOM

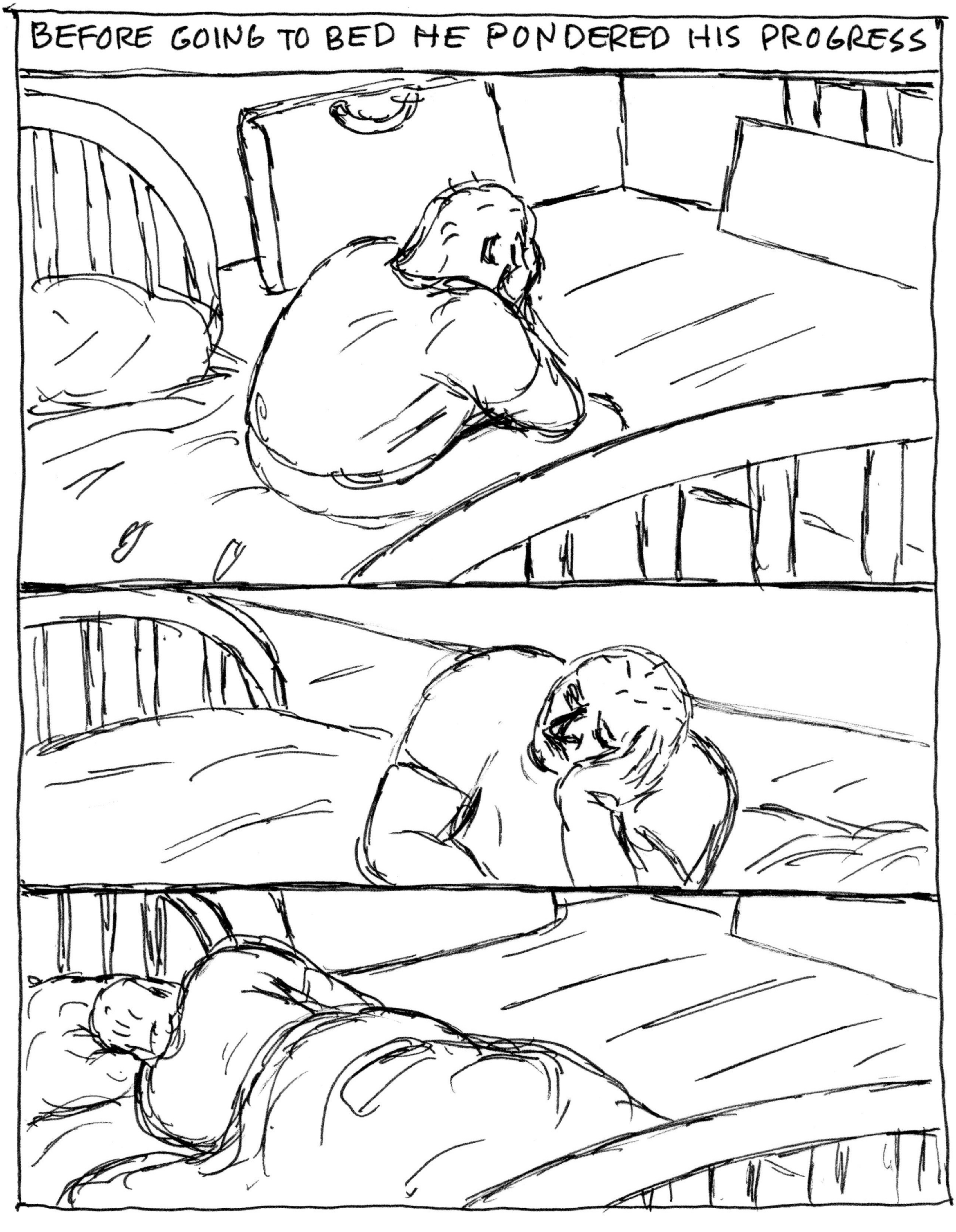
BEFORE GOING TO BED HE PONDERED HIS PROGRESS

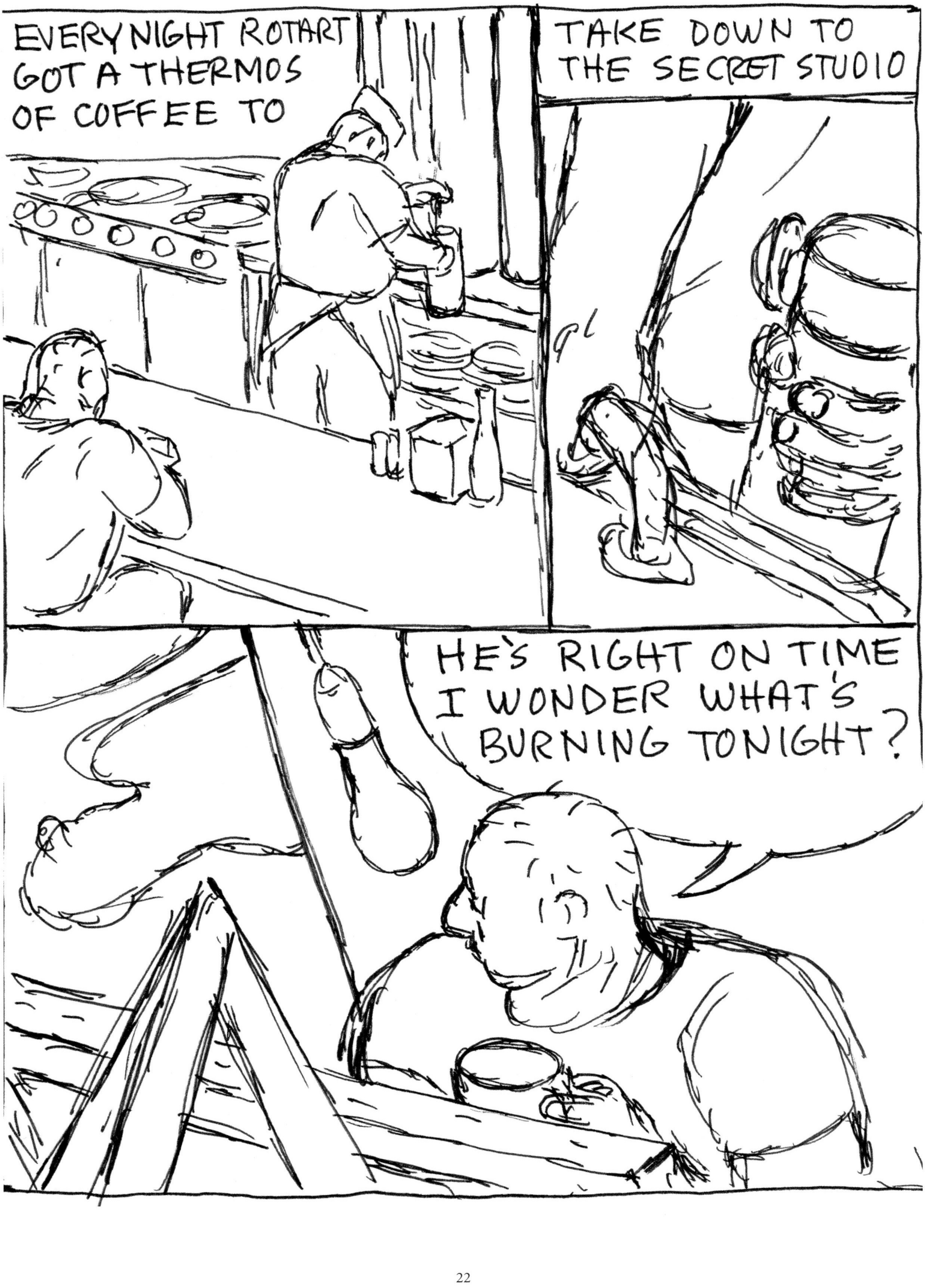
EVERY NIGHT ROTART GOT A THERMOS OF COFFEE TO
TAKE DOWN TO THE SECRET STUDIO
HE'S RIGHT ON TIME I WONDER WHAT'S BURNING TONIGHT?

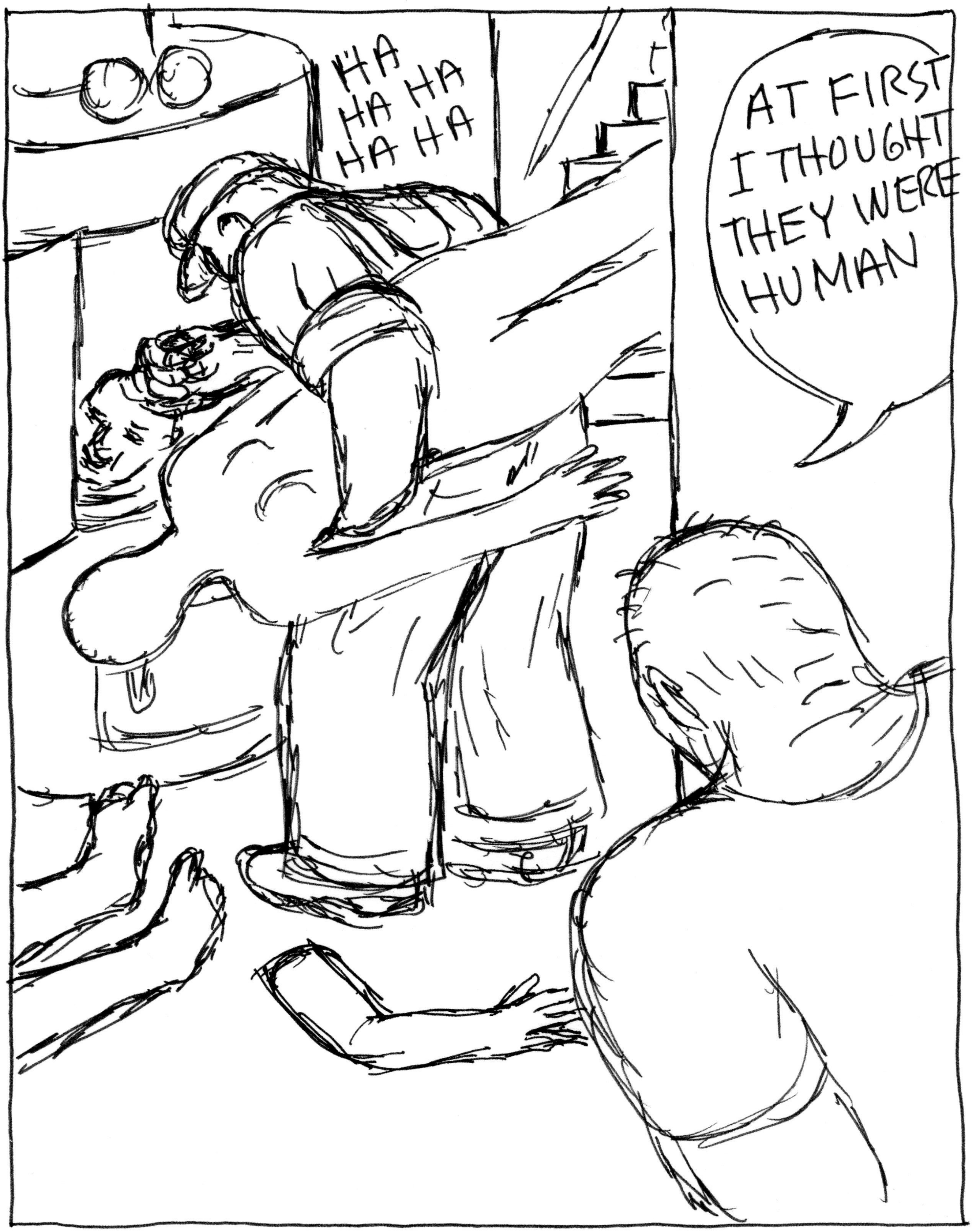
HA HA HA HA HA HA
AT FIRST I THOUGHT THEY WERE HUMAN

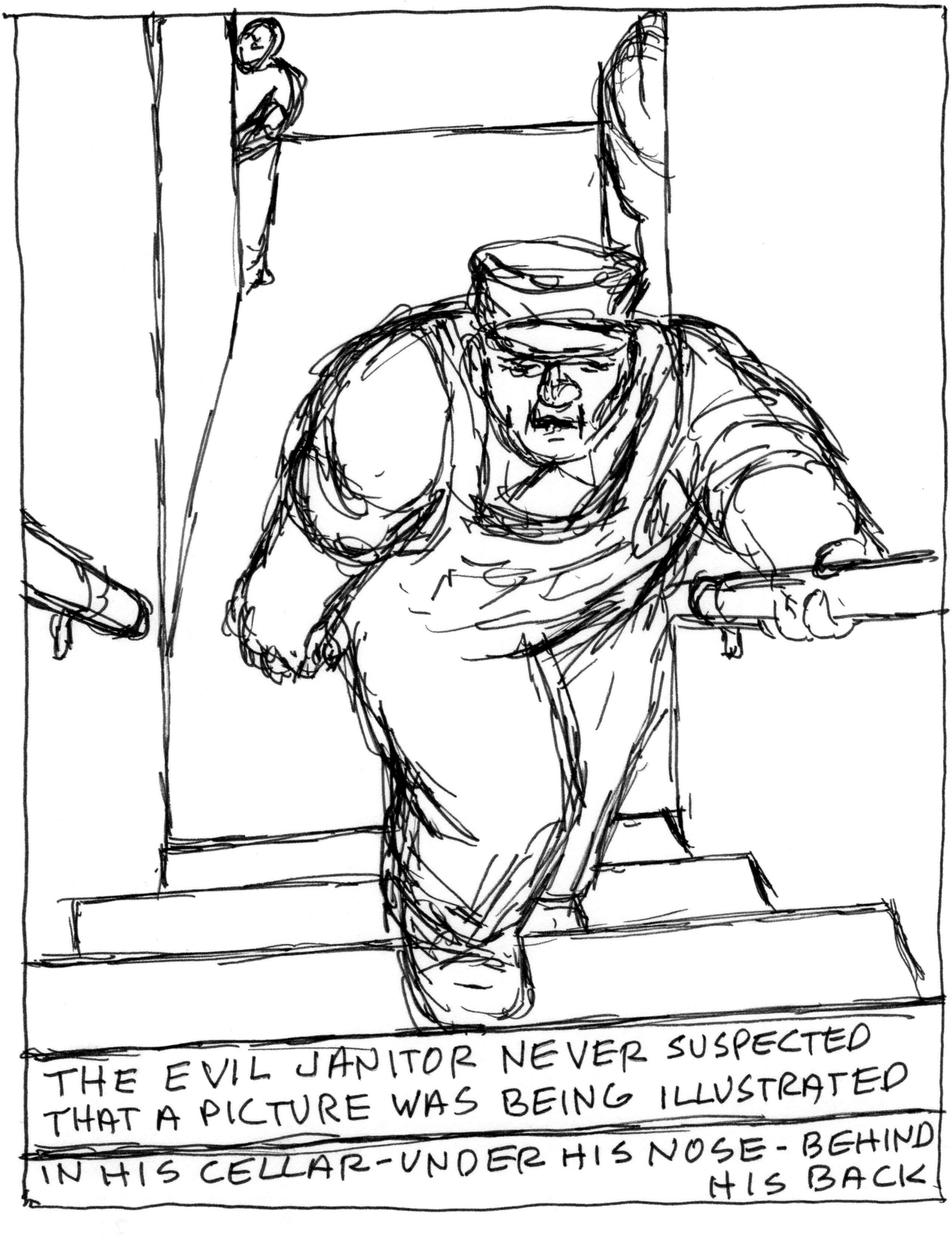
THE EVIL JANITOR NEVER SUSPECTED THAT A PICTURE WAS BEING ILLUSTRATED
IN HIS CELLAR-UNDER HIS NOSE-BEHIND HIS BACK

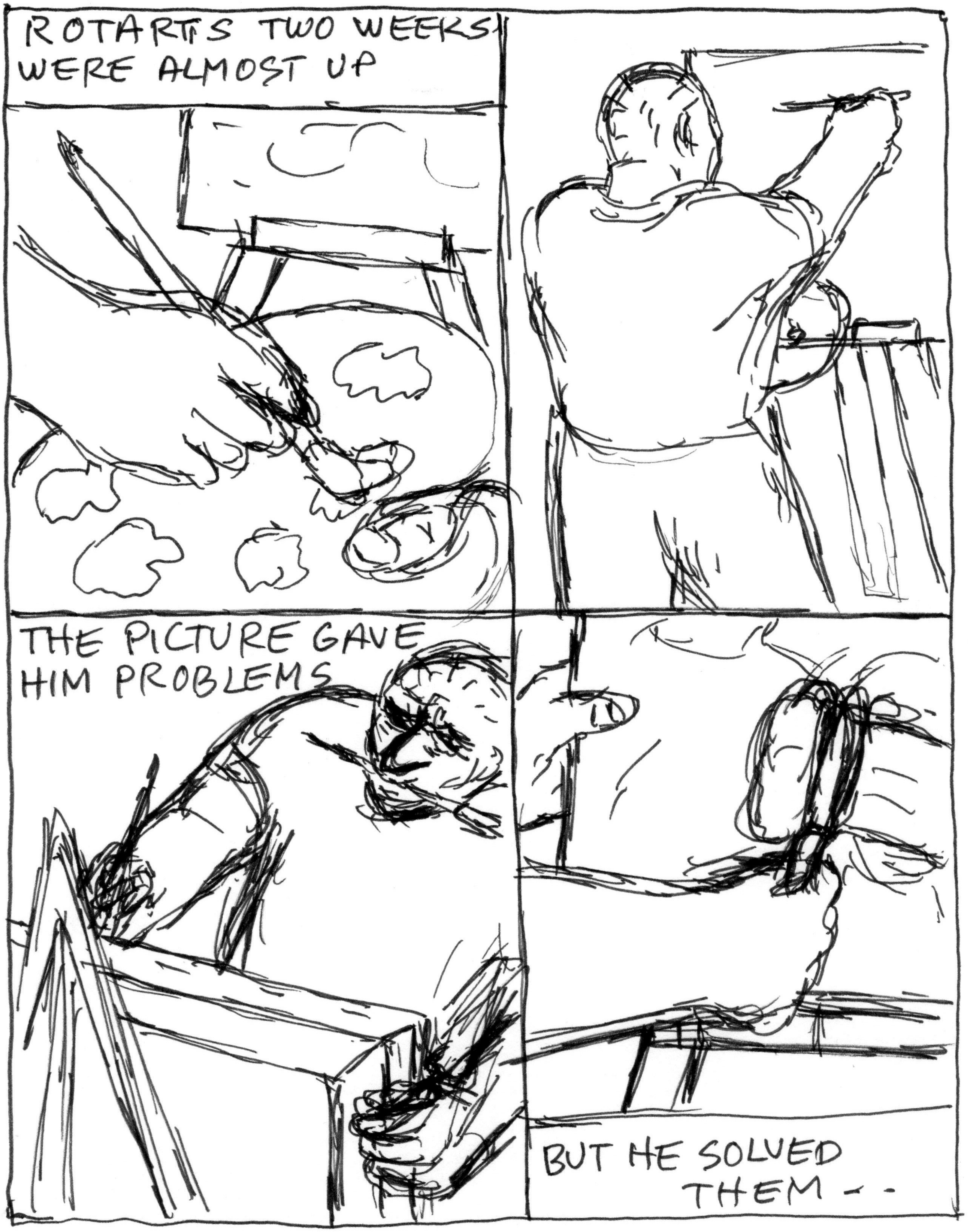
ROTART'S TWO WEEKS WERE ALMOST UP
THE PICTURE GAVE HIM PROBLEMS
BUT HE SOLVED THEM - -

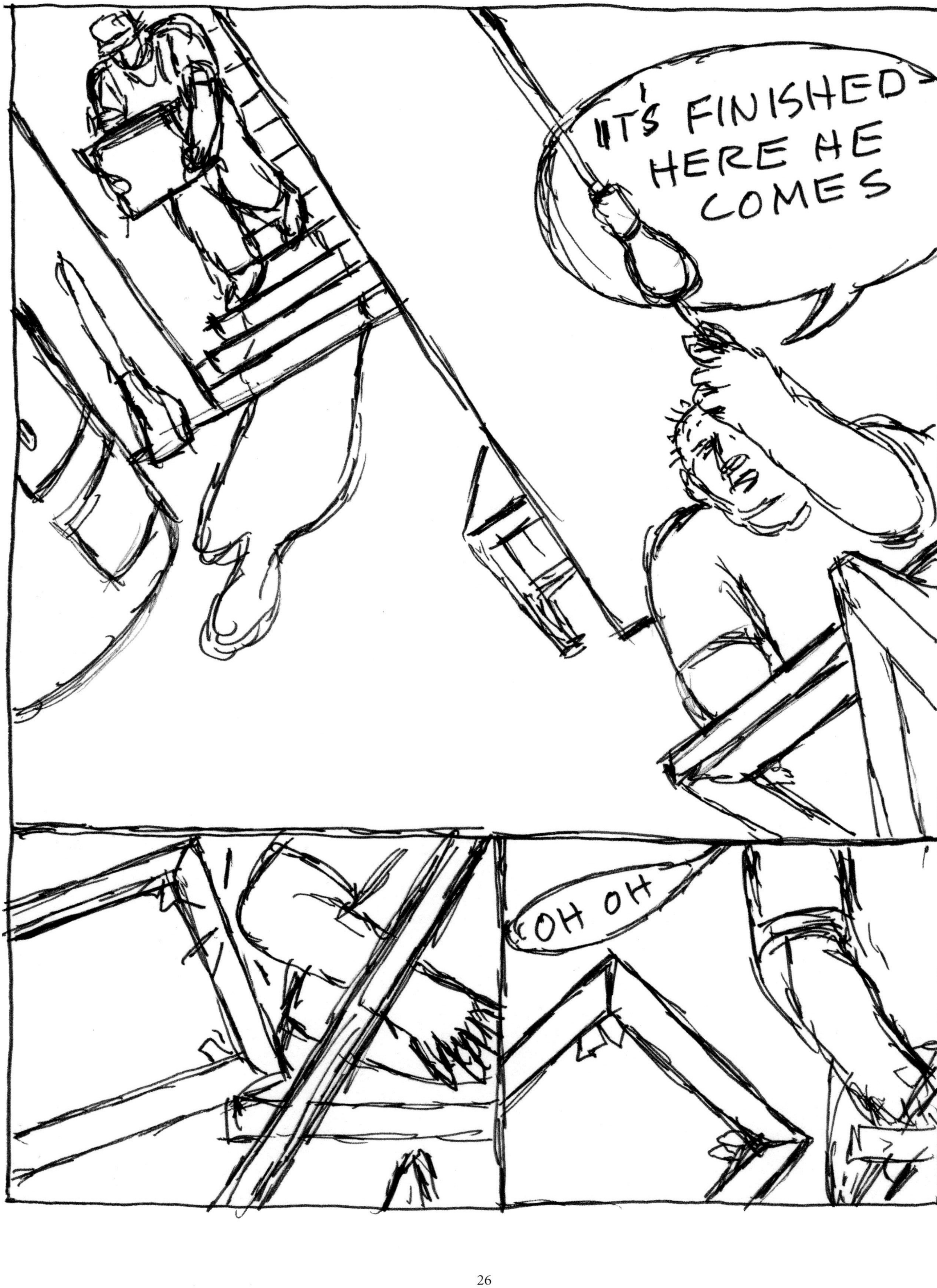
IT'S FINISHED-
HERE HE
COMES
OH OH

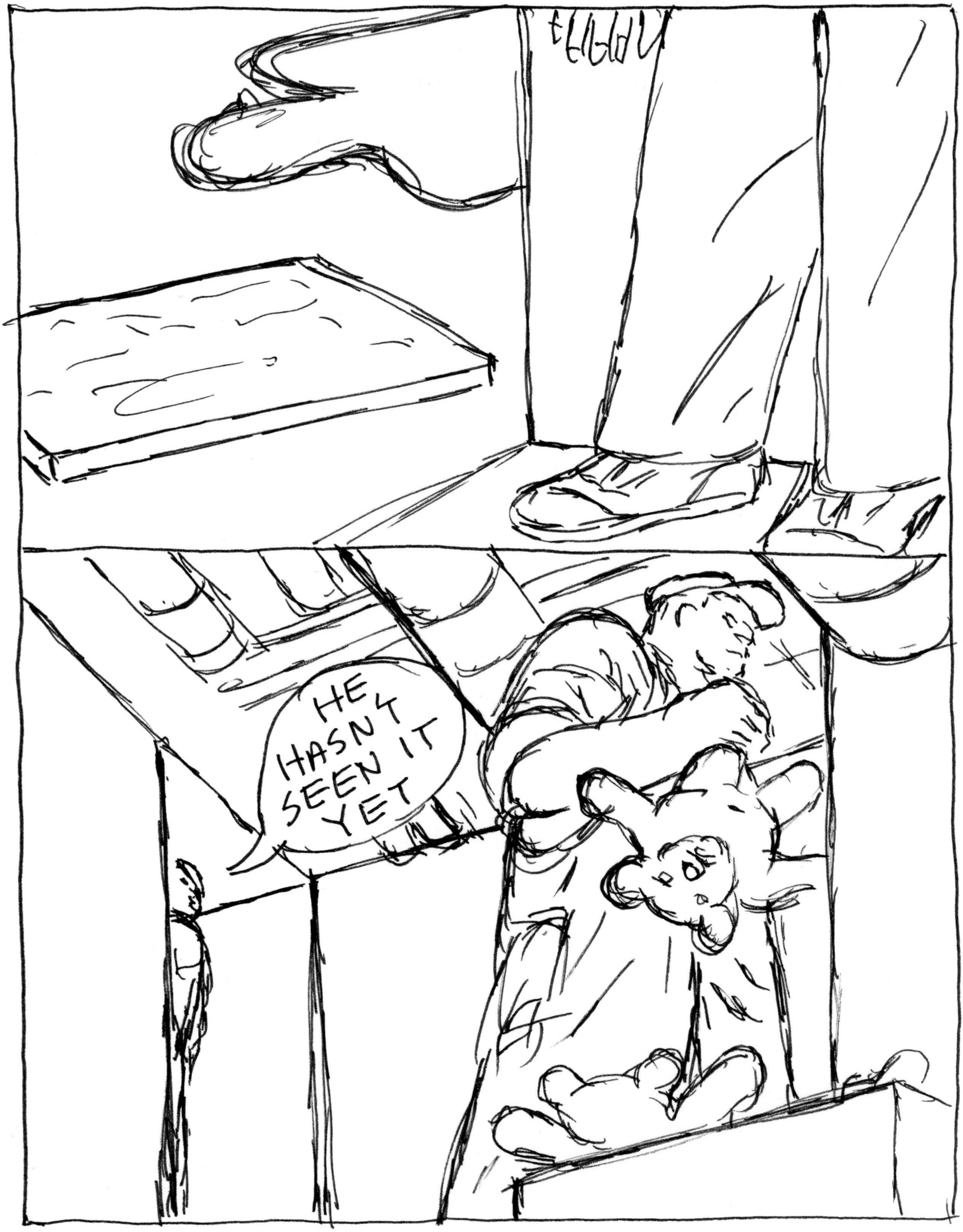
HEY HASN'T SEEN IT YET

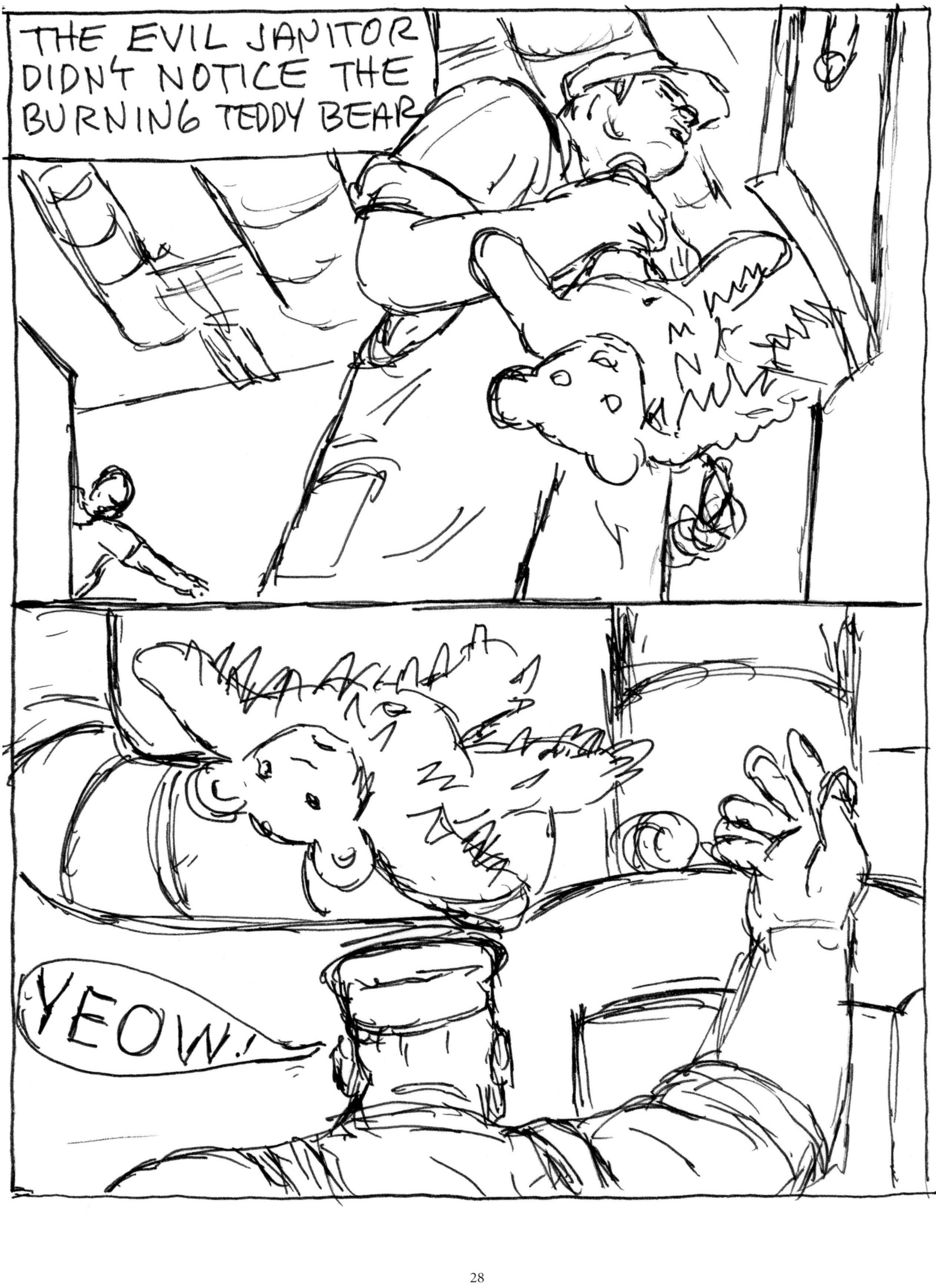
THE EVIL JANITOR DIDN'T NOTICE THE BURNING TEDDY BEAR
YEOW!

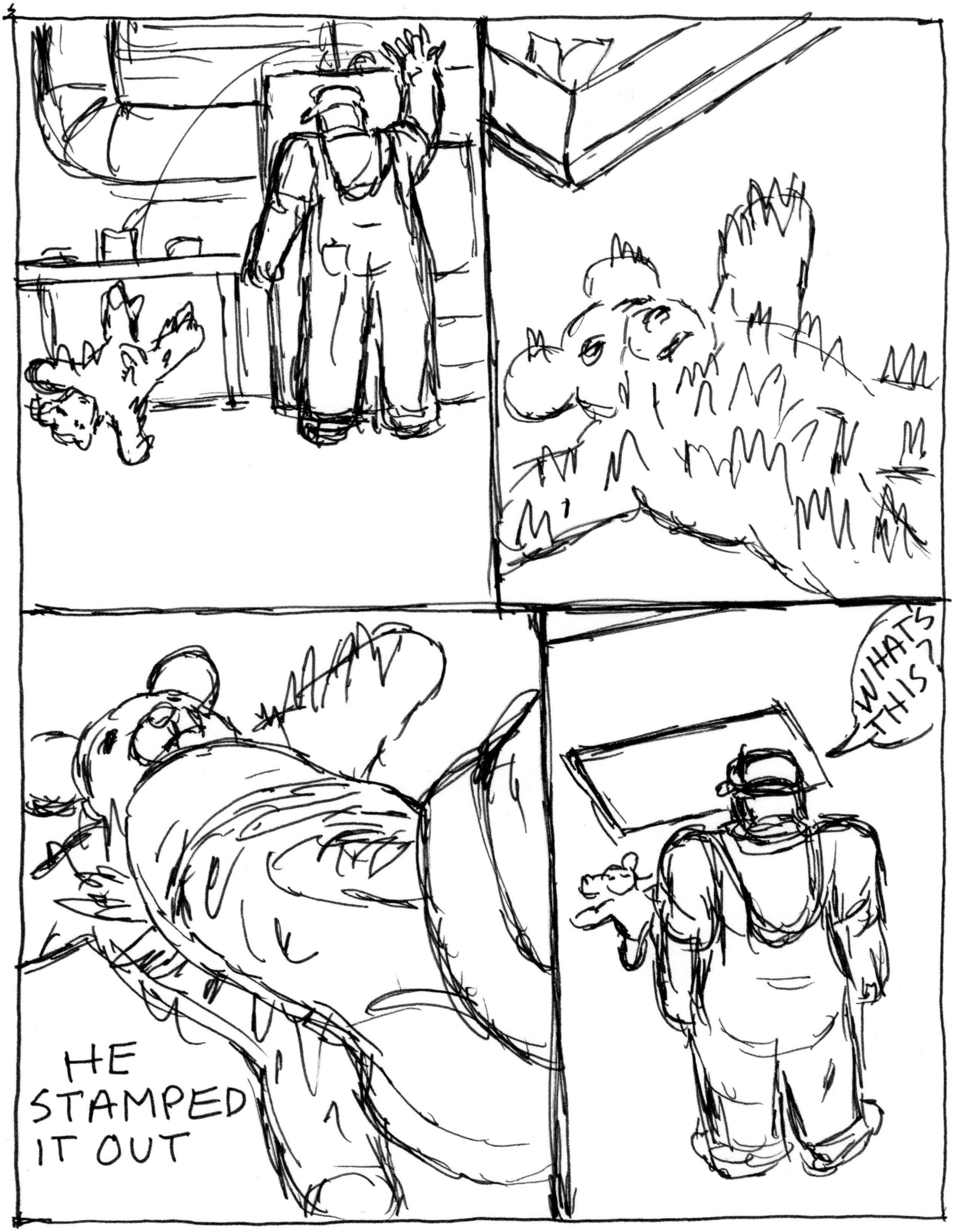
HE STAMPED IT OUT
WHAT'S THIS?

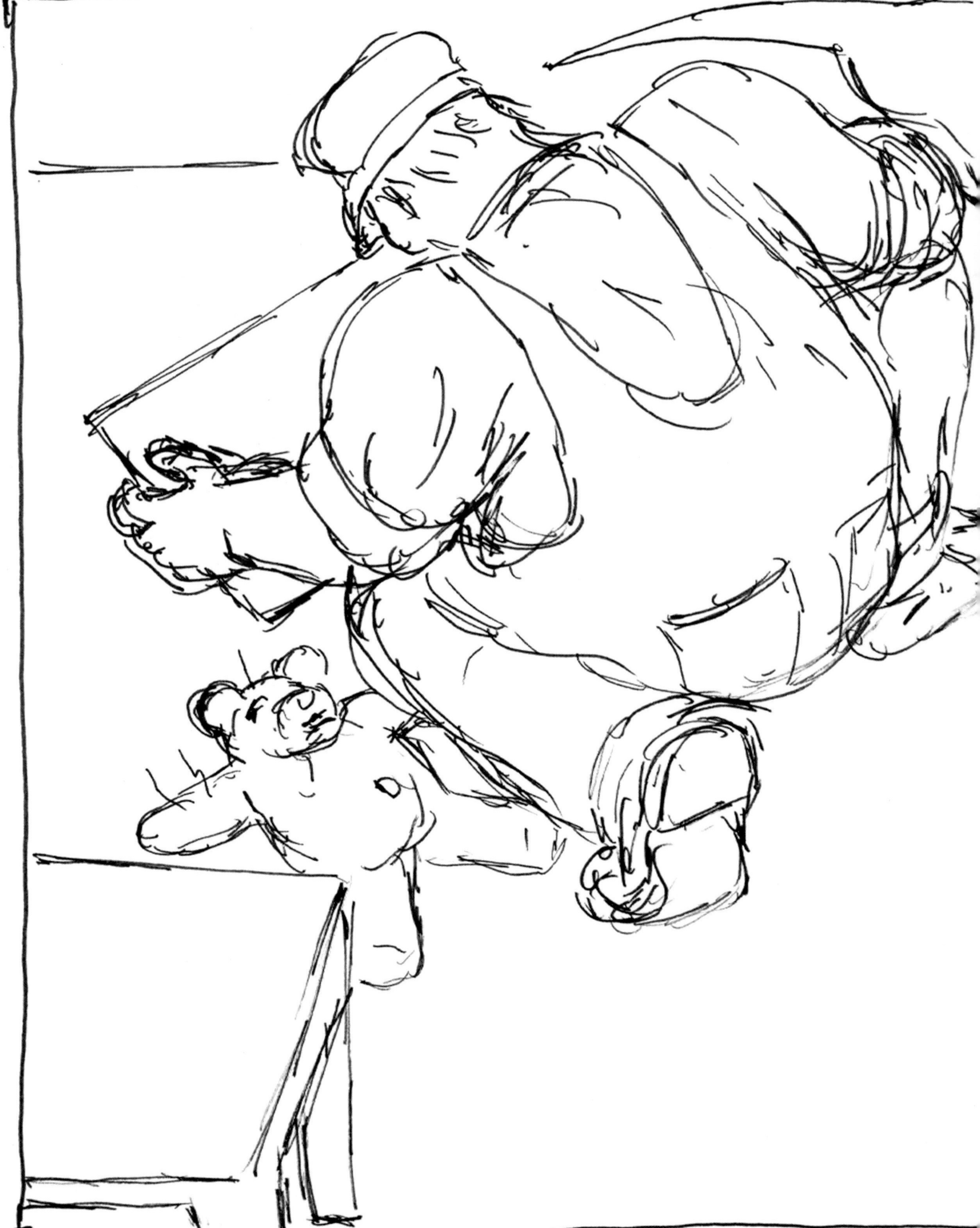

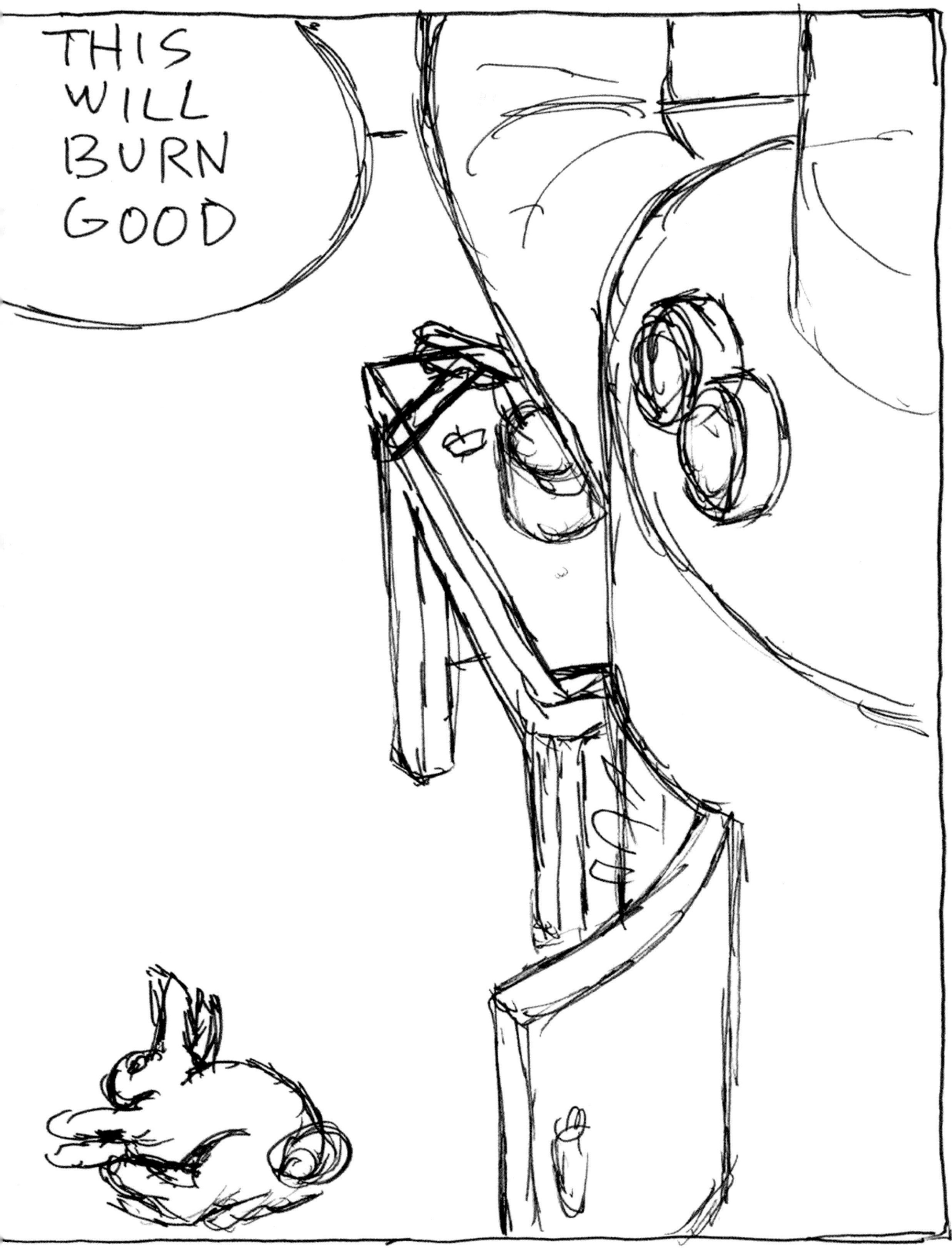
THIS WILL BURN GOOD

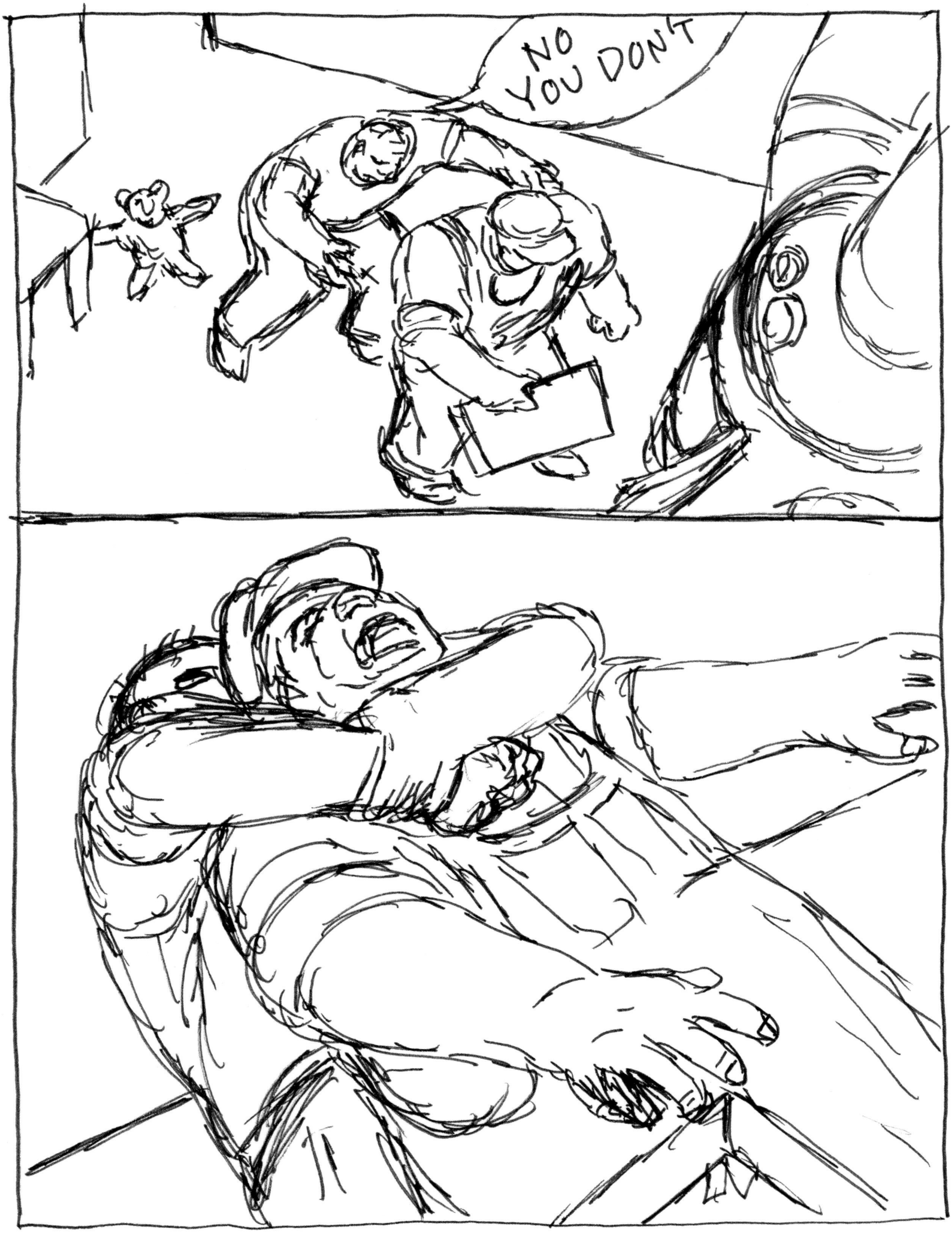
NO YOU DON'T

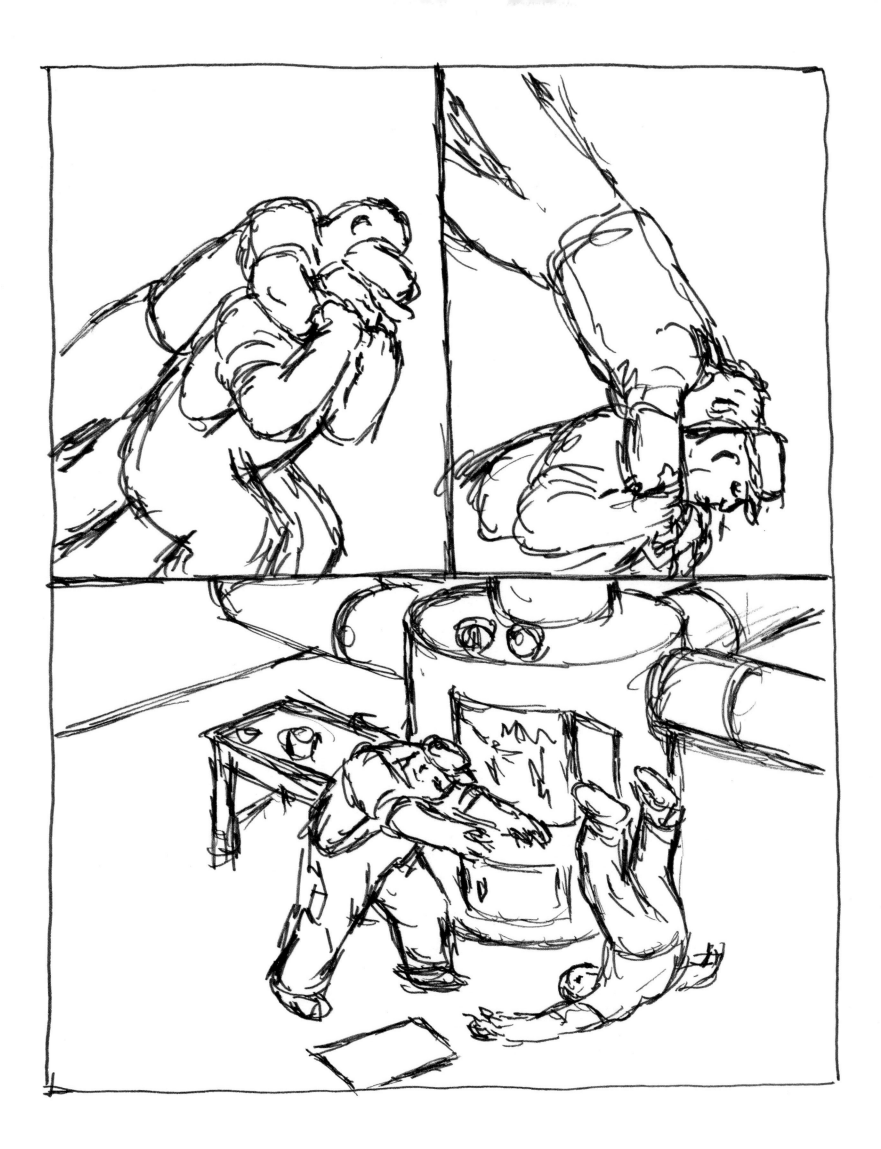

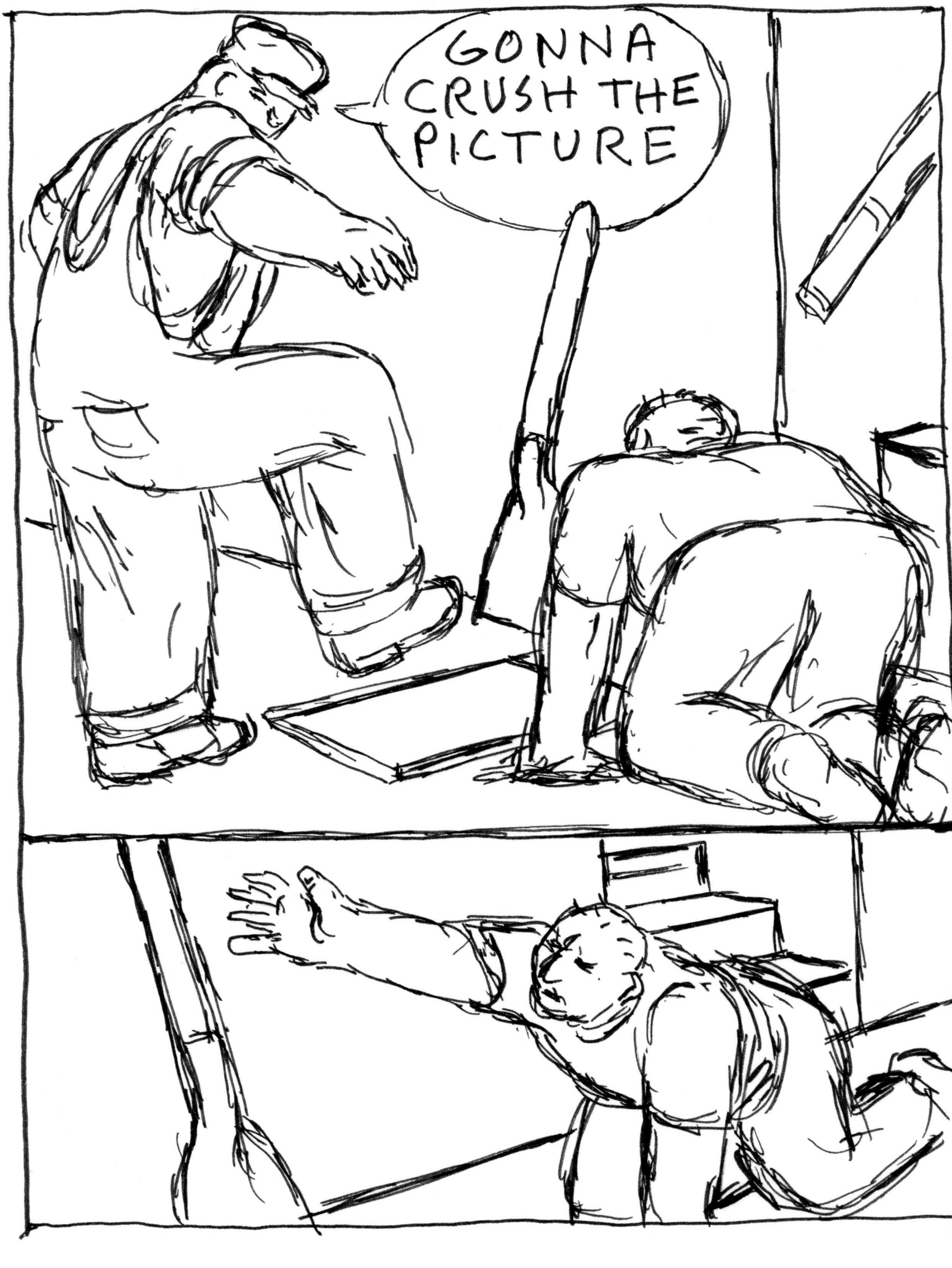
GONNA CRUSH THE PICTURE

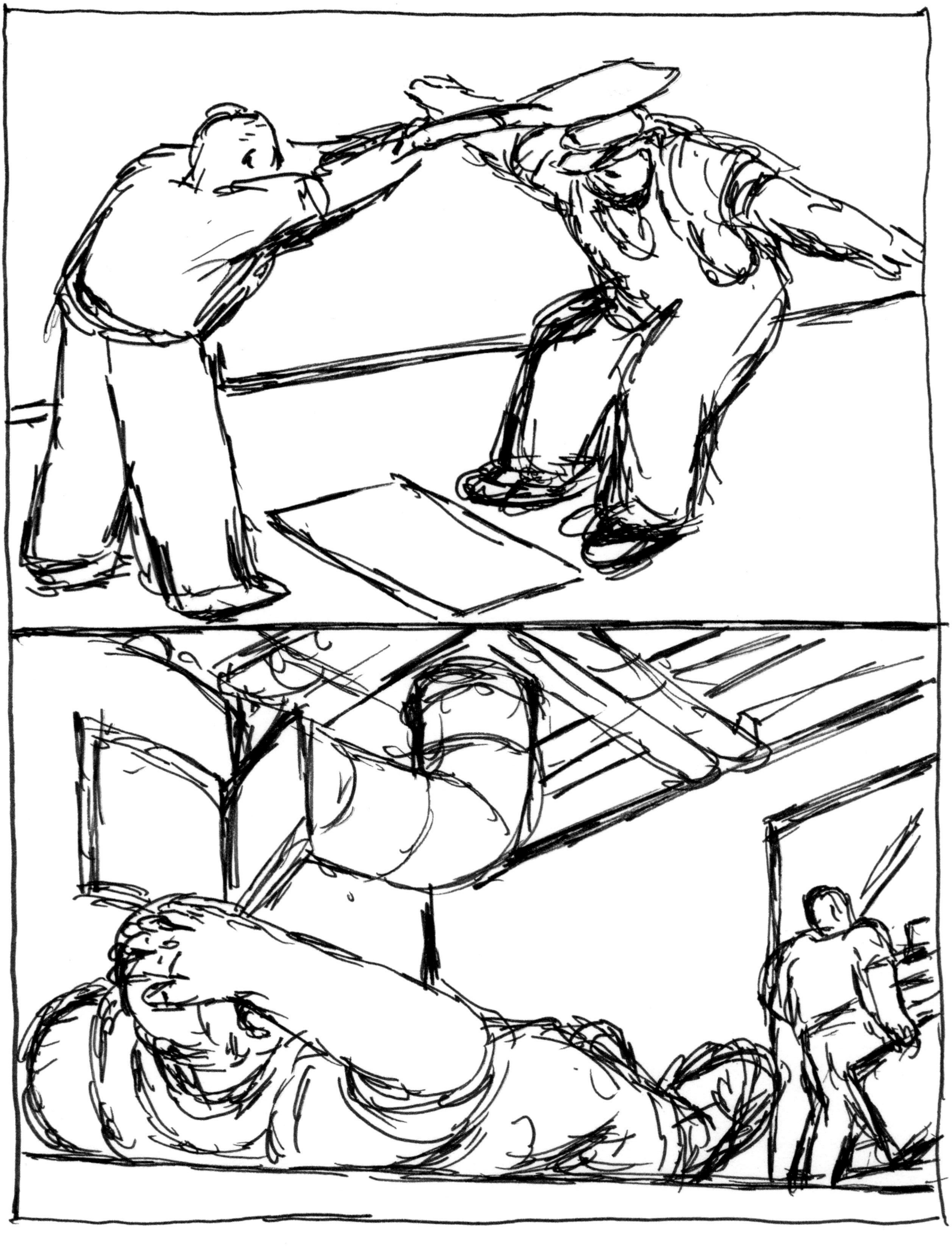

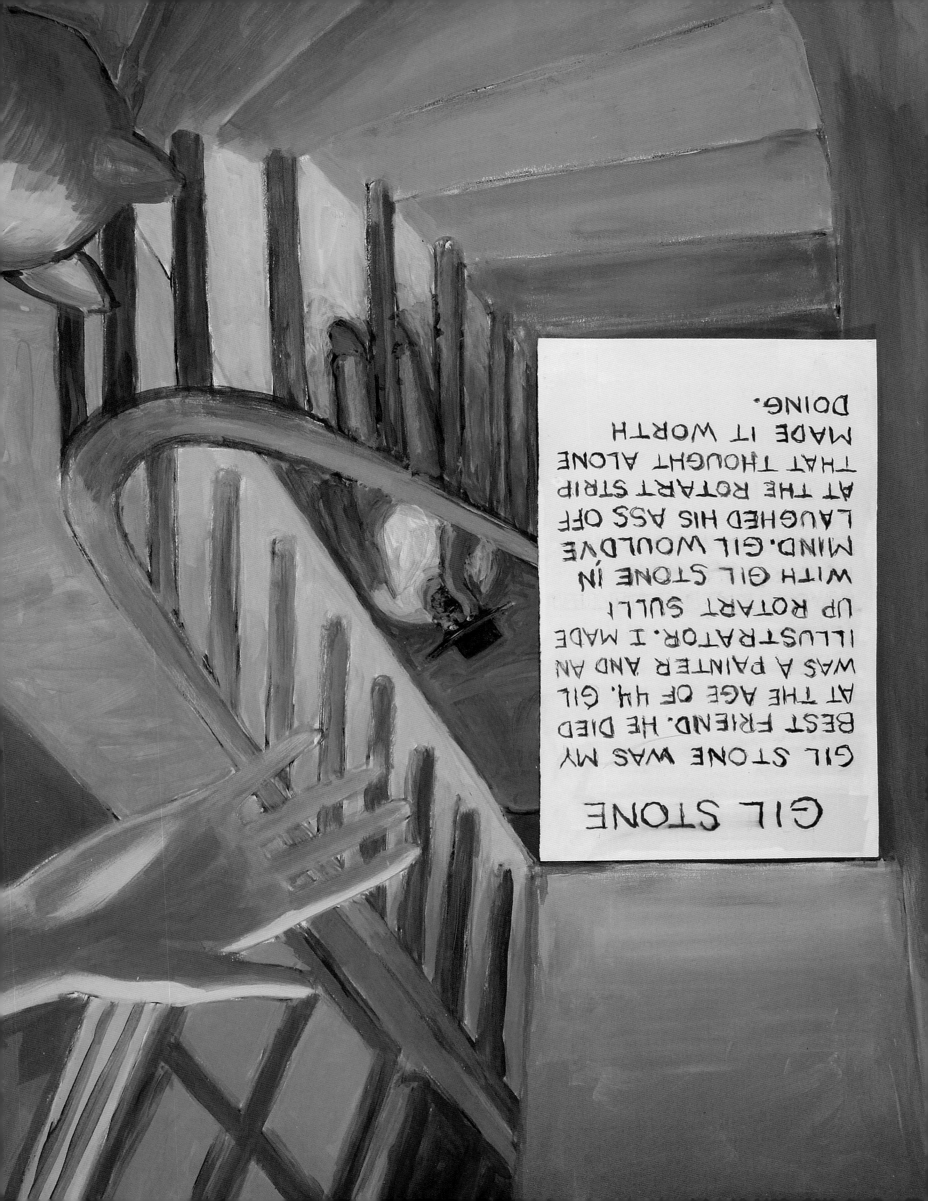

GIL STONE

GIL STONE WAS MY
BEST FRIEND. HE DIED
AT THE AGE OF 44. GIL
WAS A PAINTER AND AN
ILLUSTRATOR. I MADE
UP ROTART SULLI
WITH GIL STONE IN
MIND. GIL WOULDVE
LAUGHED HIS ASS OFF
AT THE ROTART STRIP
THAT THOUGHT ALONE
MADE IT WORTH
DOING.

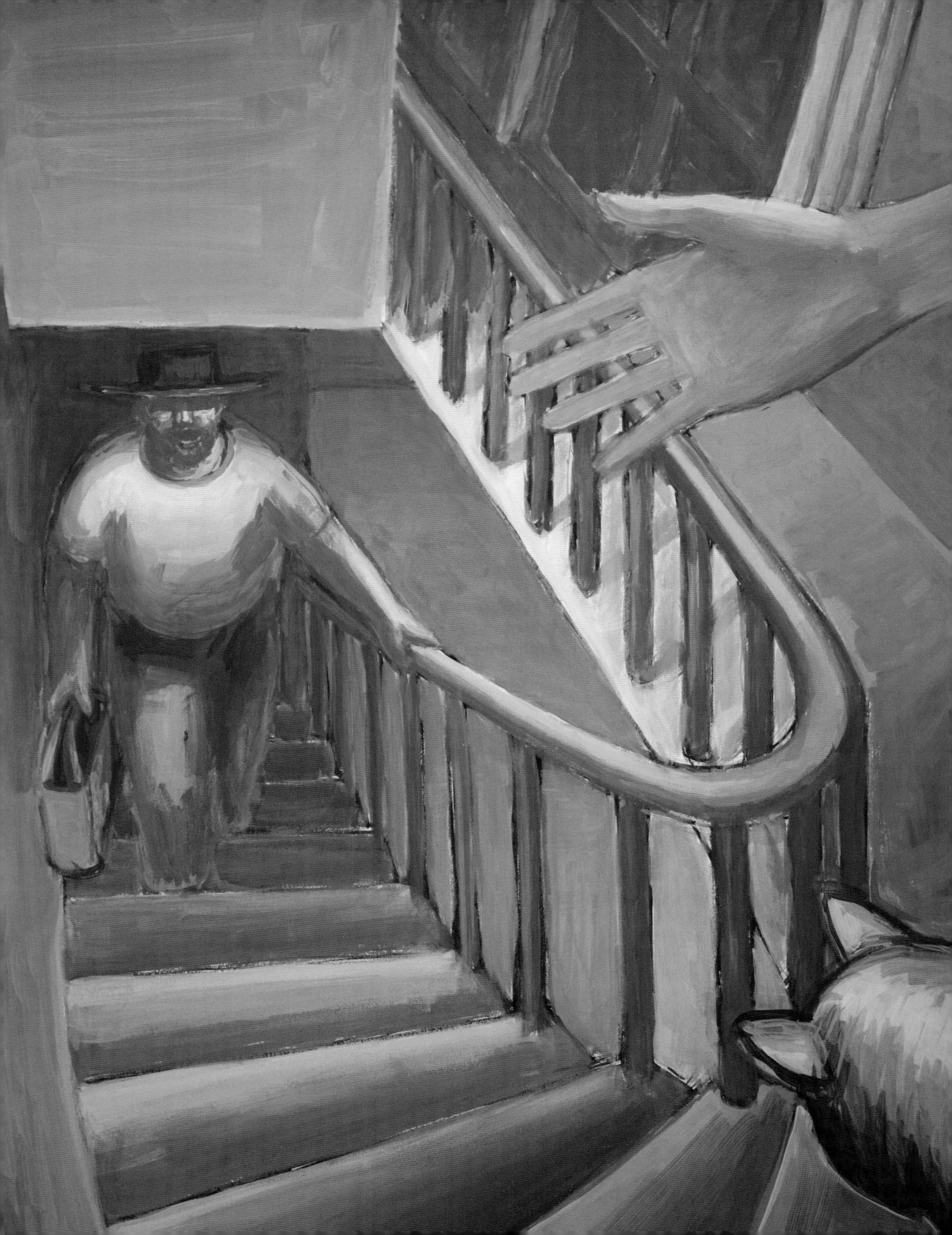

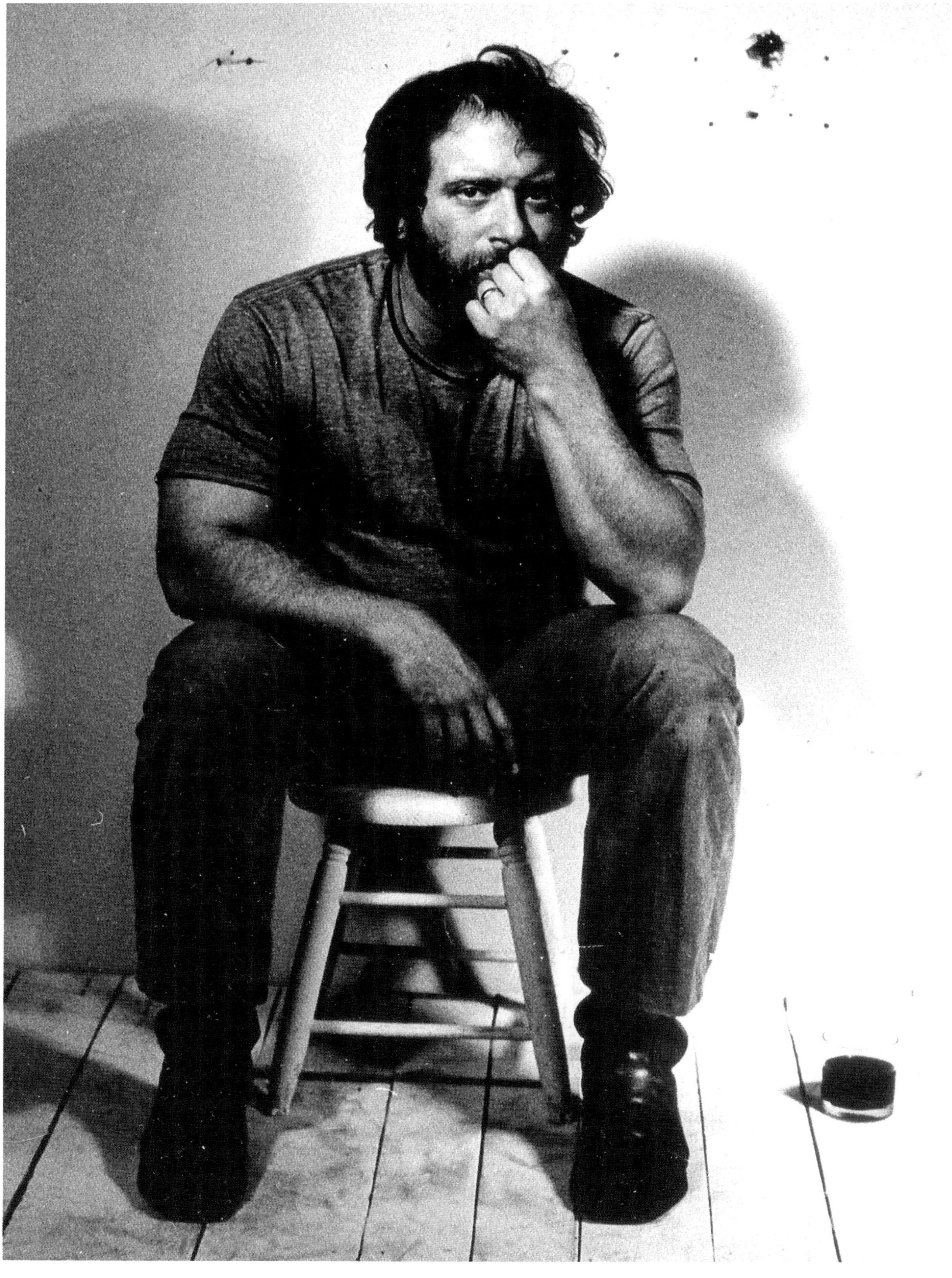

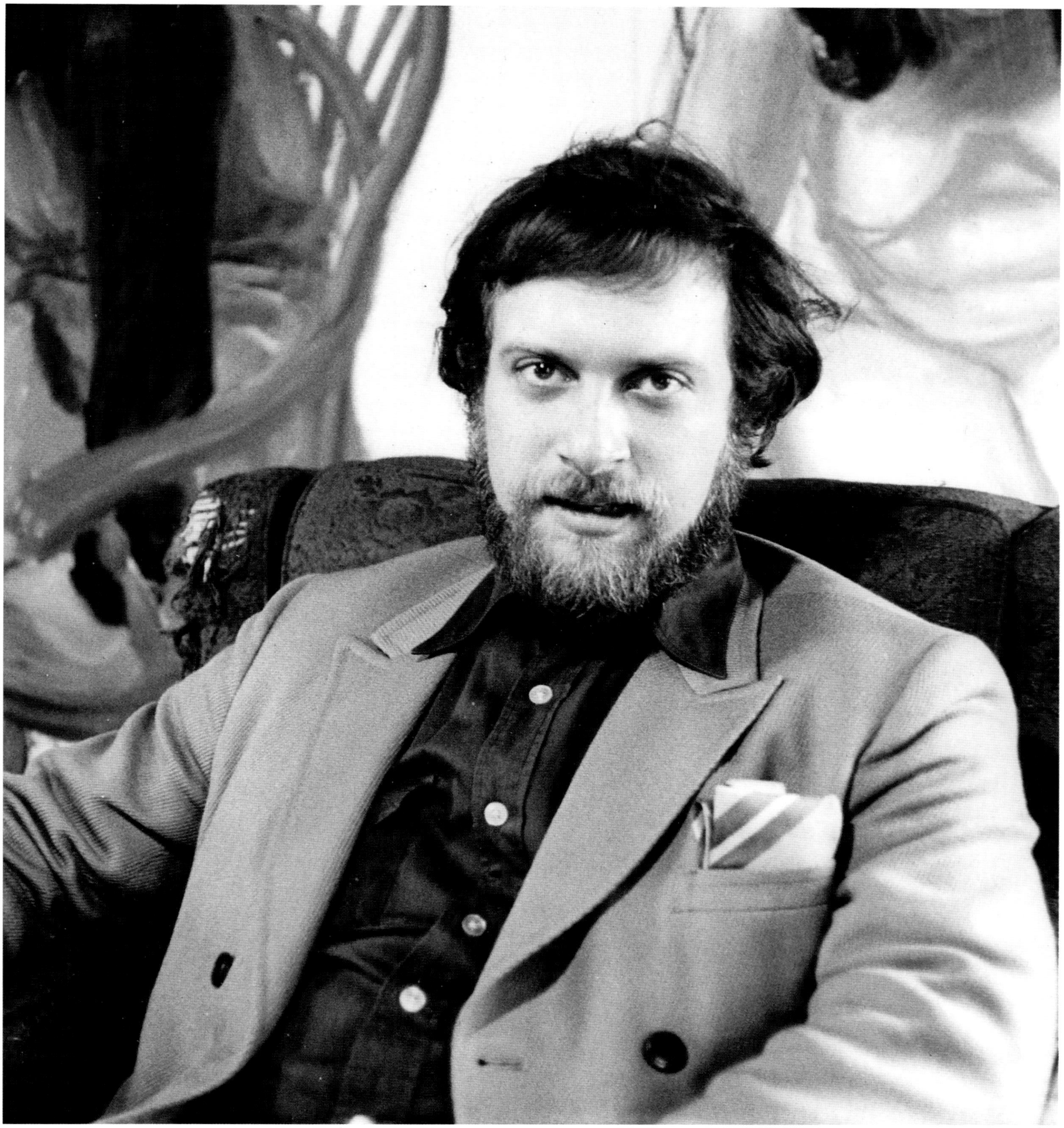

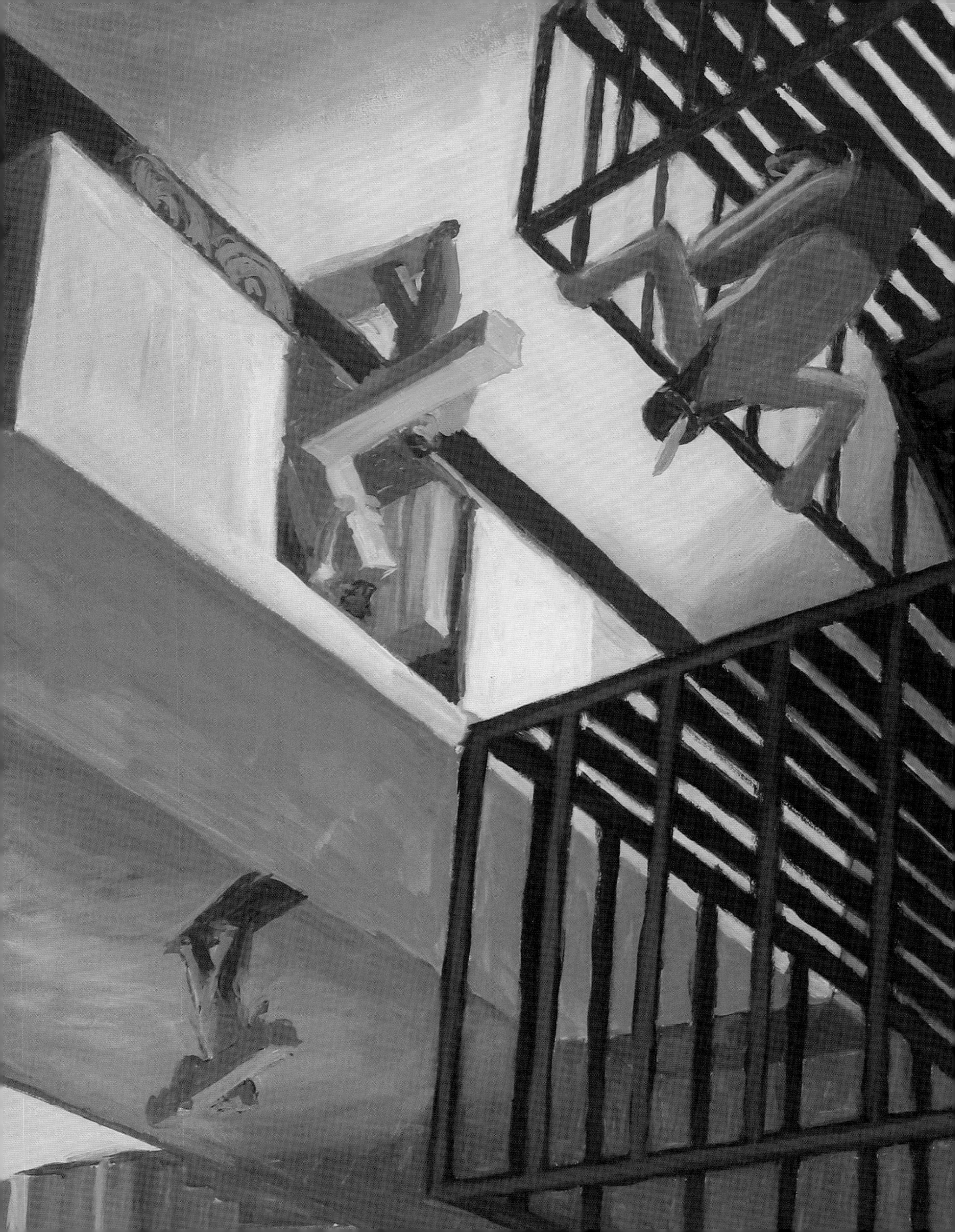

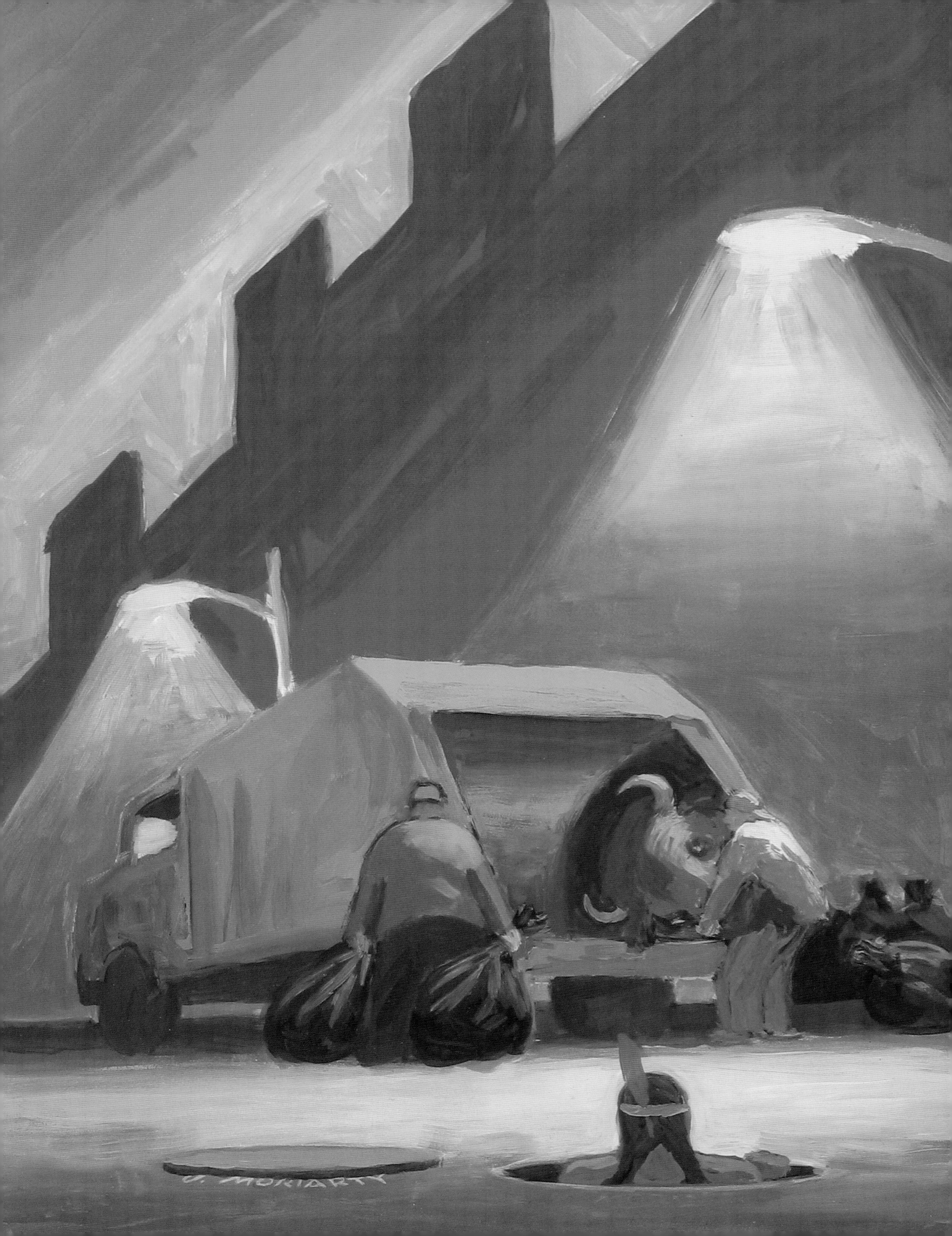
J. MORIARTY

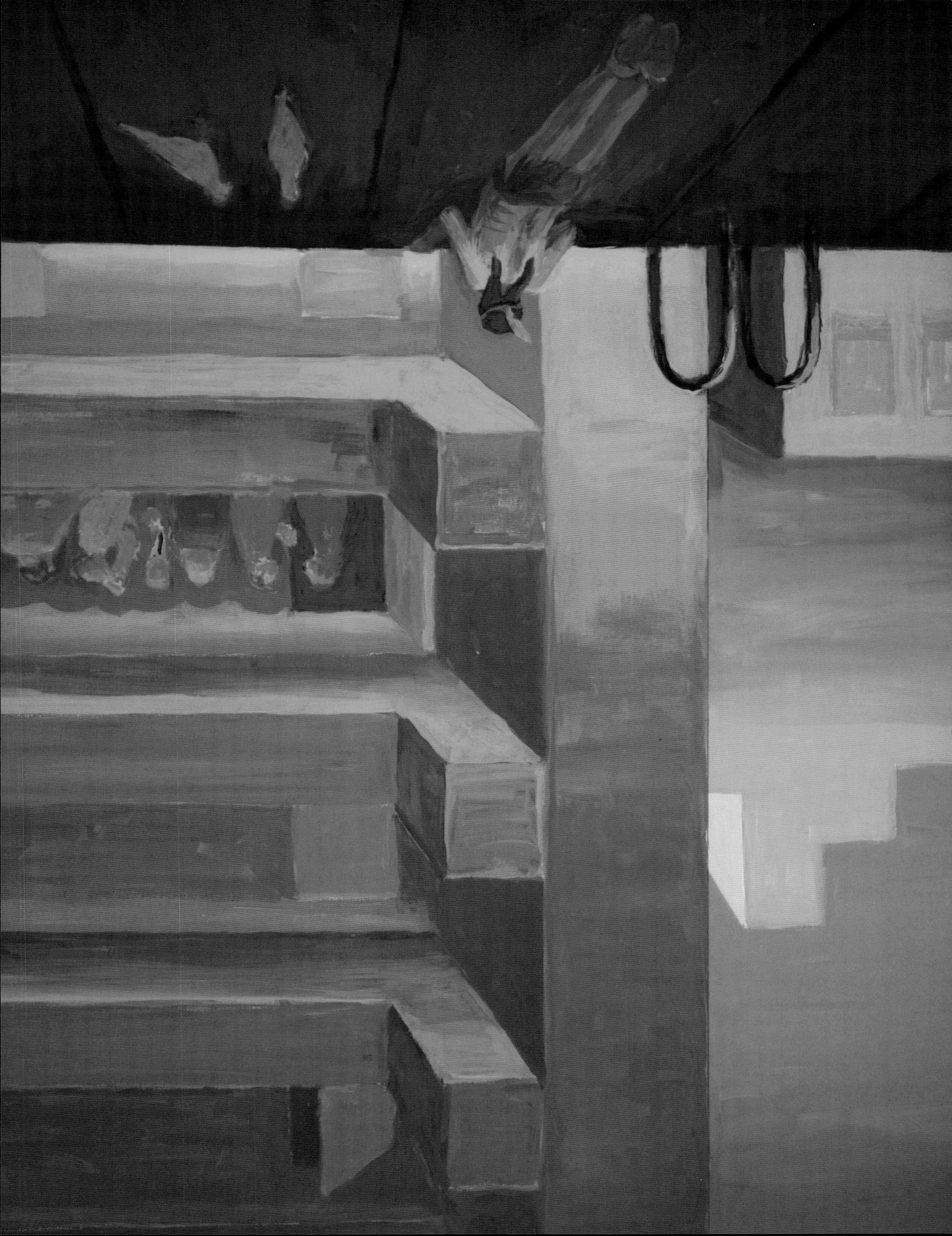

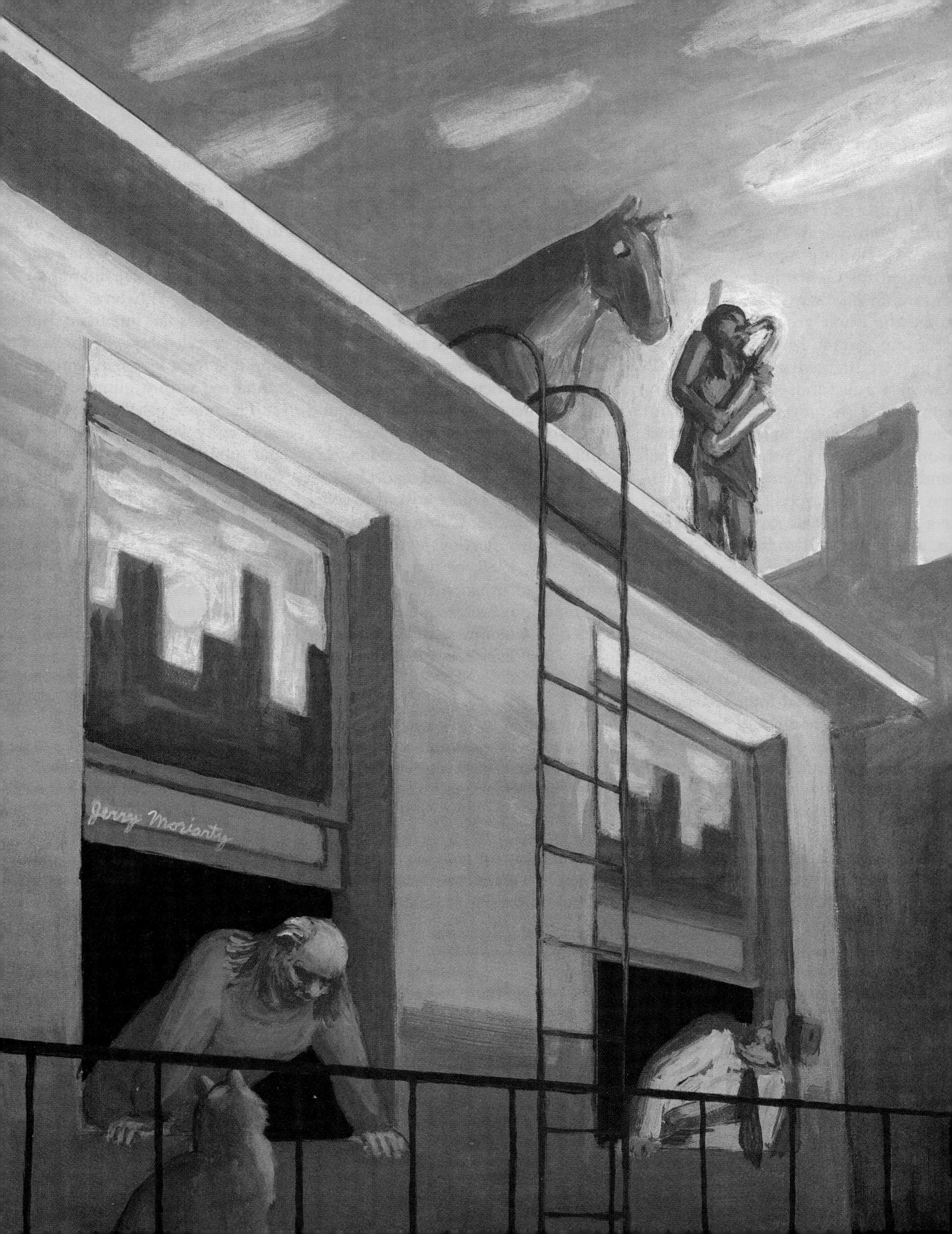
Jerry Moriarty

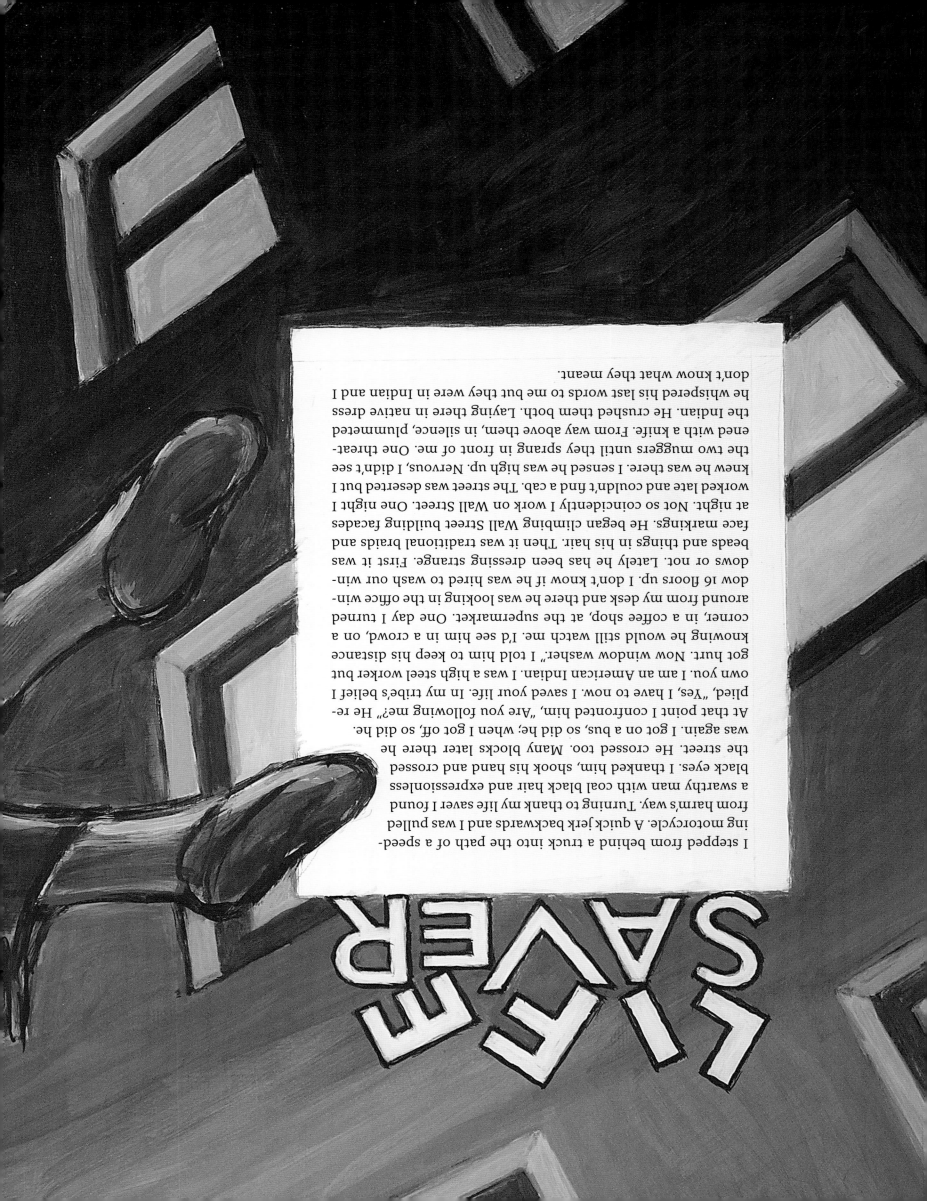

LIFE SAVER

I stepped from behind a truck into the path of a speed-ing motorcycle. A quick jerk backwards and I was pulled from harm's way. Turning to thank my life saver I found a swarthy man with coal black hair and expressionless black eyes. I thanked him, shook his hand and crossed the street. He crossed too. Many blocks later there he was again. I got on a bus, so did he; when I got off, so did he. At that point I confronted him, "Are you following me?" He re-plied, "Yes, I have to now. I saved your life. In my tribe's belief I own you. I am an American Indian. I was a high steel worker but got hurt. Now window washer." I told him to keep his distance knowing he would still watch me. I'd see him in a crowd, on a corner, in a coffee shop, at the supermarket. One day I turned around from my desk and there he was looking in the office win-dow 16 floors up. I don't know if he was hired to wash our win-dows or not. Lately he has been dressing strange. First it was beads and things in his hair. Then it was traditional braids and face markings. He began climbing Wall Street building facades at night. Not so coincidently I work on Wall Street. One night I worked late and couldn't find a cab. The street was deserted but I knew he was there. I sensed he was high up. Nervous, I didn't see the two muggers until they sprang in front of me. One threat-ened with a knife. From way above them, in silence, plummeted the Indian. He crushed them both. Laying there in native dress he whispered his last words to me but they were in Indian and I don't know what they meant.

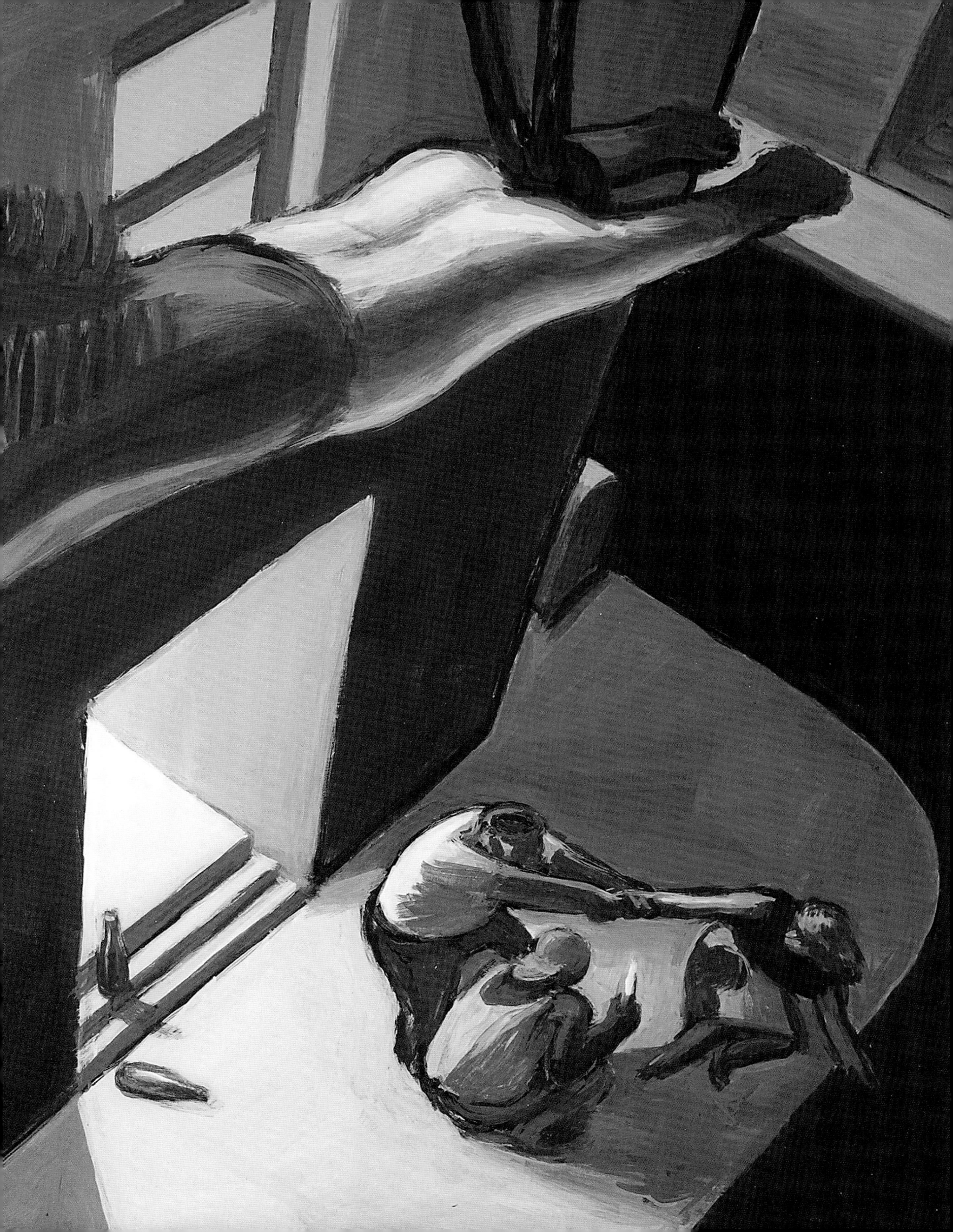

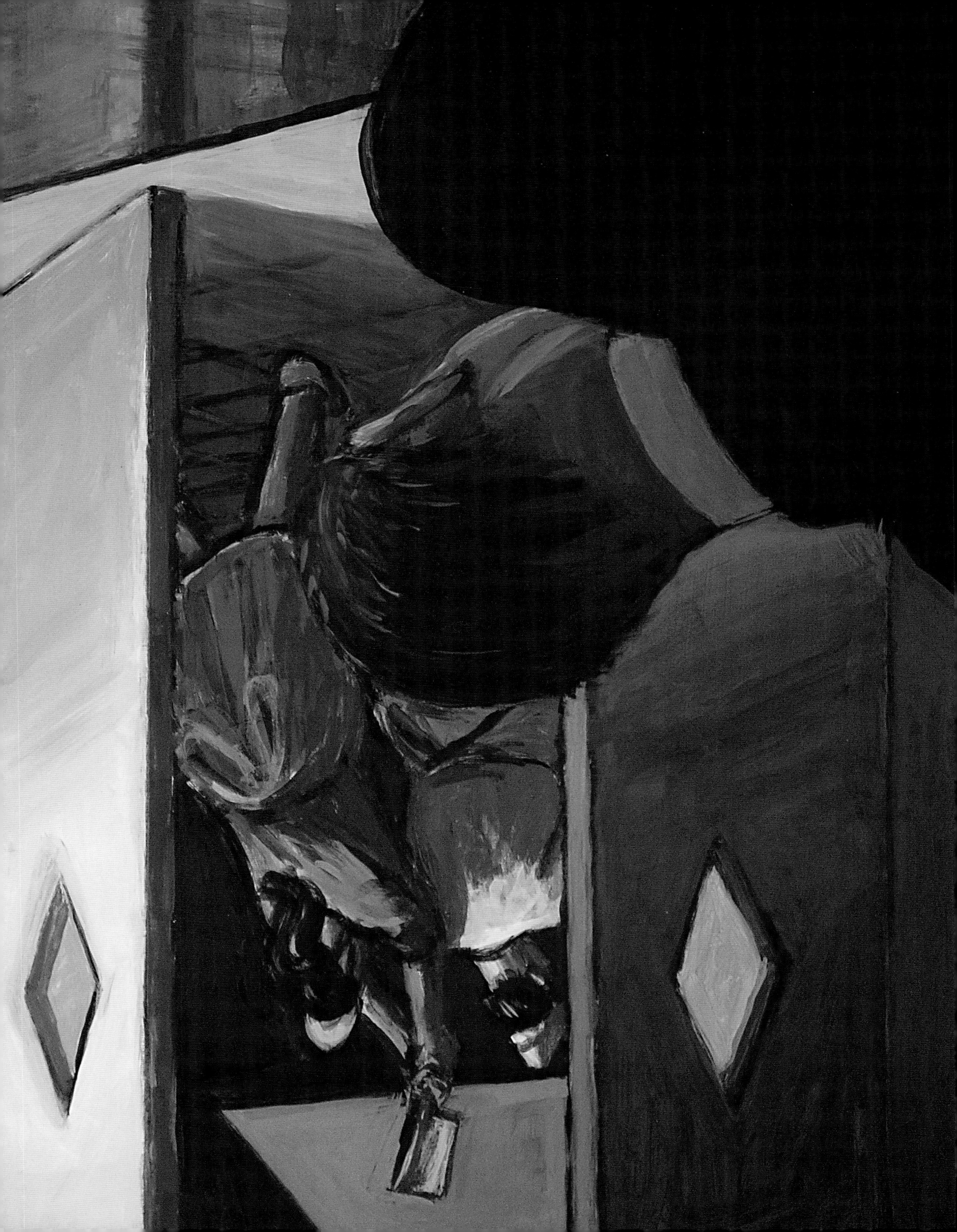

KILLER waitress

Sitting in a coffee shop with my friend discussing Wall Street and our puppet president. I happened to glance at the swinging door that went to the kitchen. It swung back and forth after a waitress left. Between the swings, to my horror, I saw a waitress creeping up behind the cook. In her raised hand was a meat cleaver. The door made small arcs showing the killer's progress like a strobe effect. I shouted desperately, "Look out! Cook out!" My friend leaped up unaware of what I was seeing. The door slammed shut. A moment passed when the killer waitress left the kitchen with an order, staring at my friend. The other waitress entered the kitchen and immediately came back out, untying her apron as she walked quickly into the street. That left my friend and I alone in the coffee shop except for the killer waitress. My friend still didn't know what caused my outburst. We had to pay her so she wrote out our check. She was cool, even pleasant. My friend and I gave good tips and left. I never went back there again and I haven't seen my friend since.

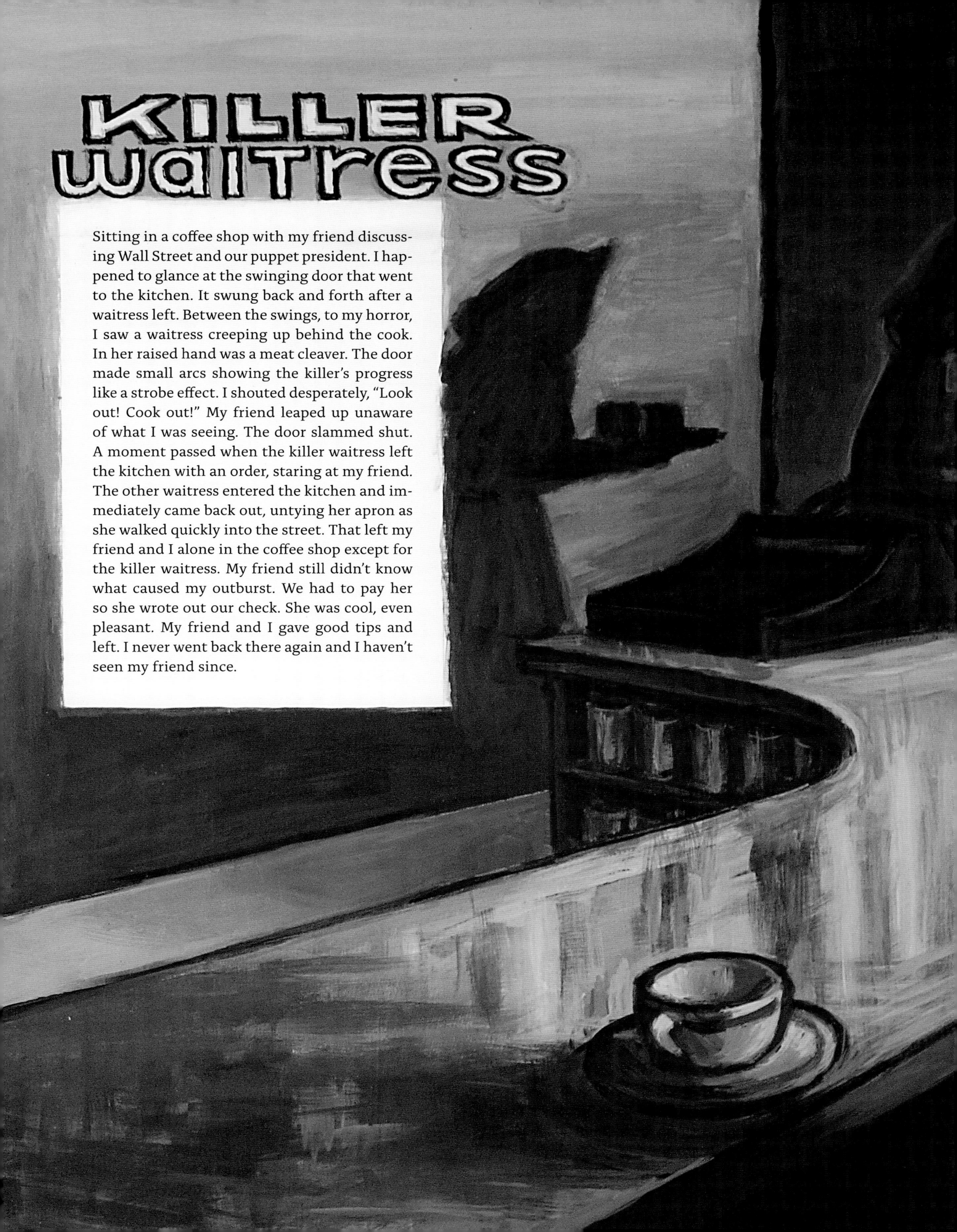

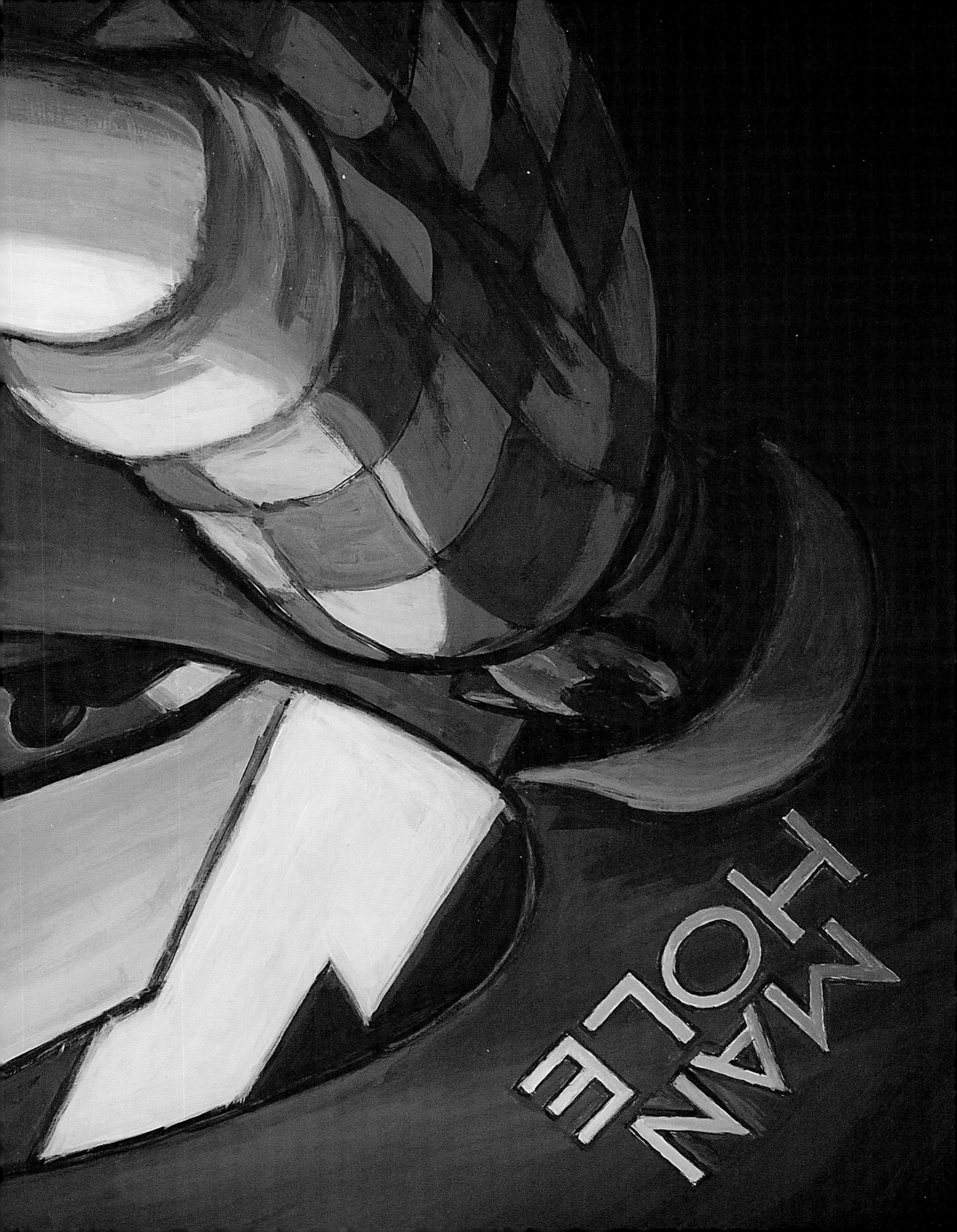
MAN
HOLE

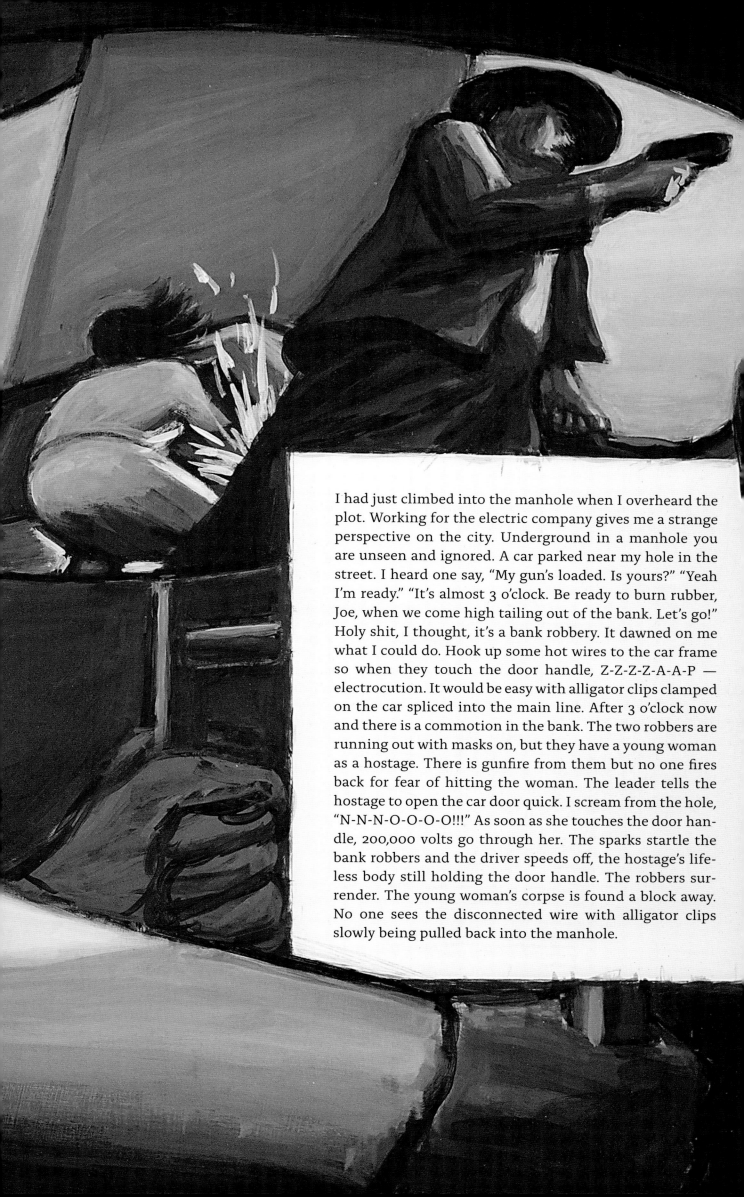

I had just climbed into the manhole when I overheard the plot. Working for the electric company gives me a strange perspective on the city. Underground in a manhole you are unseen and ignored. A car parked near my hole in the street. I heard one say, "My gun's loaded. Is yours?" "Yeah I'm ready." "It's almost 3 o'clock. Be ready to burn rubber, Joe, when we come high tailing out of the bank. Let's go!" Holy shit, I thought, it's a bank robbery. It dawned on me what I could do. Hook up some hot wires to the car frame so when they touch the door handle, Z-Z-Z-Z-A-A-P — electrocution. It would be easy with alligator clips clamped on the car spliced into the main line. After 3 o'clock now and there is a commotion in the bank. The two robbers are running out with masks on, but they have a young woman as a hostage. There is gunfire from them but no one fires back for fear of hitting the woman. The leader tells the hostage to open the car door quick. I scream from the hole, "N-N-N-O-O-O-O!!!" As soon as she touches the door handle, 200,000 volts go through her. The sparks startle the bank robbers and the driver speeds off, the hostage's lifeless body still holding the door handle. The robbers surrender. The young woman's corpse is found a block away. No one sees the disconnected wire with alligator clips slowly being pulled back into the manhole.

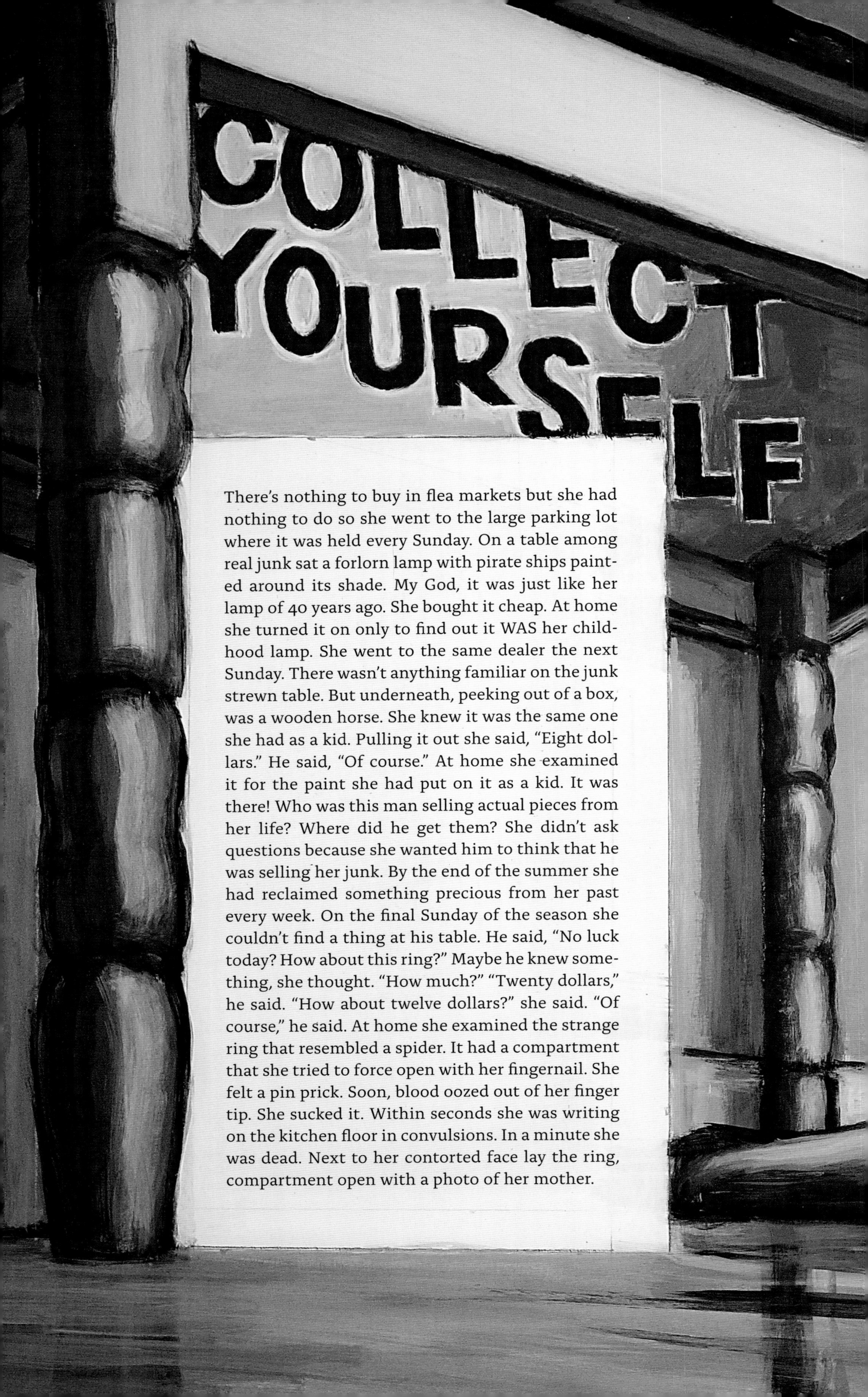
COLLECT
YOURSELF

There's nothing to buy in flea markets but she had nothing to do so she went to the large parking lot where it was held every Sunday. On a table among real junk sat a forlorn lamp with pirate ships painted around its shade. My God, it was just like her lamp of 40 years ago. She bought it cheap. At home she turned it on only to find out it WAS her childhood lamp. She went to the same dealer the next Sunday. There wasn't anything familiar on the junk strewn table. But underneath, peeking out of a box, was a wooden horse. She knew it was the same one she had as a kid. Pulling it out she said, "Eight dollars." He said, "Of course." At home she examined it for the paint she had put on it as a kid. It was there! Who was this man selling actual pieces from her life? Where did he get them? She didn't ask questions because she wanted him to think that he was selling her junk. By the end of the summer she had reclaimed something precious from her past every week. On the final Sunday of the season she couldn't find a thing at his table. He said, "No luck today? How about this ring?" Maybe he knew something, she thought. "How much?" "Twenty dollars," he said. "How about twelve dollars?" she said. "Of course," he said. At home she examined the strange ring that resembled a spider. It had a compartment that she tried to force open with her fingernail. She felt a pin prick. Soon, blood oozed out of her finger tip. She sucked it. Within seconds she was writing on the kitchen floor in convulsions. In a minute she was dead. Next to her contorted face lay the ring, compartment open with a photo of her mother.

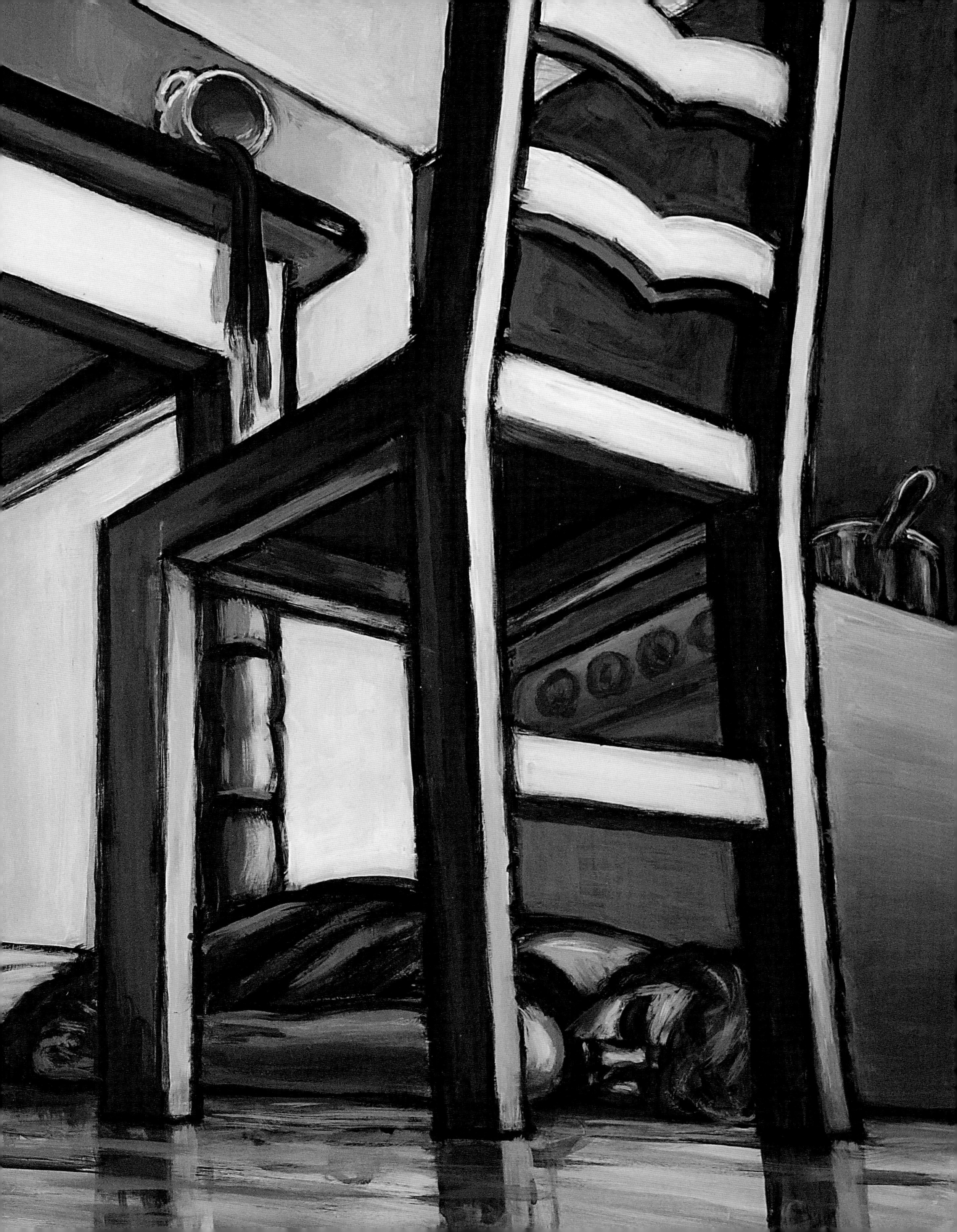

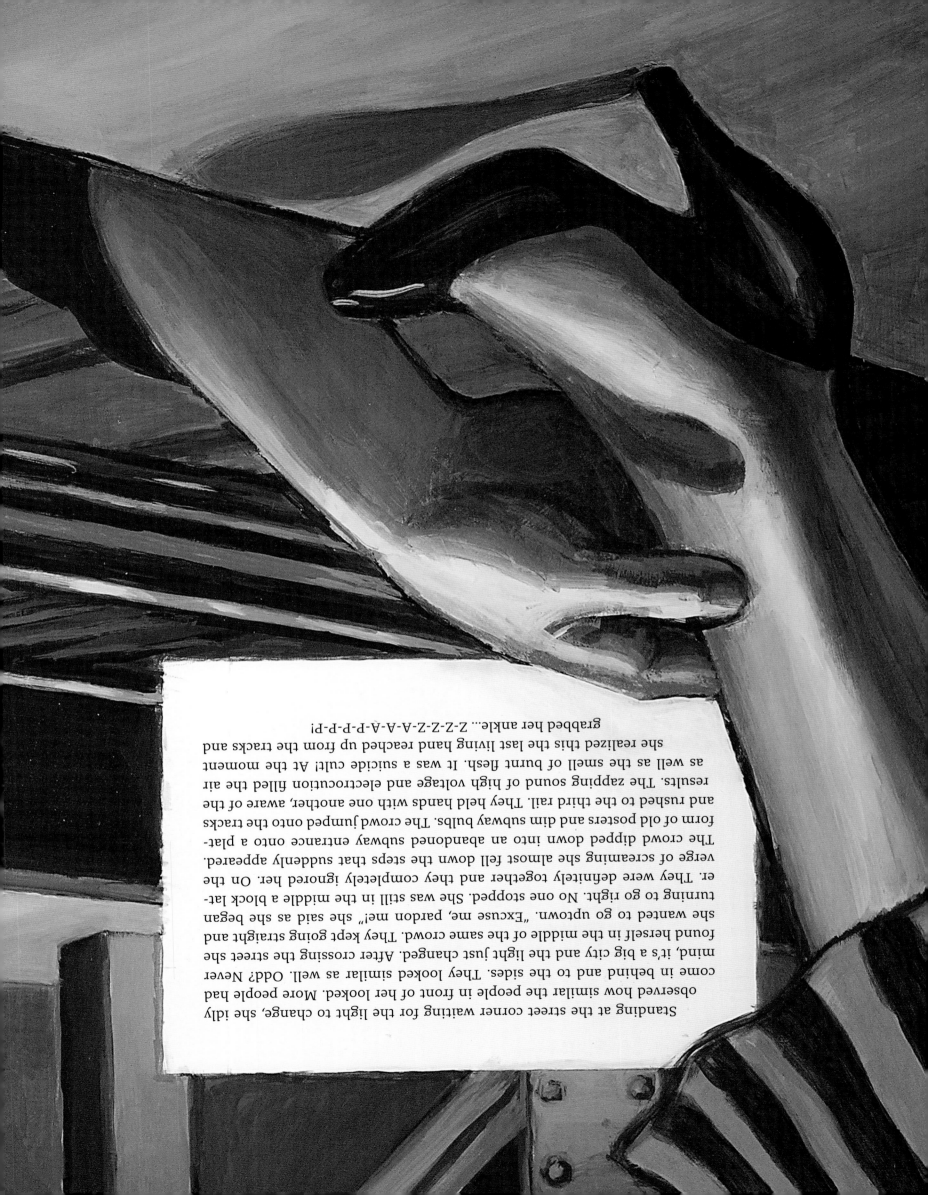

Standing at the street corner waiting for the light to change, she idly observed how similar the people in front of her looked. More people had come in behind and to the sides. They looked similar as well. Odd? Never mind, it's a big city and the light just changed. After crossing the street she found herself in the middle of the same crowd. They kept going straight and she wanted to go uptown. "Excuse me, pardon me!" she said as she began turning to go right. No one stopped. She was still in the middle a block later. They were definitely together and they completely ignored her. On the verge of screaming she almost fell down the steps that suddenly appeared. The crowd dipped down into an abandoned subway entrance onto a plat-form of old posters and dim subway bulbs. The crowd jumped onto the tracks and rushed to the third rail. They held hands with one another, aware of the results. The zapping sound of high voltage and electrocution filled the air as well as the smell of burnt flesh. It was a suicide cult! At the moment she realized this the last living hand reached up from the tracks and grabbed her ankle. Z-Z-Z-A-A-A-P-P-p-p-i...

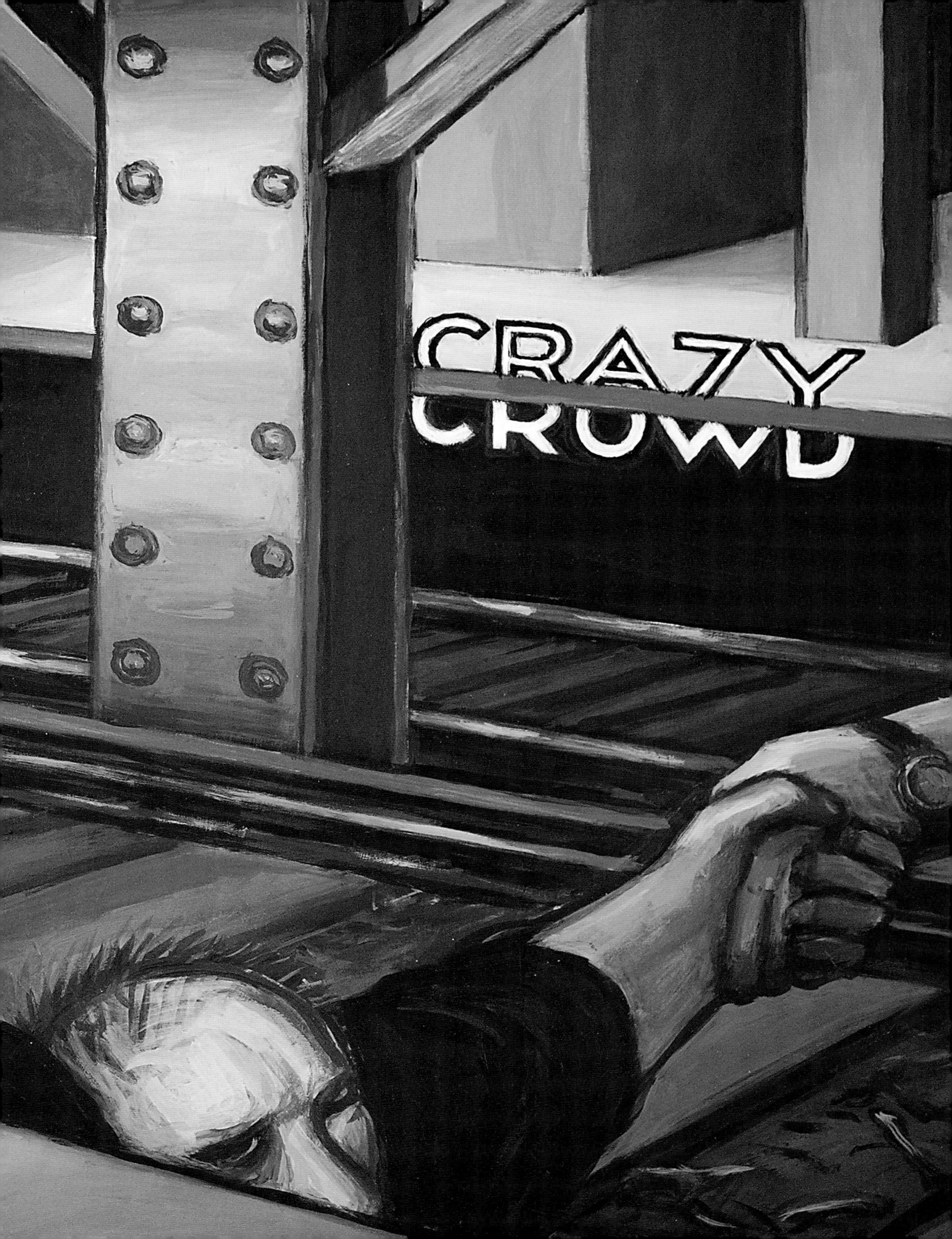
CRAZY
CROWD

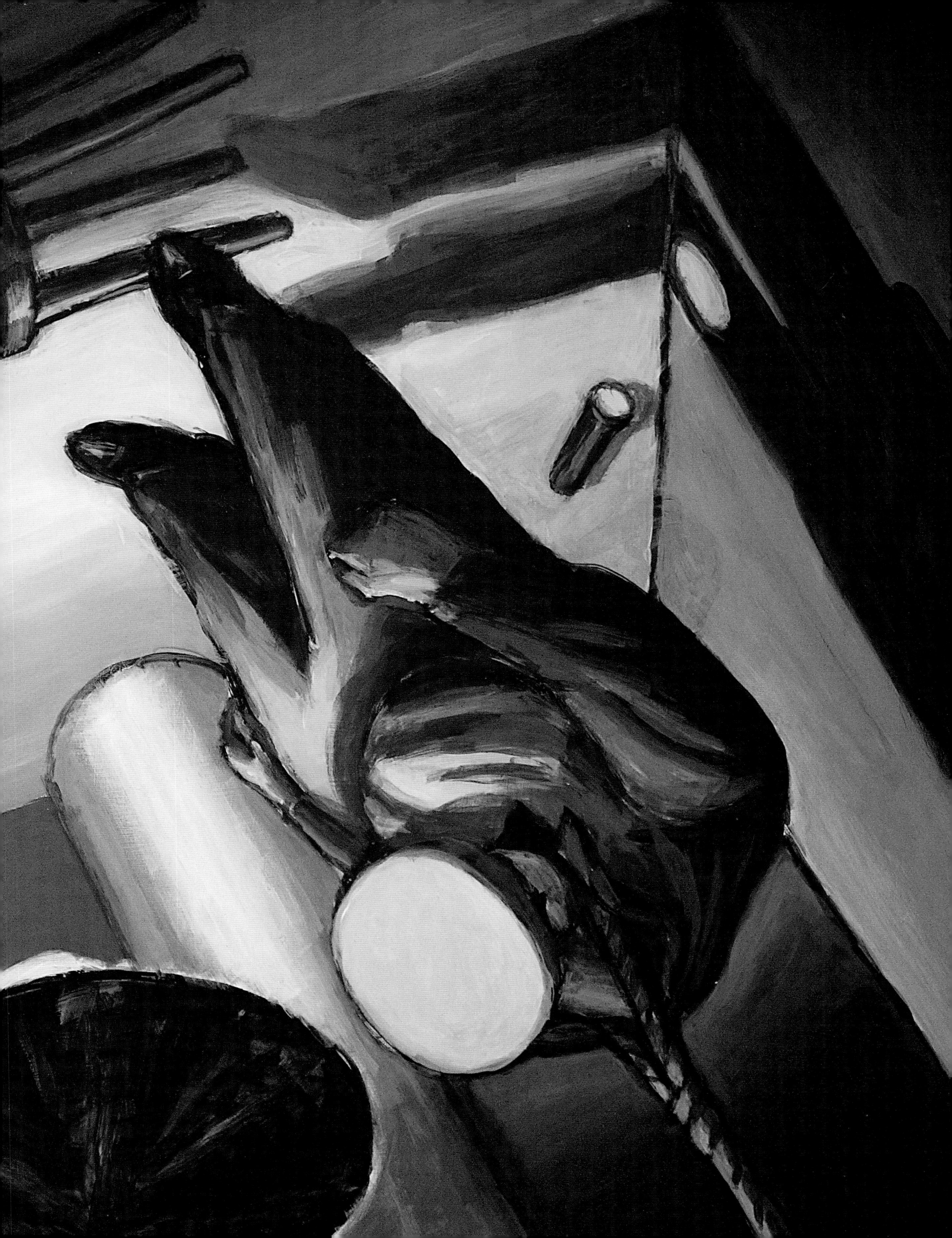

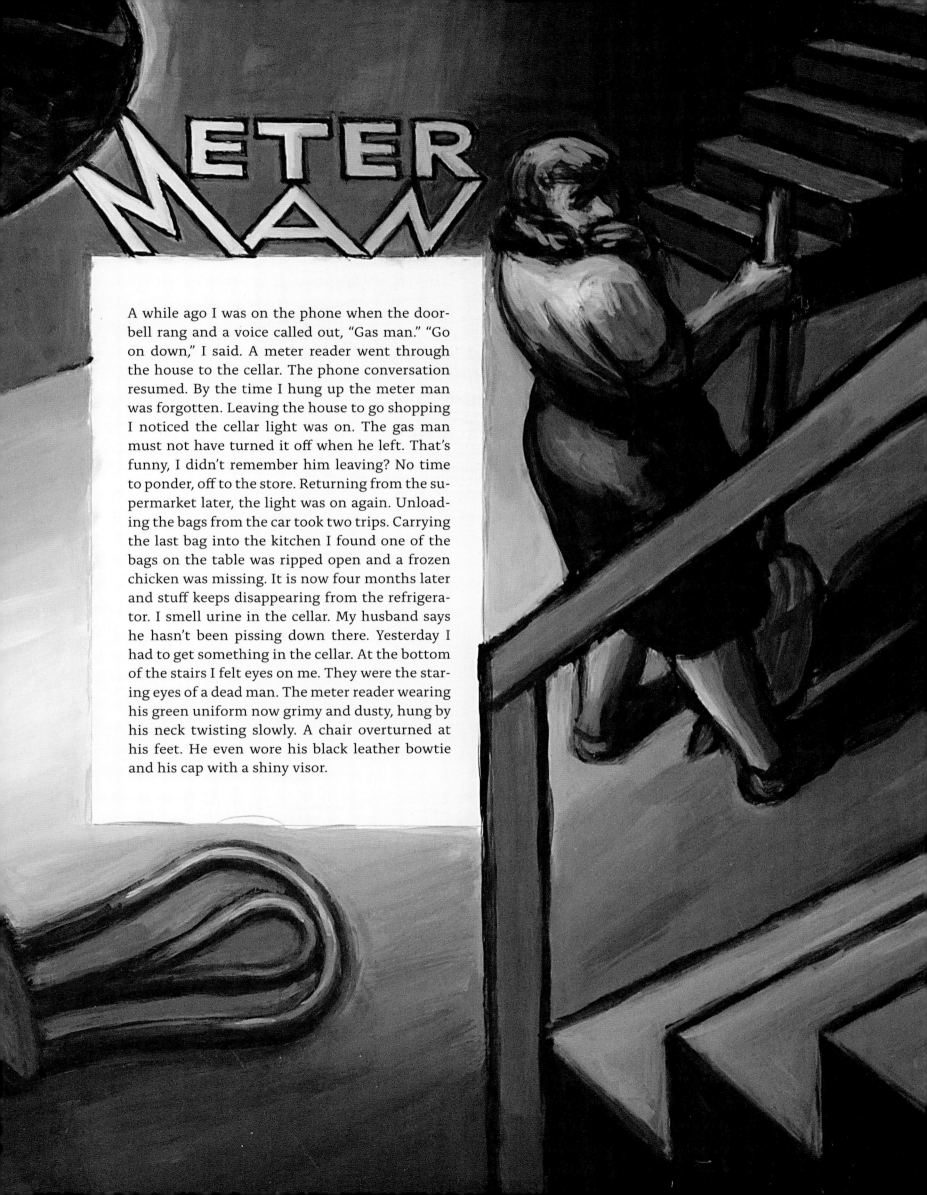

METER MAN

A while ago I was on the phone when the doorbell rang and a voice called out, "Gas man." "Go on down," I said. A meter reader went through the house to the cellar. The phone conversation resumed. By the time I hung up the meter man was forgotten. Leaving the house to go shopping I noticed the cellar light was on. The gas man must not have turned it off when he left. That's funny, I didn't remember him leaving? No time to ponder, off to the store. Returning from the supermarket later, the light was on again. Unloading the bags from the car took two trips. Carrying the last bag into the kitchen I found one of the bags on the table was ripped open and a frozen chicken was missing. It is now four months later and stuff keeps disappearing from the refrigerator. I smell urine in the cellar. My husband says he hasn't been pissing down there. Yesterday I had to get something in the cellar. At the bottom of the stairs I felt eyes on me. They were the staring eyes of a dead man. The meter reader wearing his green uniform now grimy and dusty, hung by his neck twisting slowly. A chair overturned at his feet. He even wore his black leather bowtie and his cap with a shiny visor.

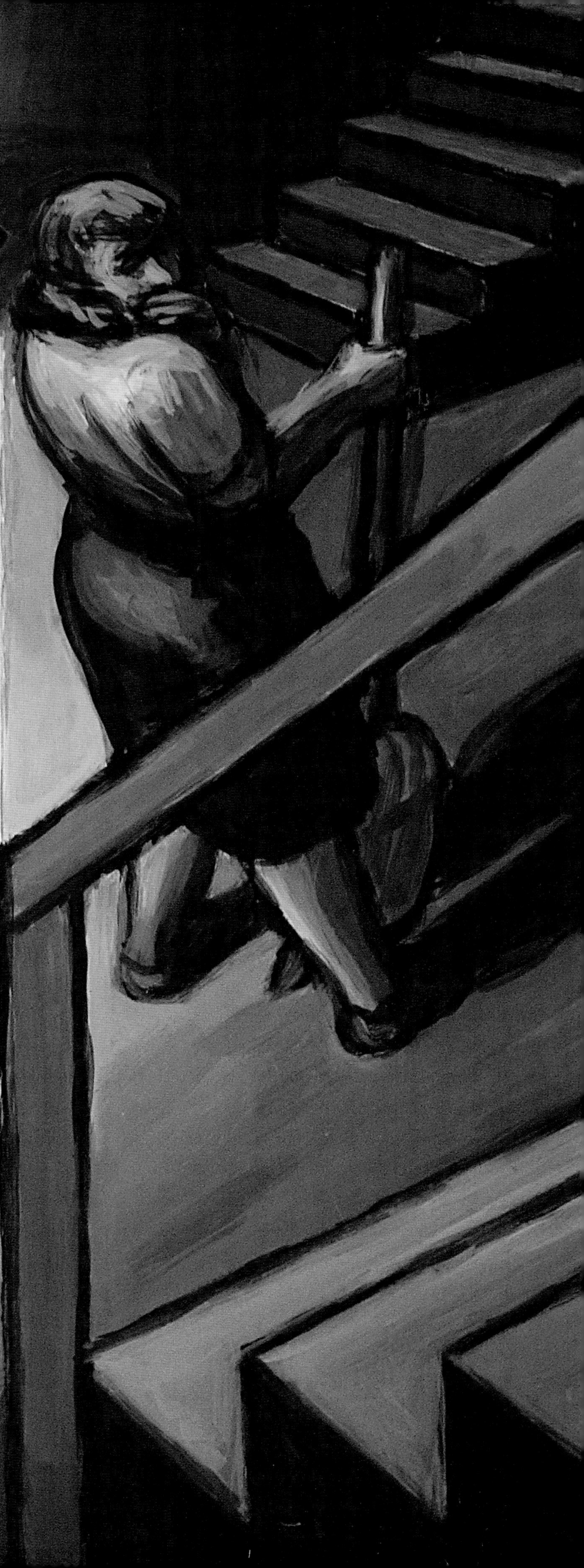

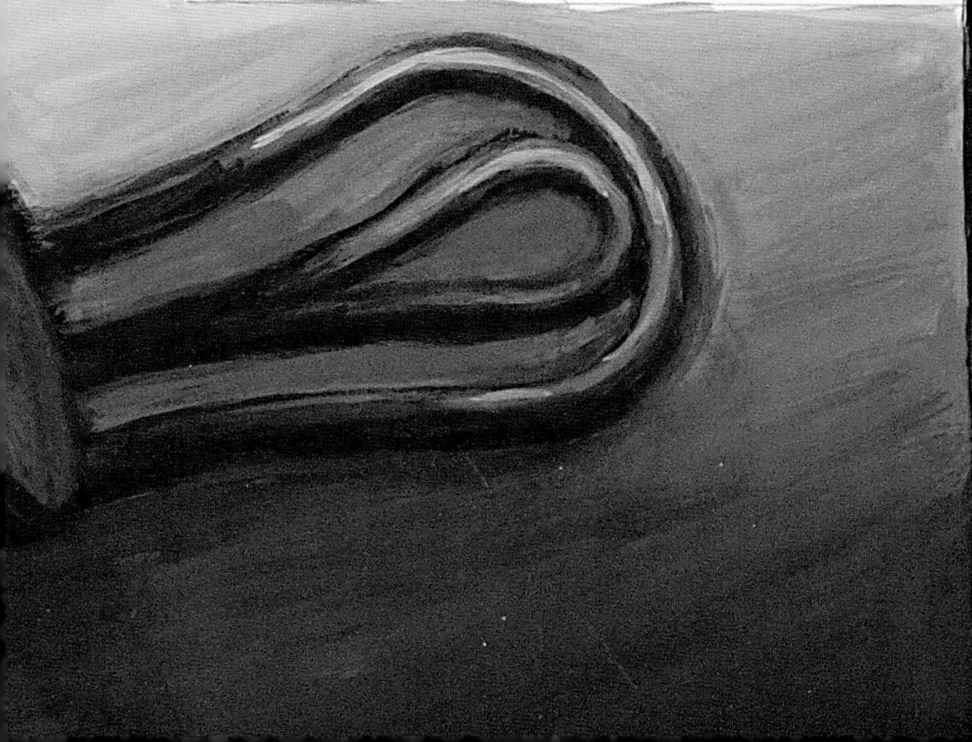

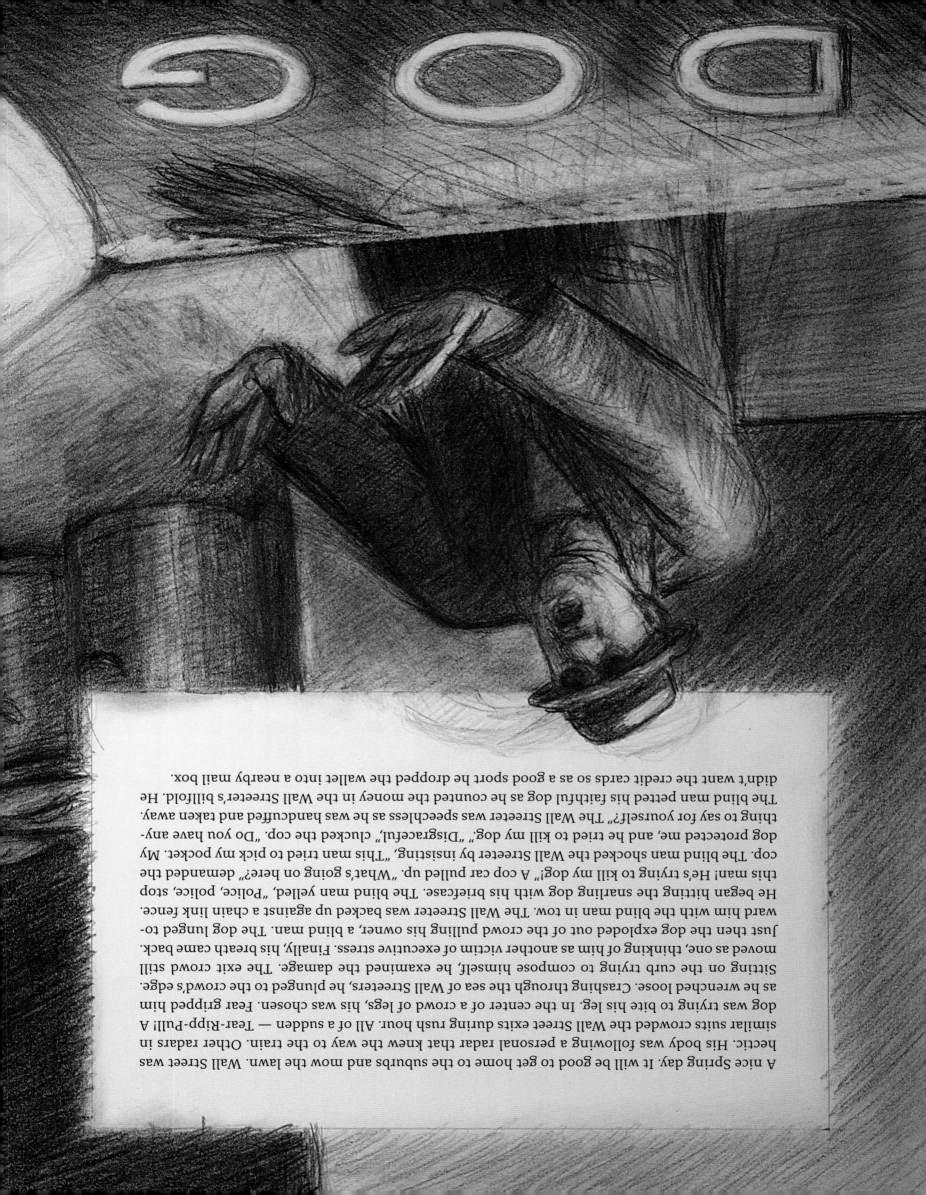

DOG

A nice Spring day. It will be good to get home to the suburbs and mow the lawn. Wall Street was hectic. His body was following a personal radar that knew the way to the train. Other radars in similar suits crowded the Wall Street exits during rush hour. All of a sudden — Tear-Ripp-Pull! A dog was trying to bite his leg. In the center of a crowd of legs, his was chosen. Fear gripped him as he wrenched loose. Crashing through the sea of Wall Streeters, he plunged to the crowd's edge. Sitting on the curb trying to compose himself, he examined the damage. The exit crowd still moved as one, thinking of him as another victim of executive stress. Finally, his breath came back. Just then the dog exploded out of the crowd pulling his owner, a blind man. The dog lunged toward him with the blind man in tow. The Wall Streeter was backed up against a chain link fence. He began hitting the snarling dog with his briefcase. The blind man yelled, "Police, police, stop this man! He's trying to kill my dog!" A cop car pulled up. "What's going on here?" demanded the cop. The blind man shocked the Wall Streeter by insisting, "This man tried to pick my pocket. My dog protected me, and he tried to kill my dog." "Disgraceful," clucked the cop. "Do you have anything to say for yourself?" The Wall Streeter was speechless as he was handcuffed and taken away. The blind man petted his faithful dog as he counted the money in the Wall Streeter's billfold. He didn't want the credit cards so as a good sport he dropped the wallet into a nearby mail box.

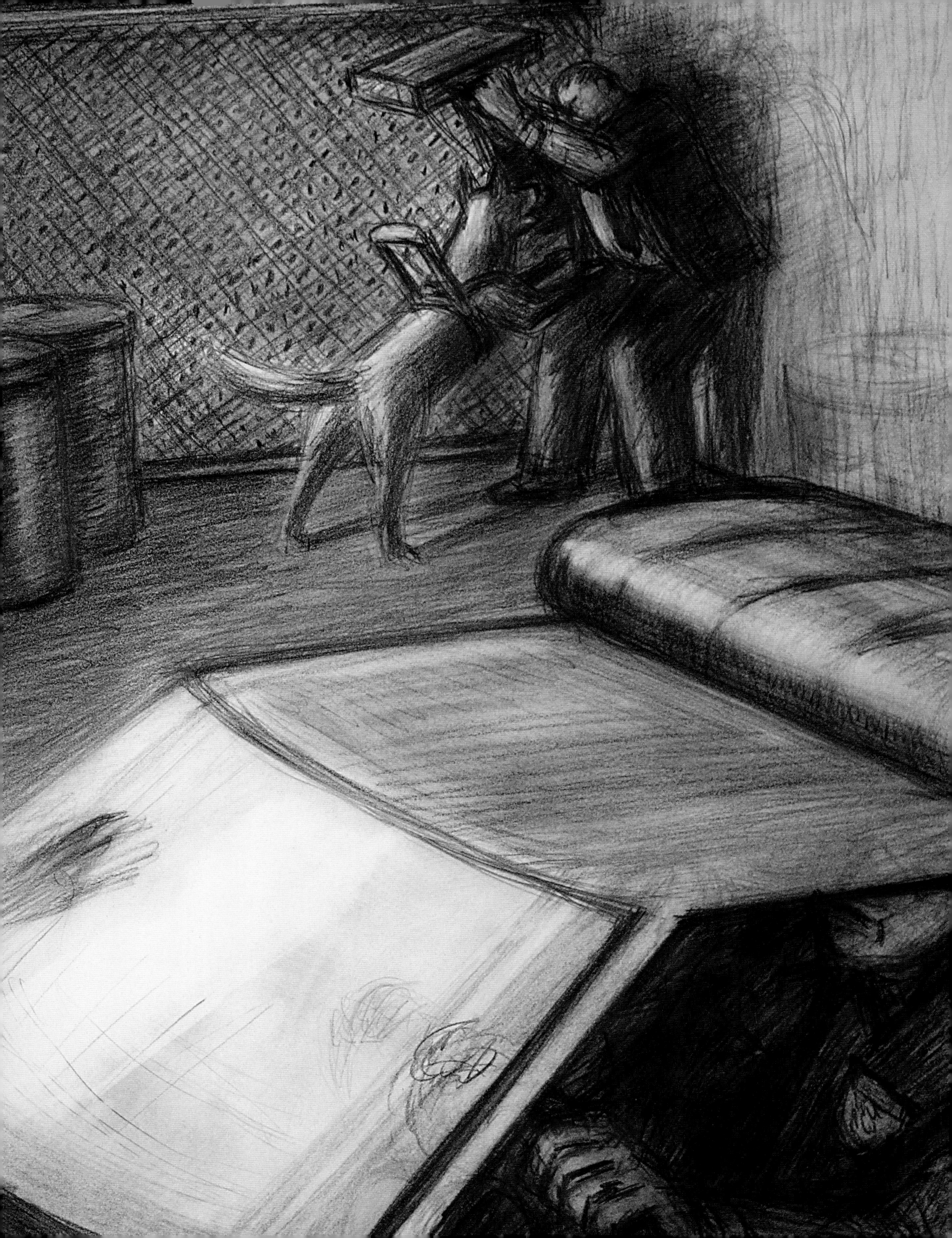

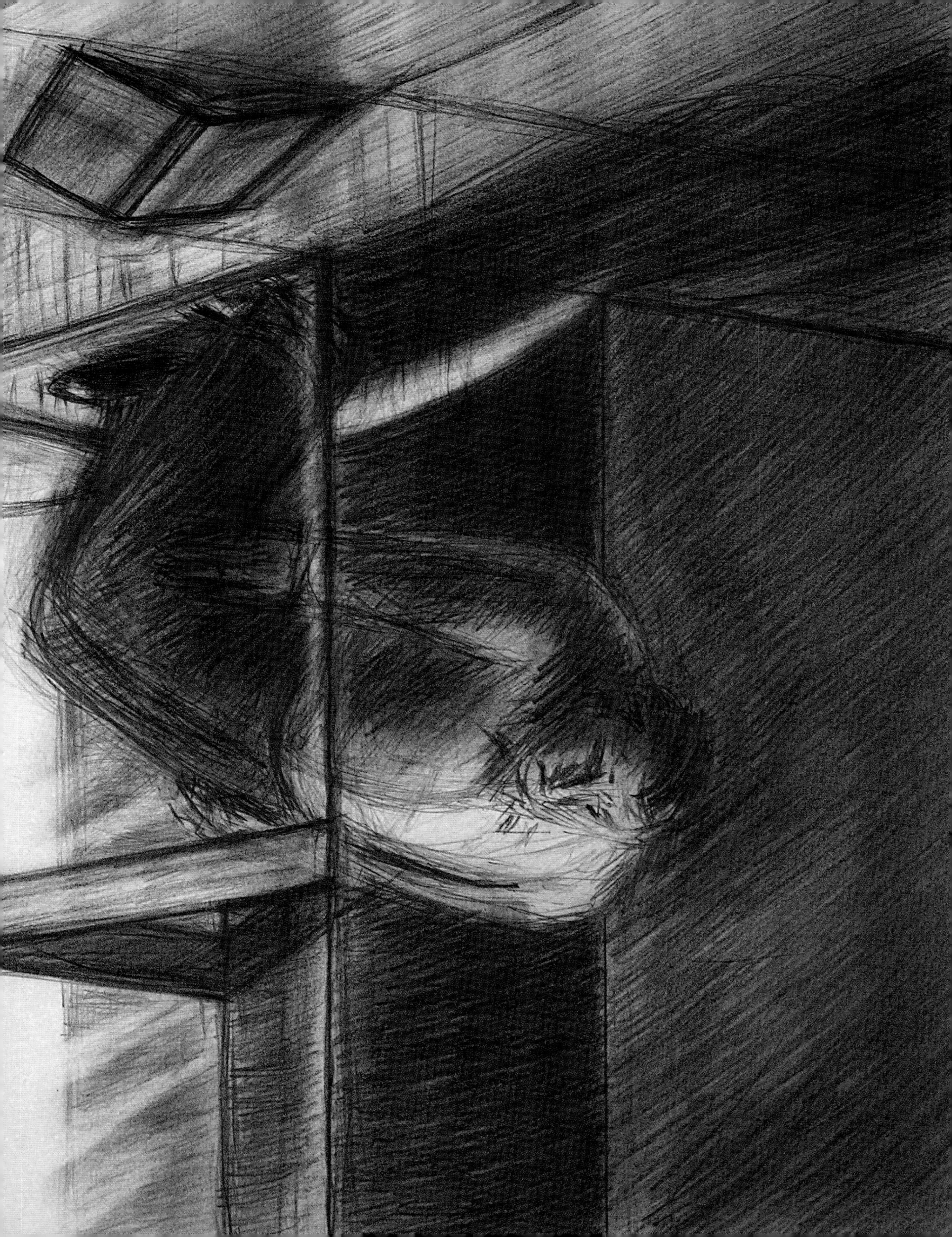

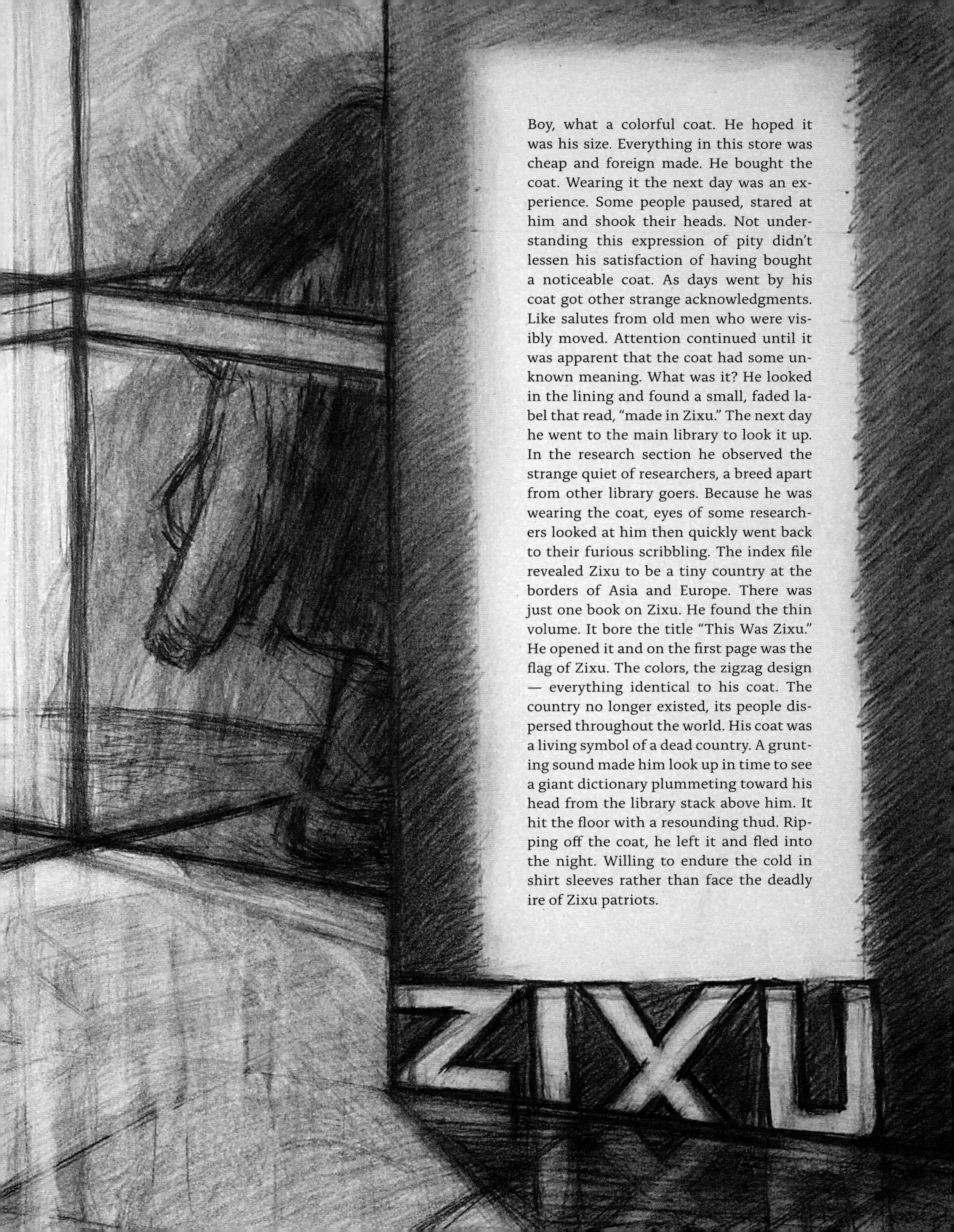
ZIXU

Boy, what a colorful coat. He hoped it was his size. Everything in this store was cheap and foreign made. He bought the coat. Wearing it the next day was an experience. Some people paused, stared at him and shook their heads. Not understanding this expression of pity didn't lessen his satisfaction of having bought a noticeable coat. As days went by his coat got other strange acknowledgments. Like salutes from old men who were visibly moved. Attention continued until it was apparent that the coat had some unknown meaning. What was it? He looked in the lining and found a small, faded label that read, "made in Zixu." The next day he went to the main library to look it up. In the research section he observed the strange quiet of researchers, a breed apart from other library goers. Because he was wearing the coat, eyes of some researchers looked at him then quickly went back to their furious scribbling. The index file revealed Zixu to be a tiny country at the borders of Asia and Europe. There was just one book on Zixu. He found the thin volume. It bore the title "This Was Zixu." He opened it and on the first page was the flag of Zixu. The colors, the zigzag design — everything identical to his coat. The country no longer existed, its people dispersed throughout the world. His coat was a living symbol of a dead country. A grunting sound made him look up in time to see a giant dictionary plummeting toward his head from the library stack above him. It hit the floor with a resounding thud. Ripping off the coat, he left it and fled into the night. Willing to endure the cold in shirt sleeves rather than face the deadly ire of Zixu patriots.

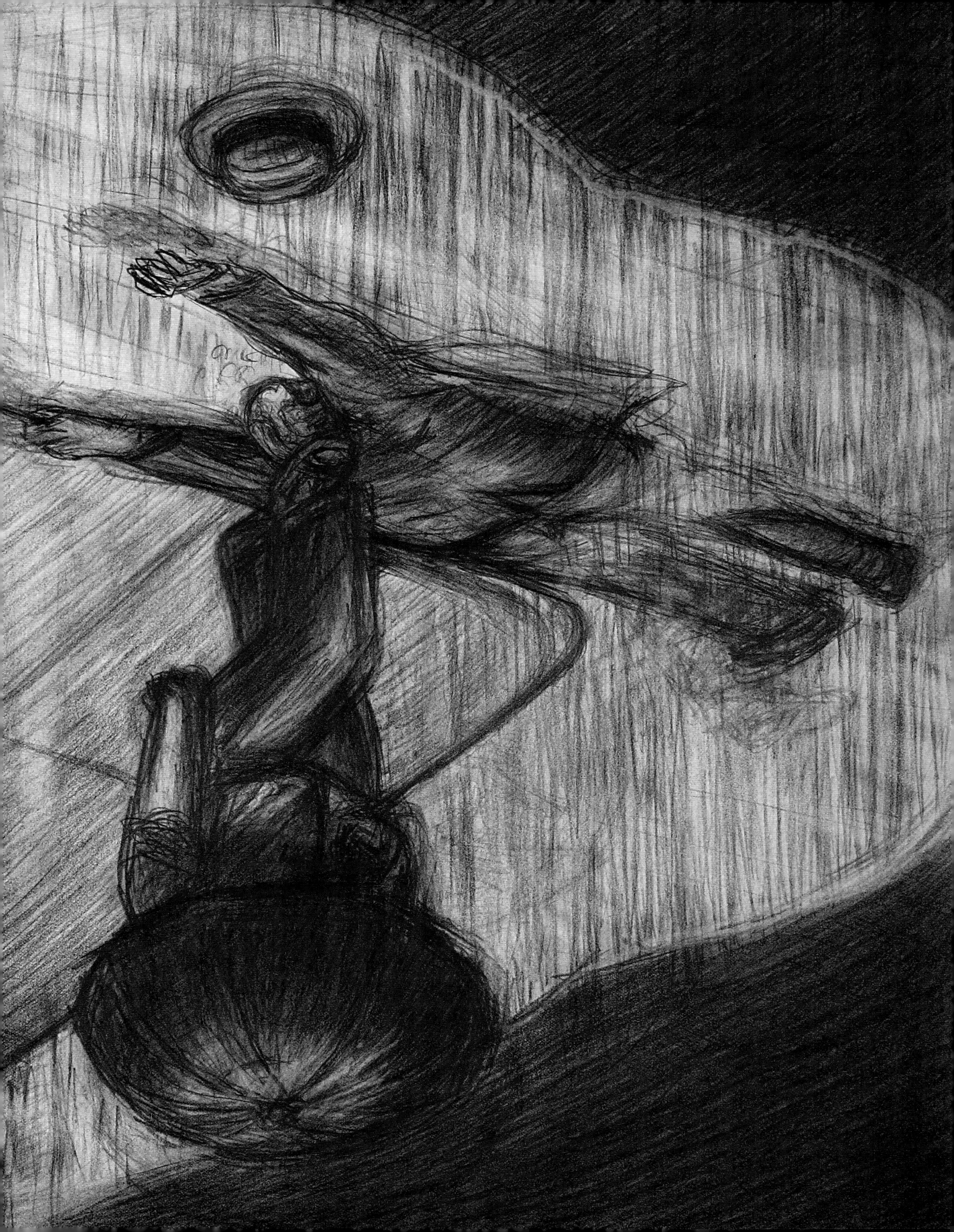

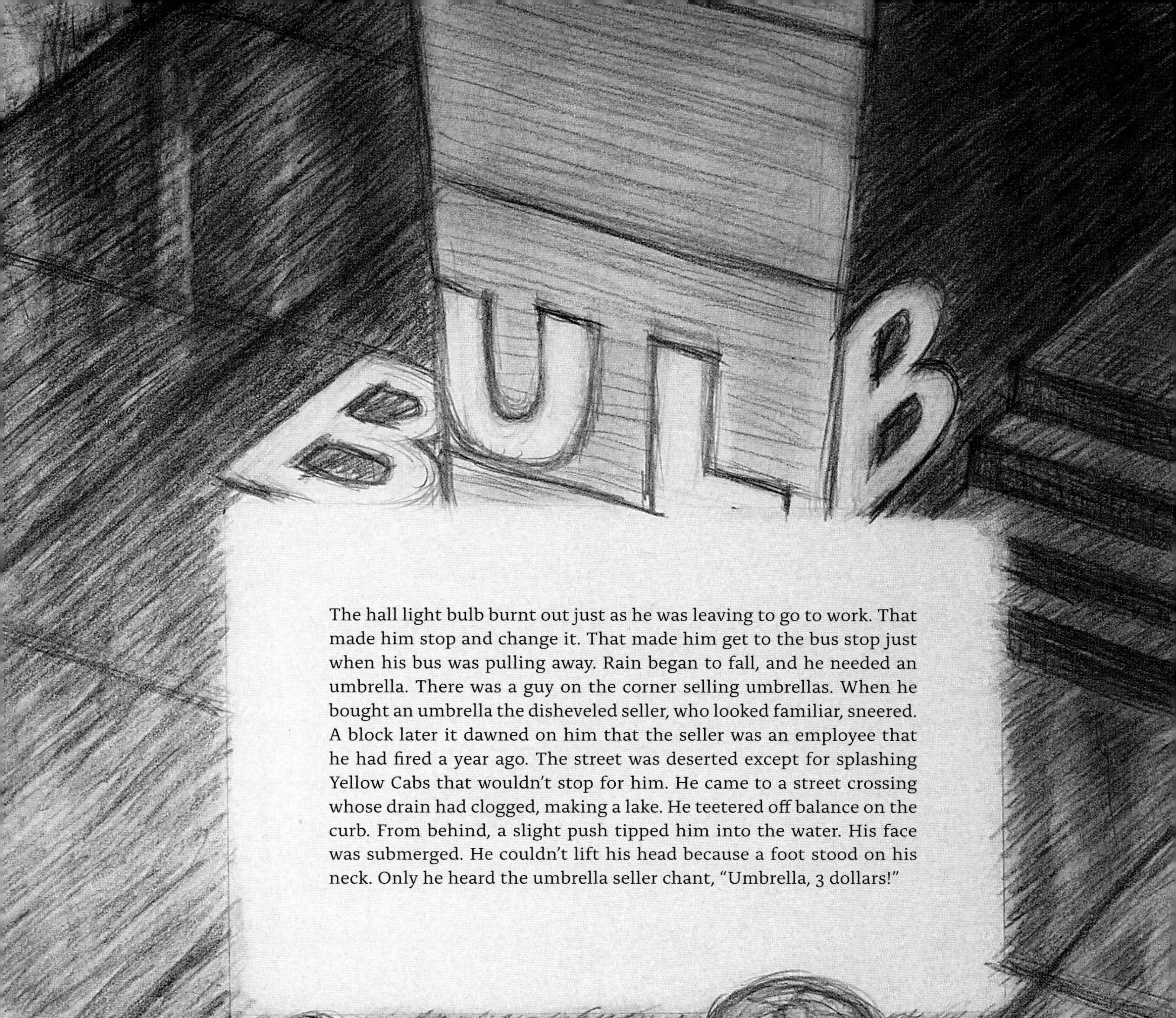
BULB

The hall light bulb burnt out just as he was leaving to go to work. That made him stop and change it. That made him get to the bus stop just when his bus was pulling away. Rain began to fall, and he needed an umbrella. There was a guy on the corner selling umbrellas. When he bought an umbrella the disheveled seller, who looked familiar, sneered. A block later it dawned on him that the seller was an employee that he had fired a year ago. The street was deserted except for splashing Yellow Cabs that wouldn't stop for him. He came to a street crossing whose drain had clogged, making a lake. He teetered off balance on the curb. From behind, a slight push tipped him into the water. His face was submerged. He couldn't lift his head because a foot stood on his neck. Only he heard the umbrella seller chant, "Umbrella, 3 dollars!"

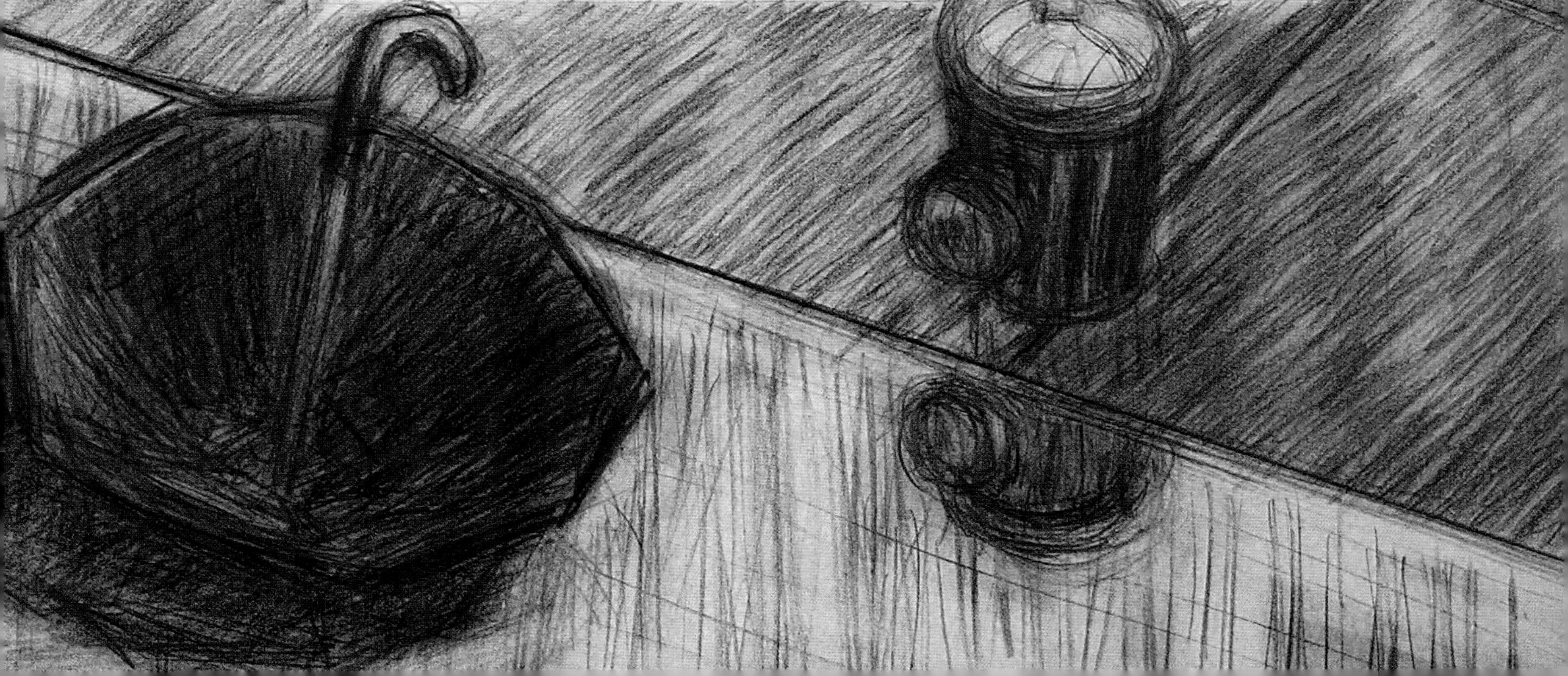

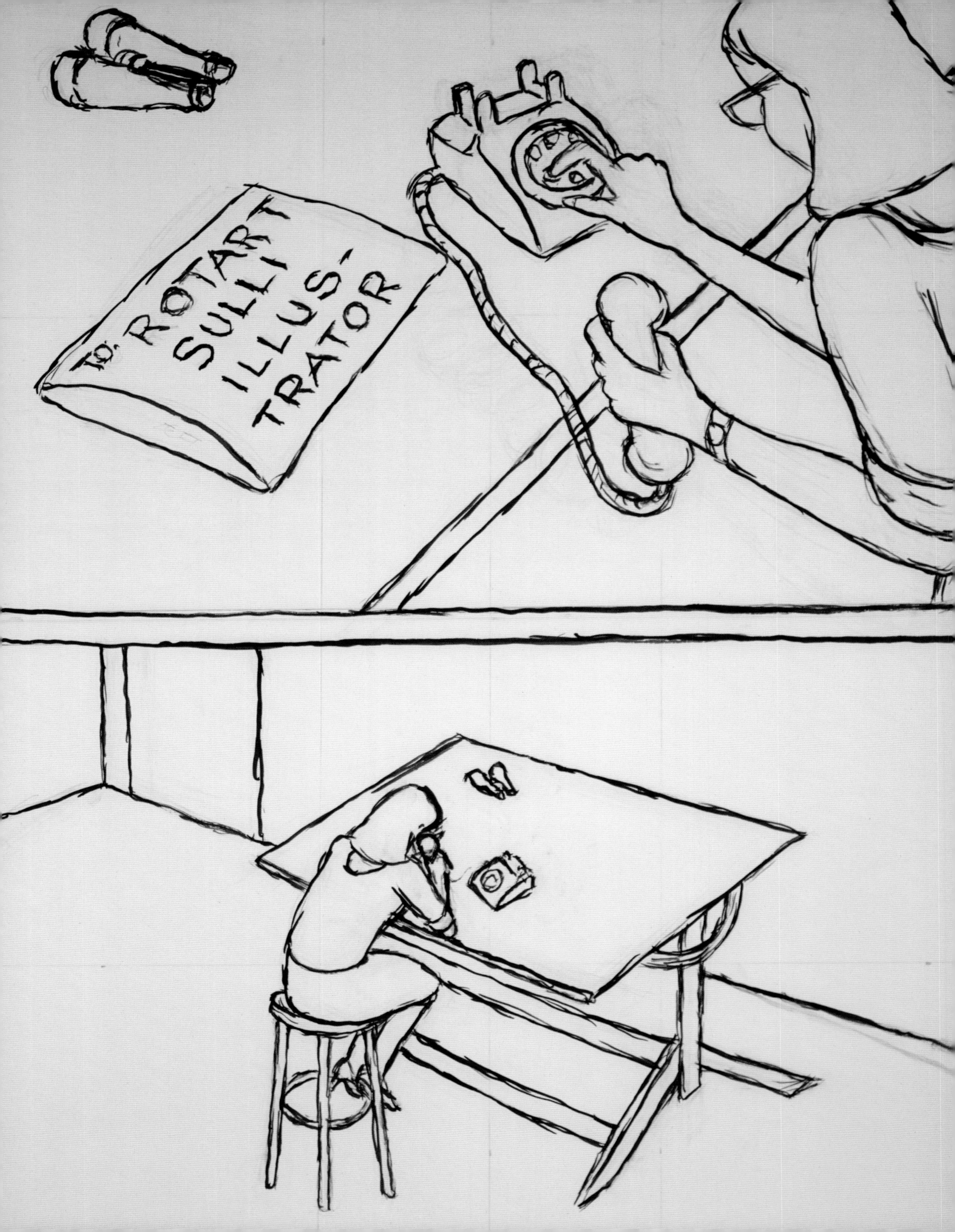
TO: ROTART SULLI ILLUS-TRATOR

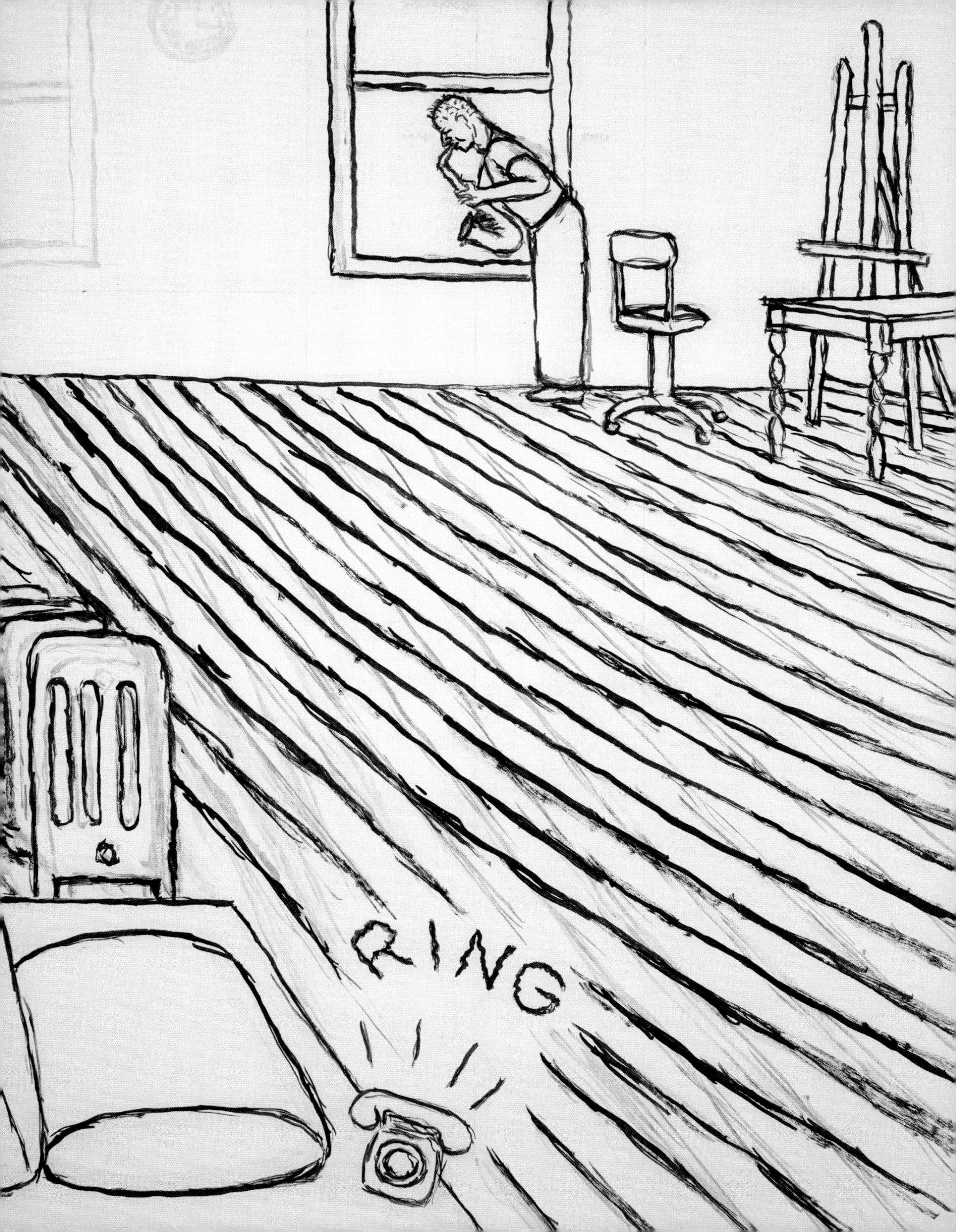
RING

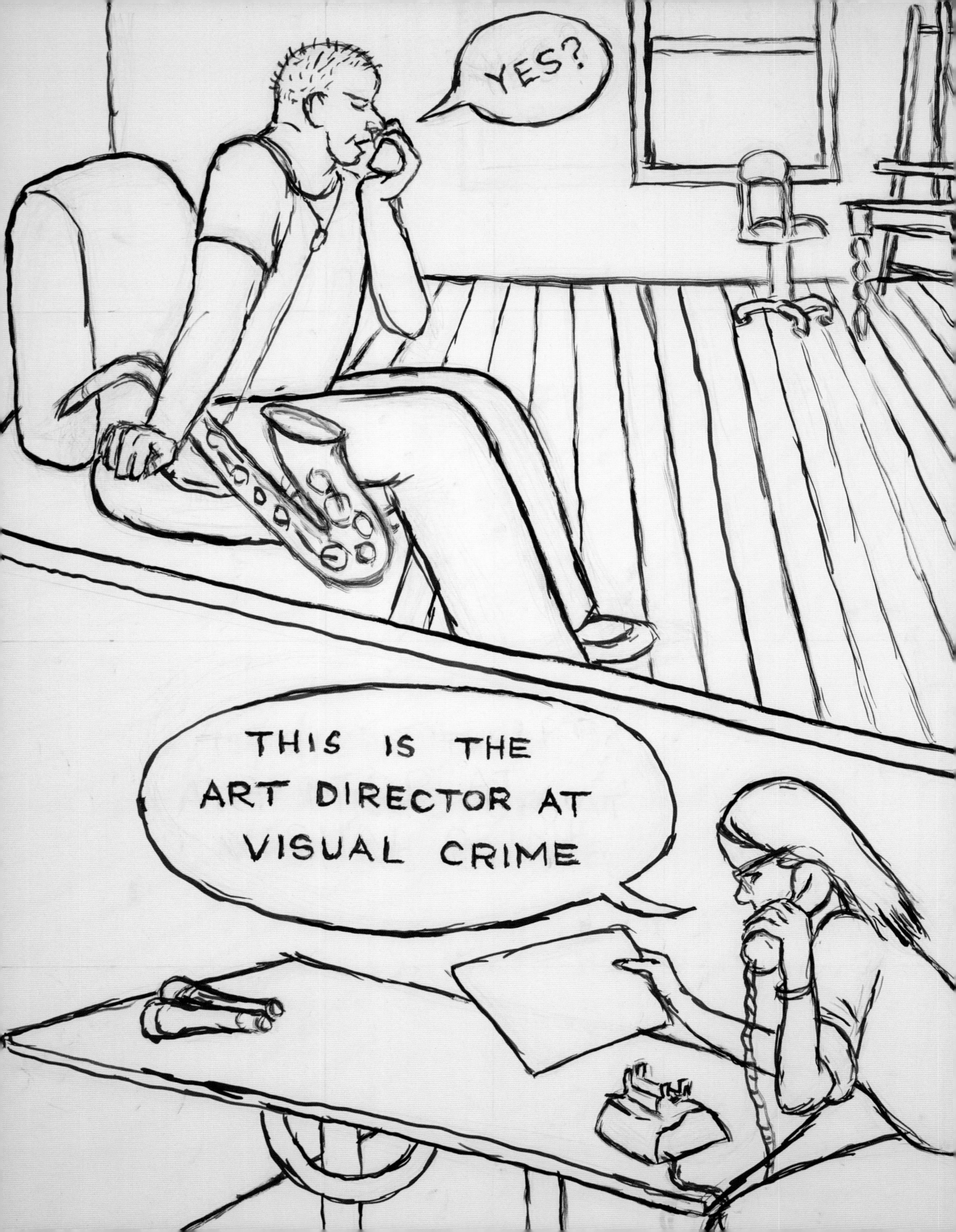
YES?
THIS IS THE ART DIRECTOR AT VISUAL CRIME

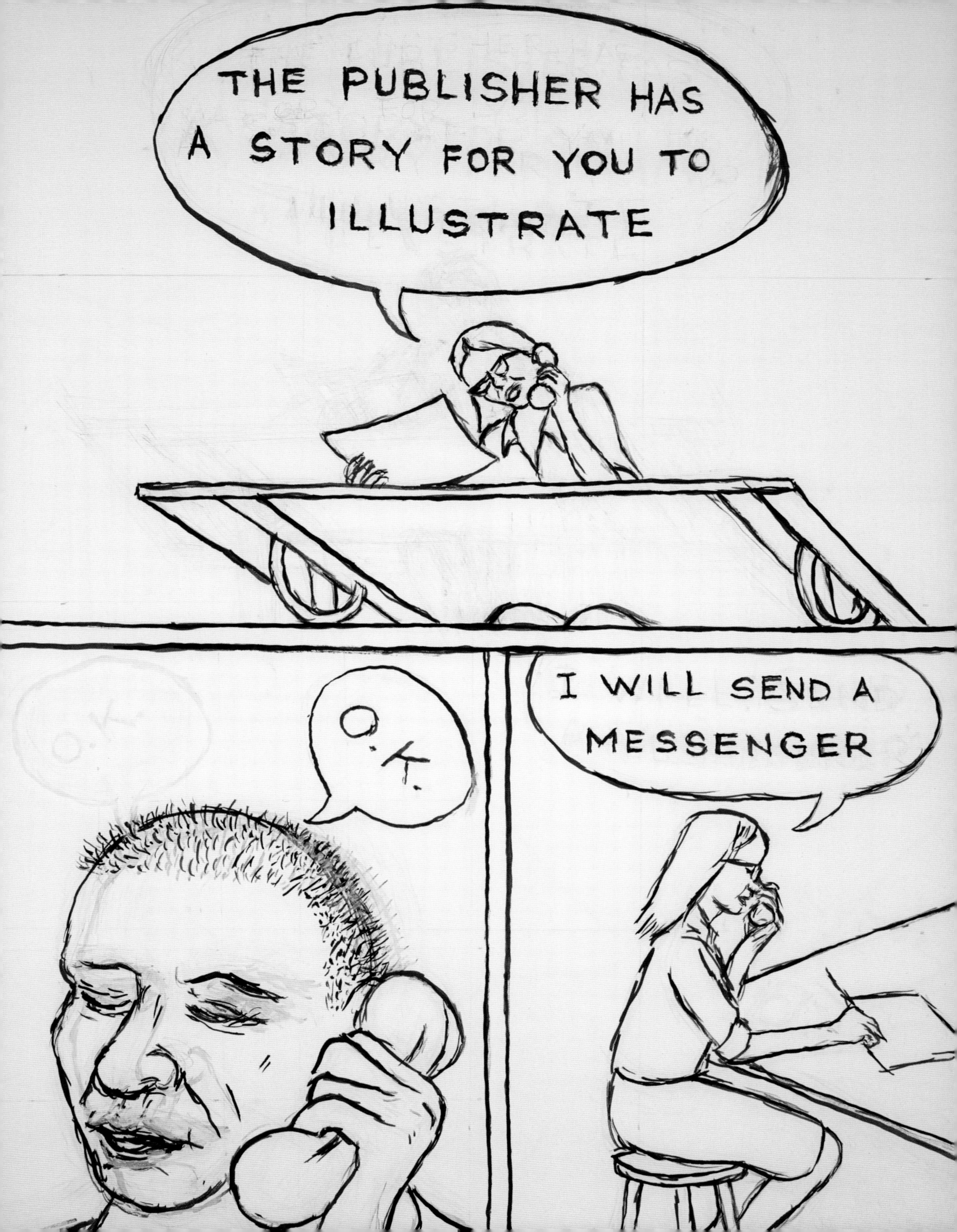
THE PUBLISHER HAS A STORY FOR YOU TO ILLUSTRATE
O.K.
I WILL SEND A MESSENGER

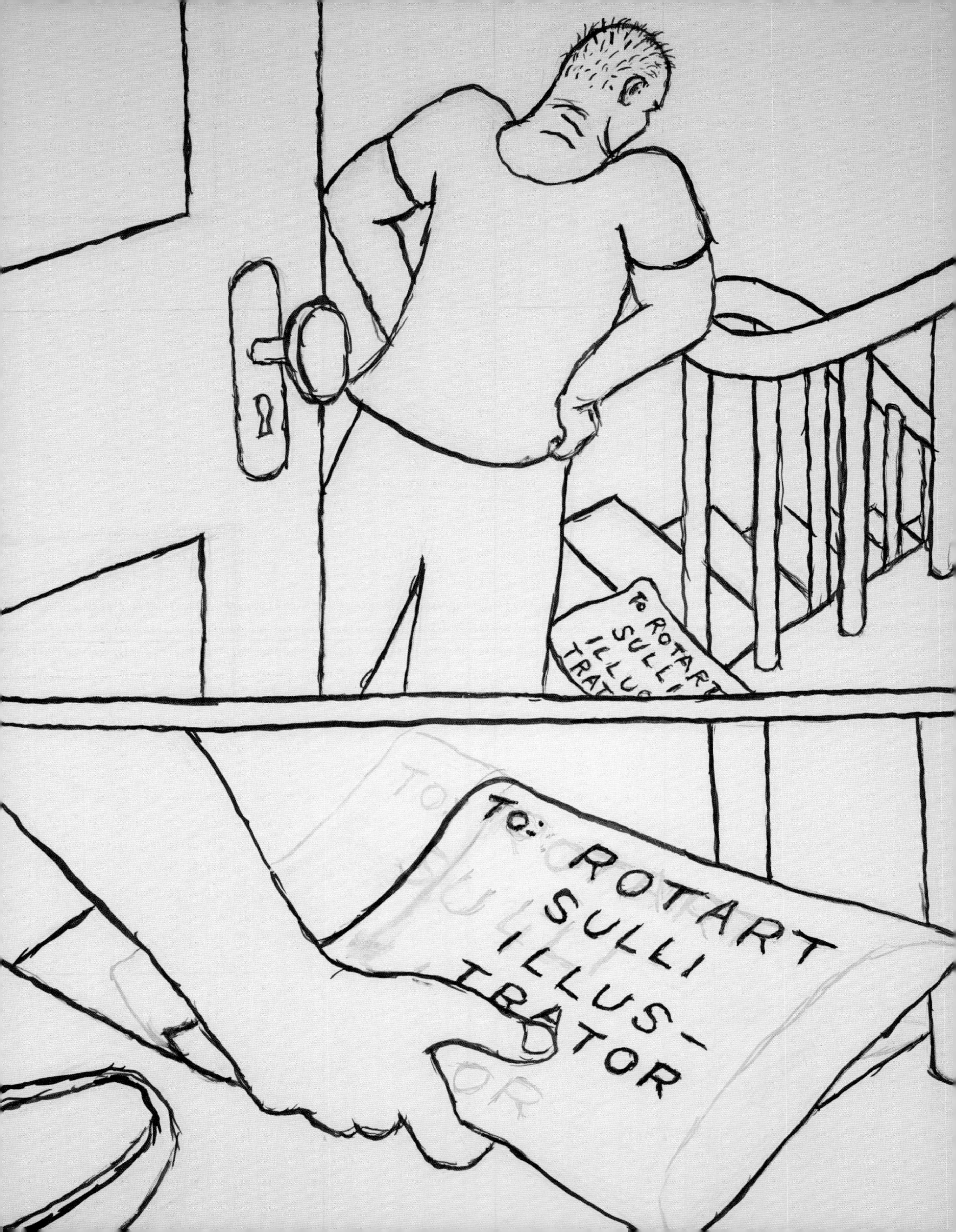
To ROTART
SULLI
To: ROTART
SULLI
ILLUS-
TRATOR

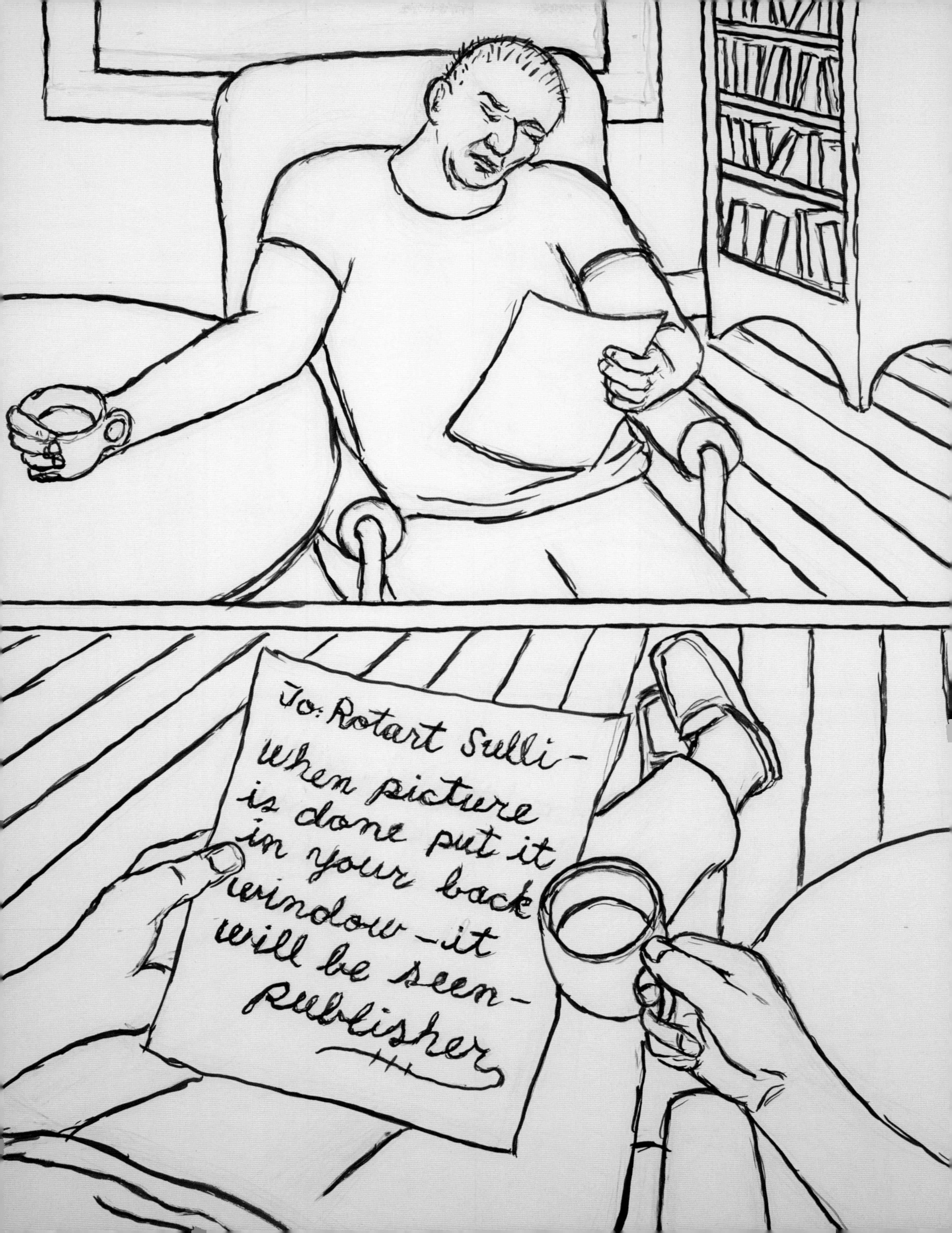
To: Rotart Sulli-
When picture
is done put it
in your back
window-it
will be seen-
Publisher

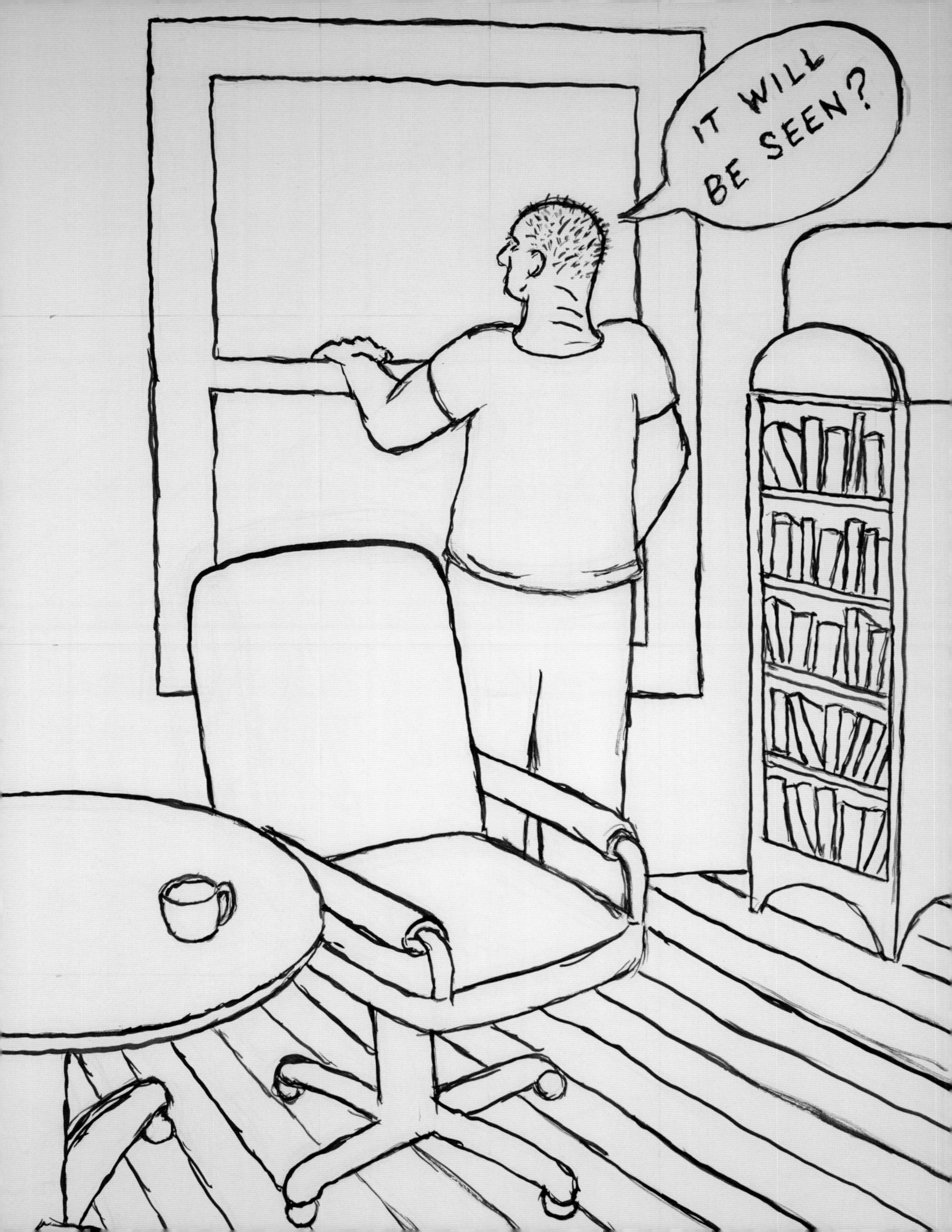
IT WILL BE SEEN?

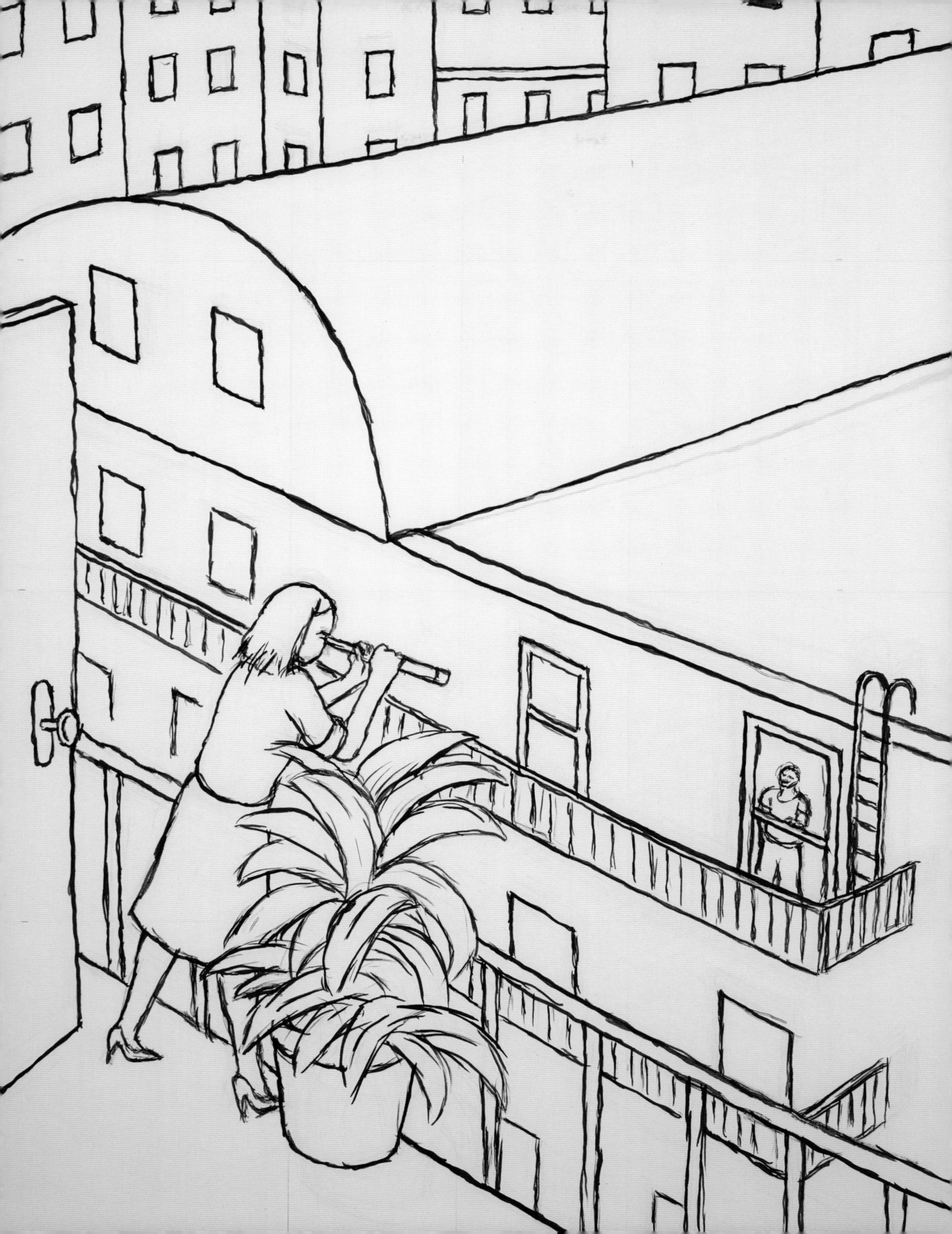

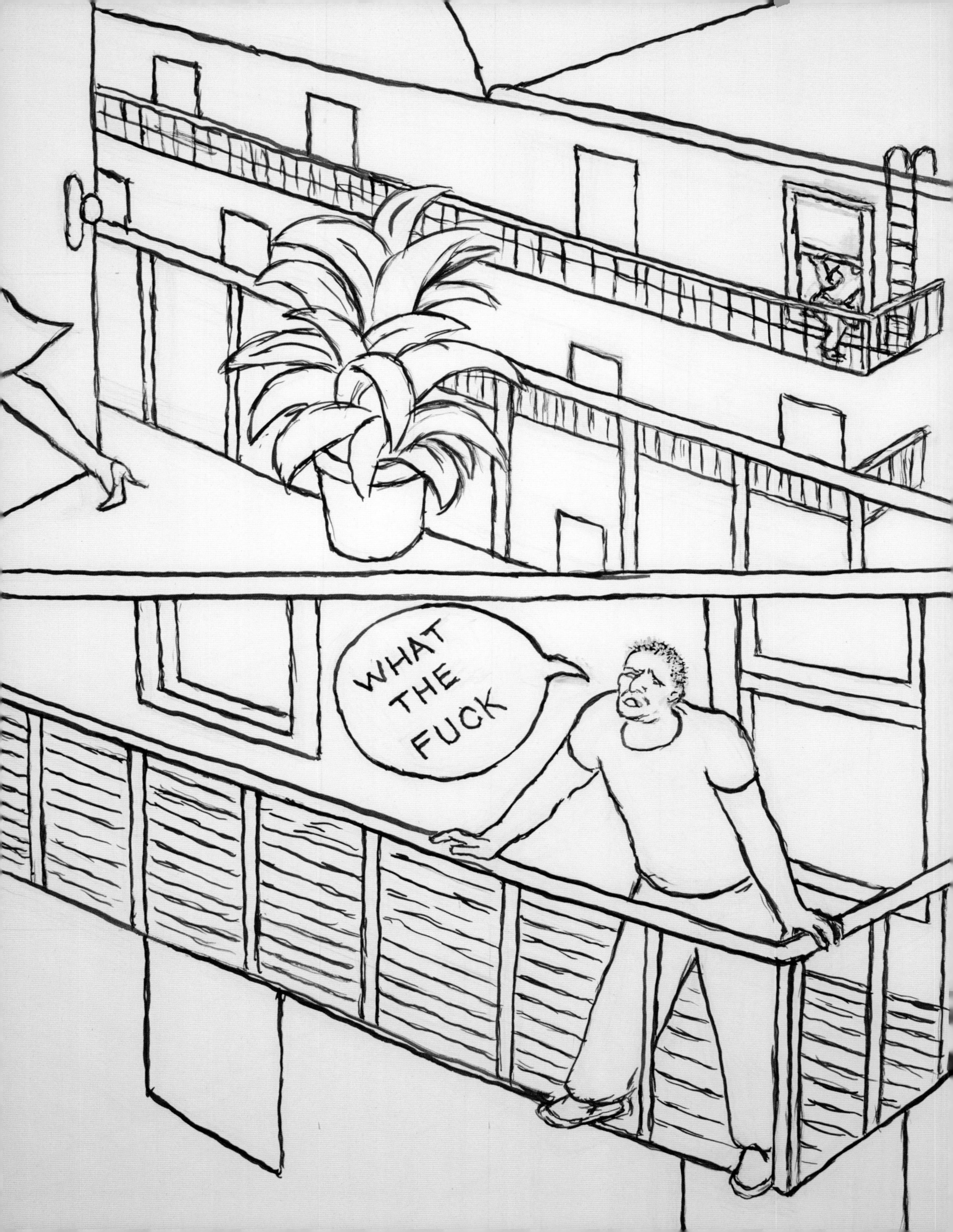
WHAT THE FUCK

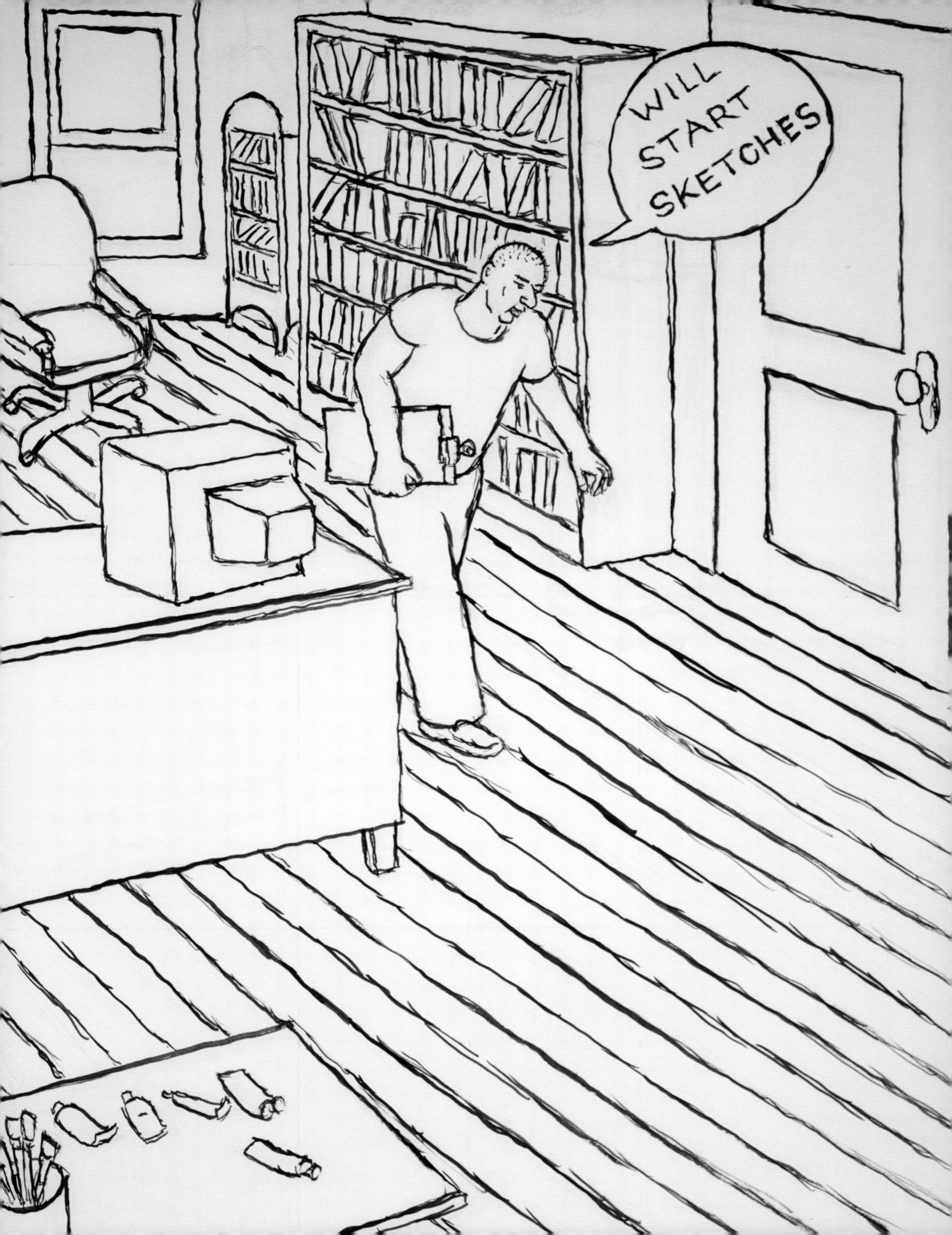
WILL START SKETCHES

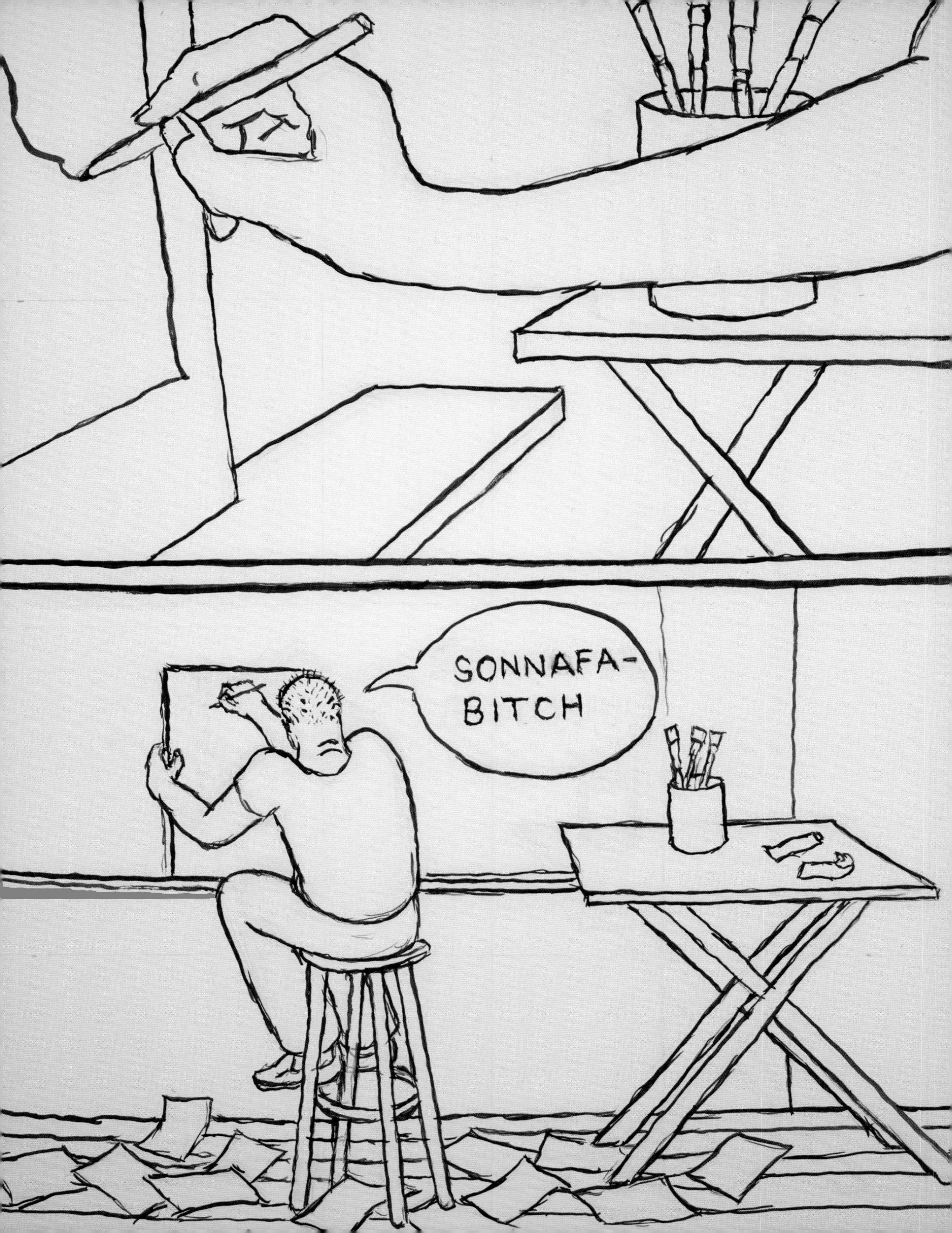
SONNAFA-
BITCH

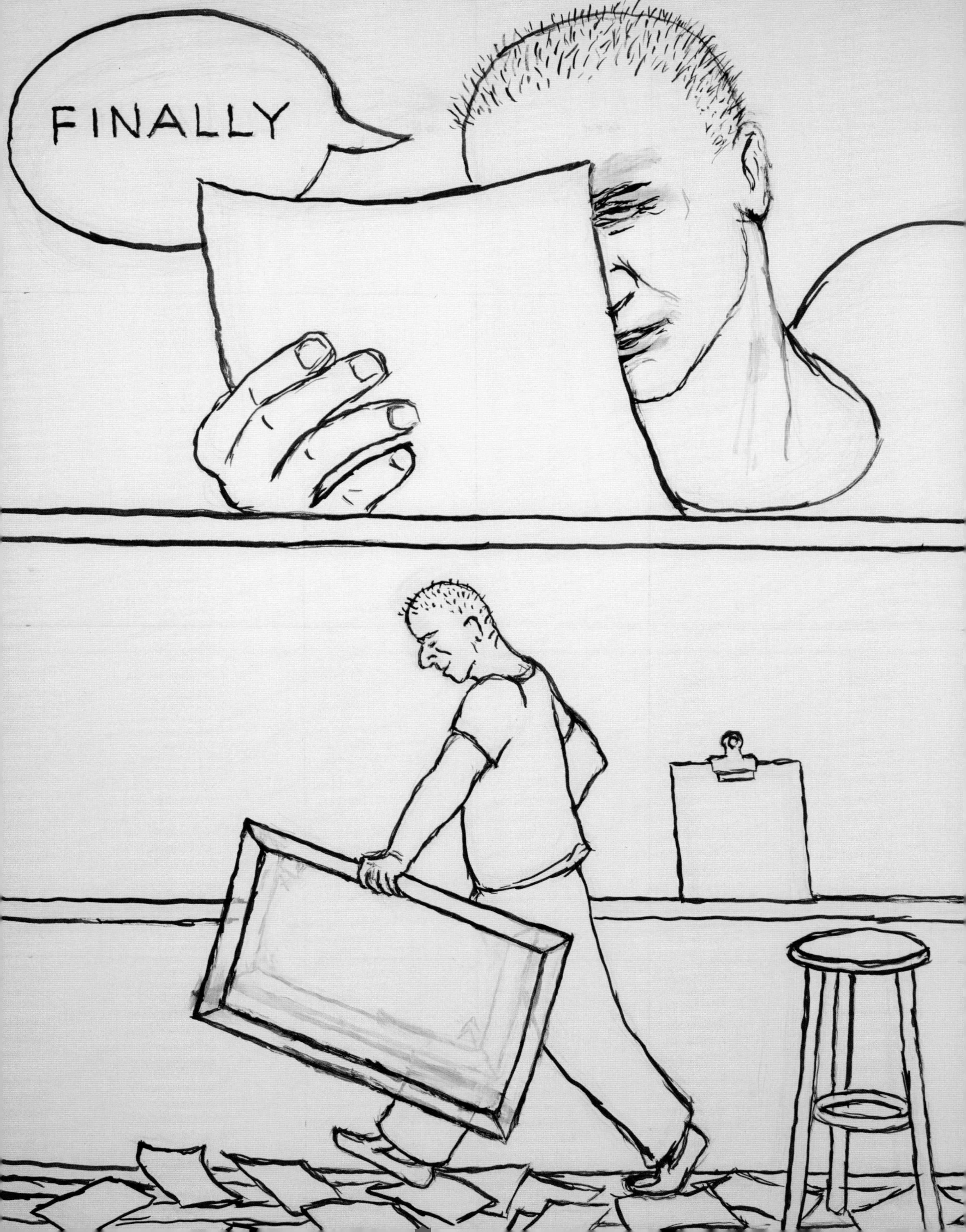
FINALLY

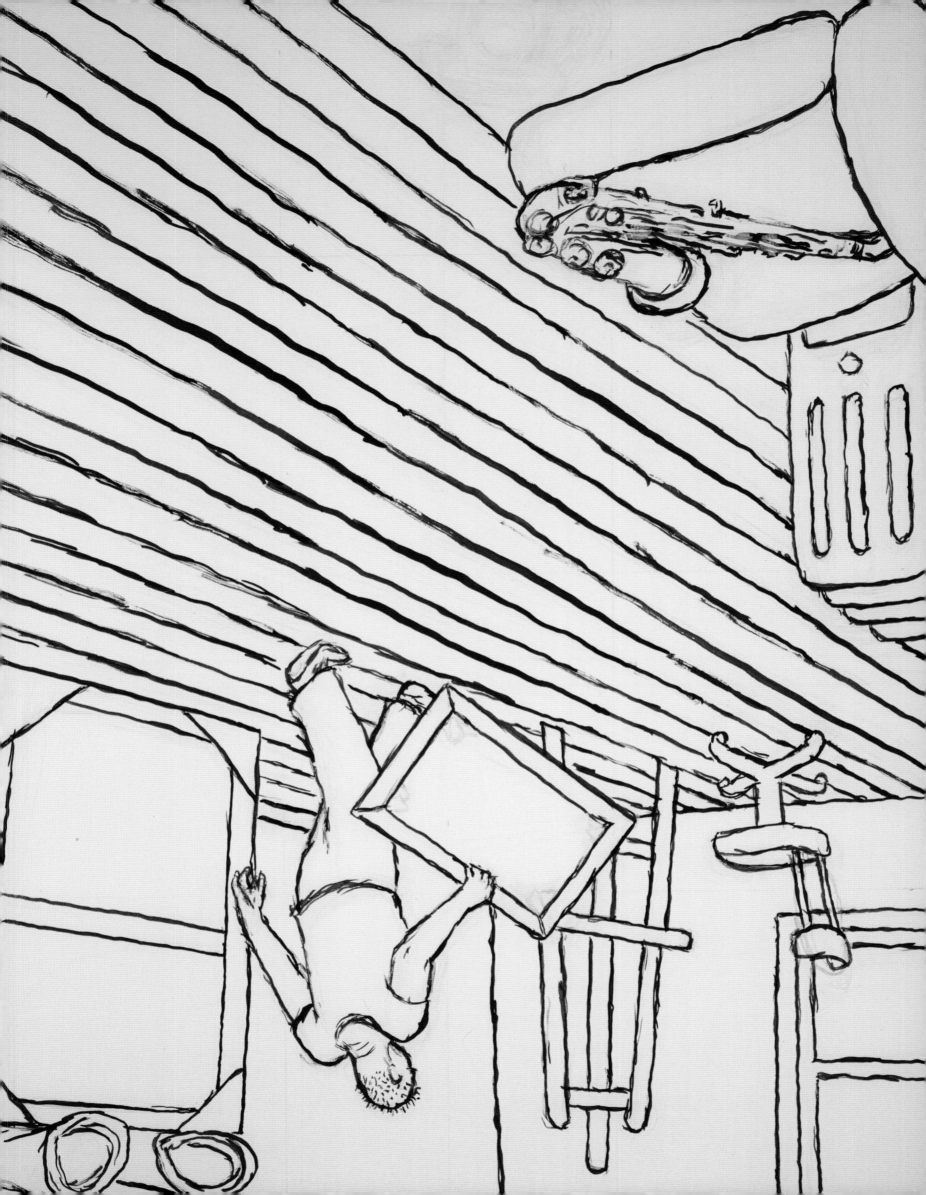

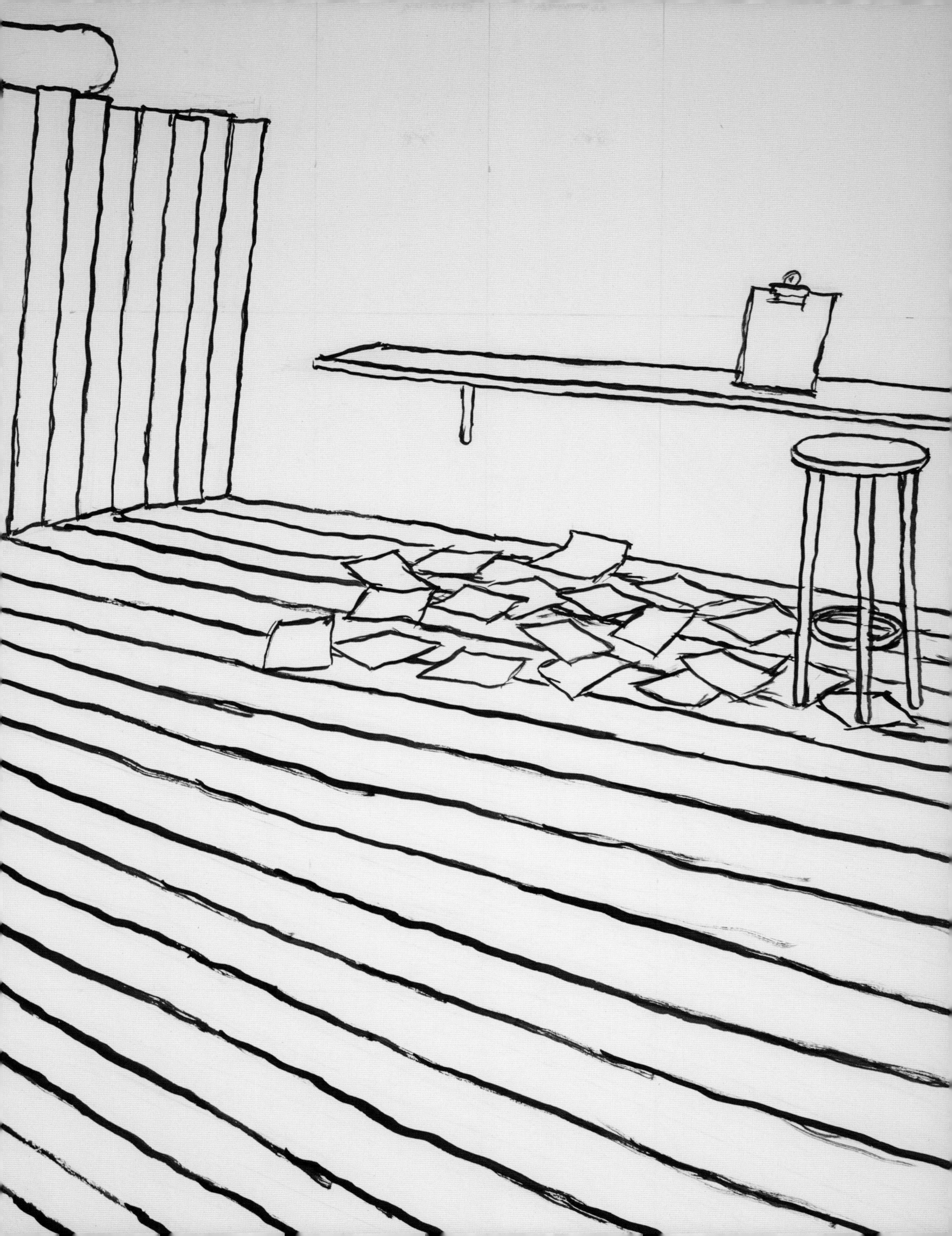

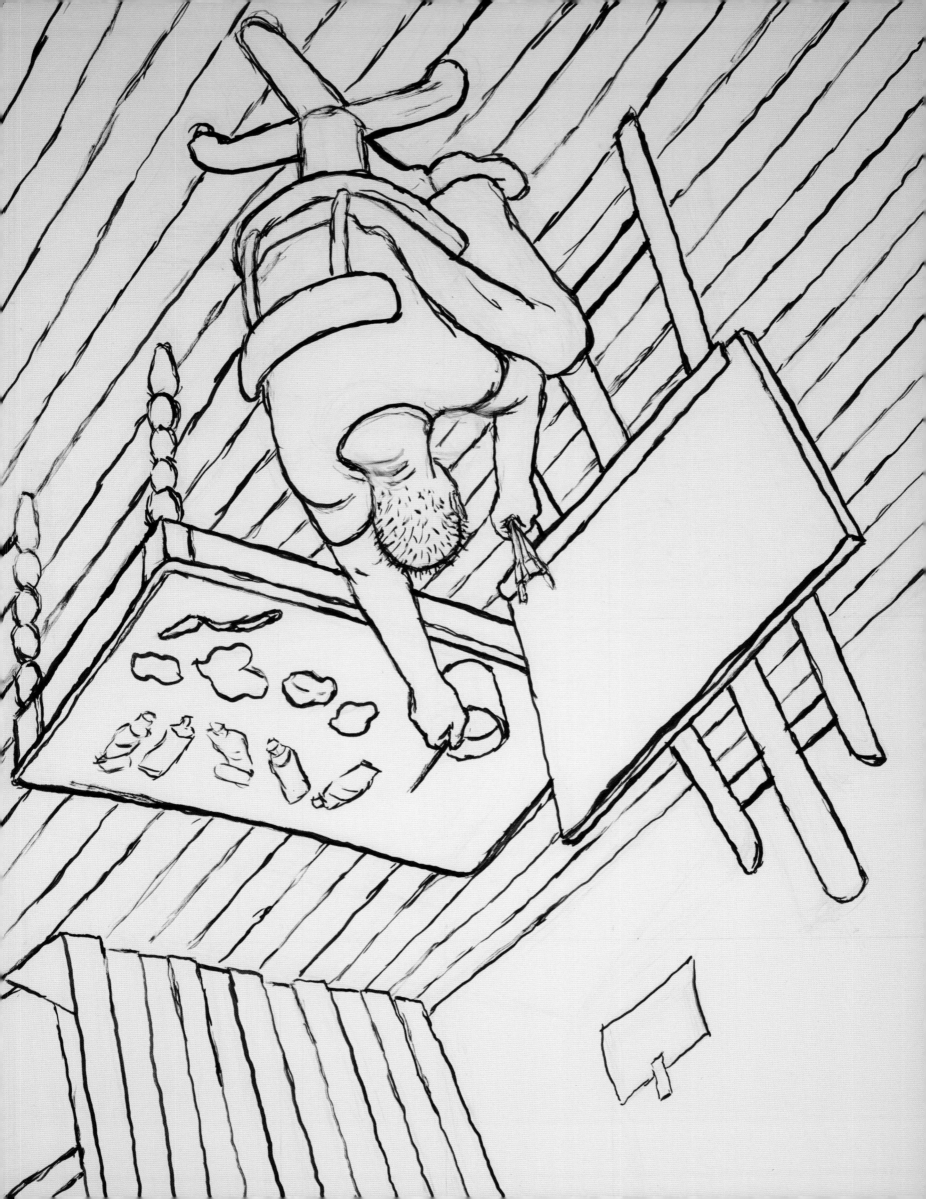

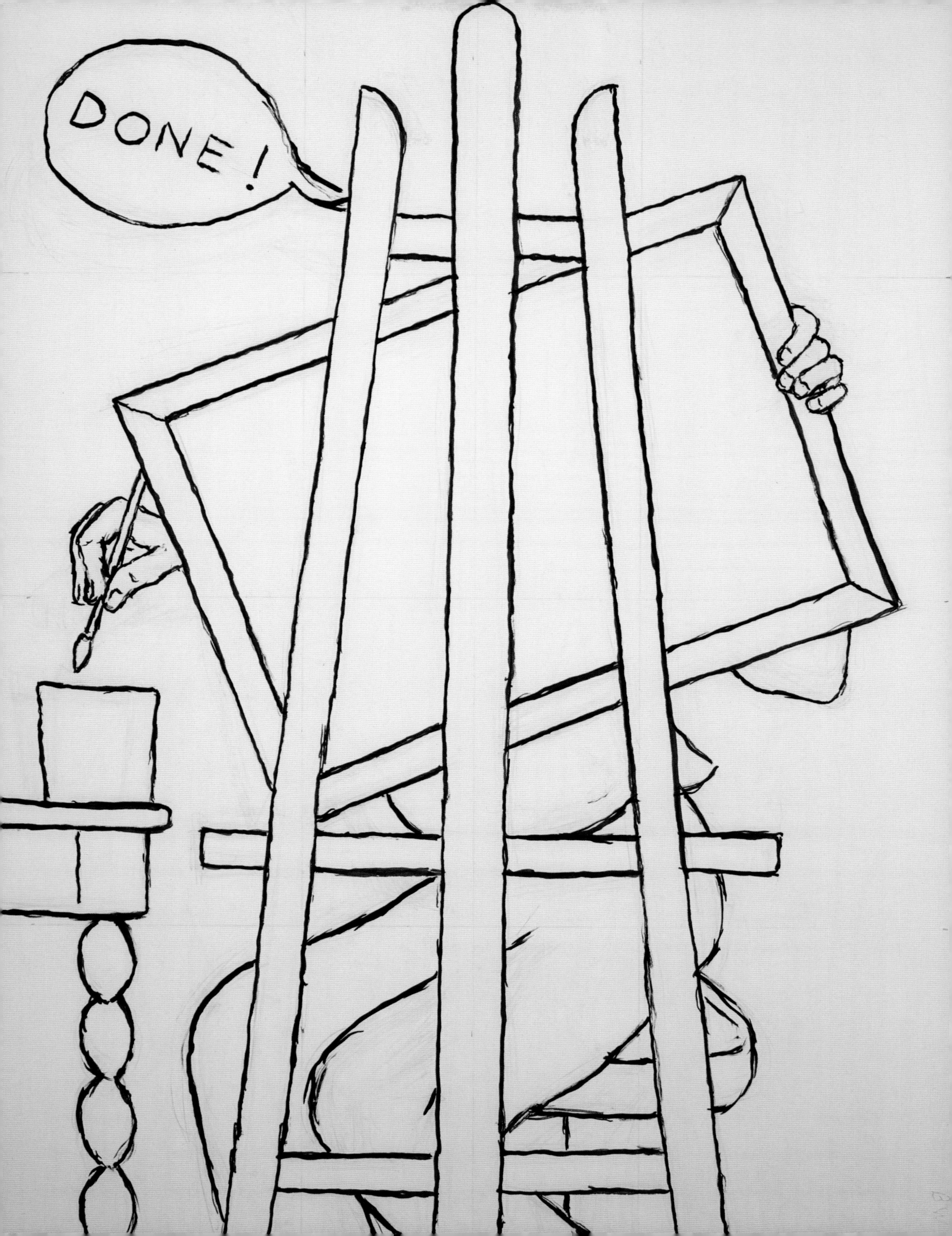
DONE!

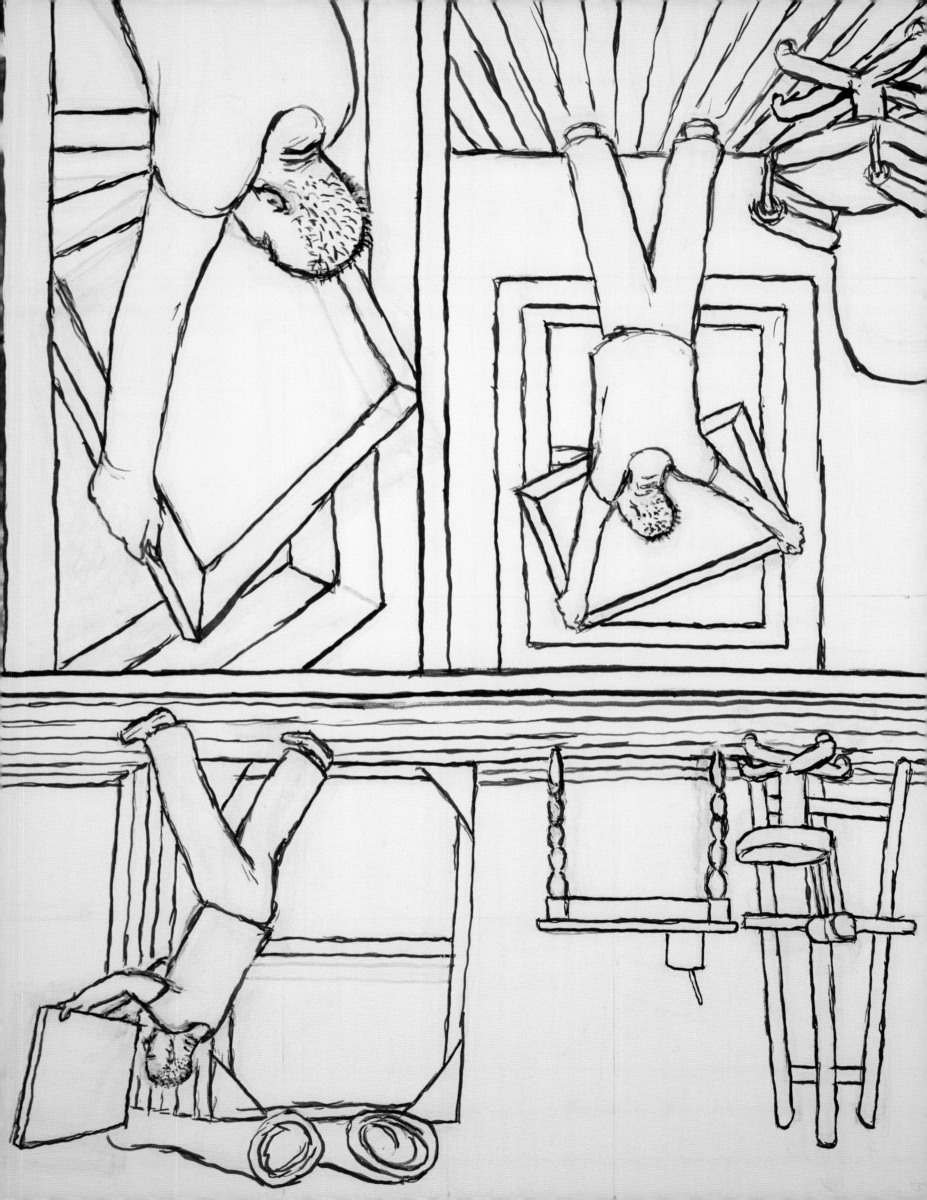

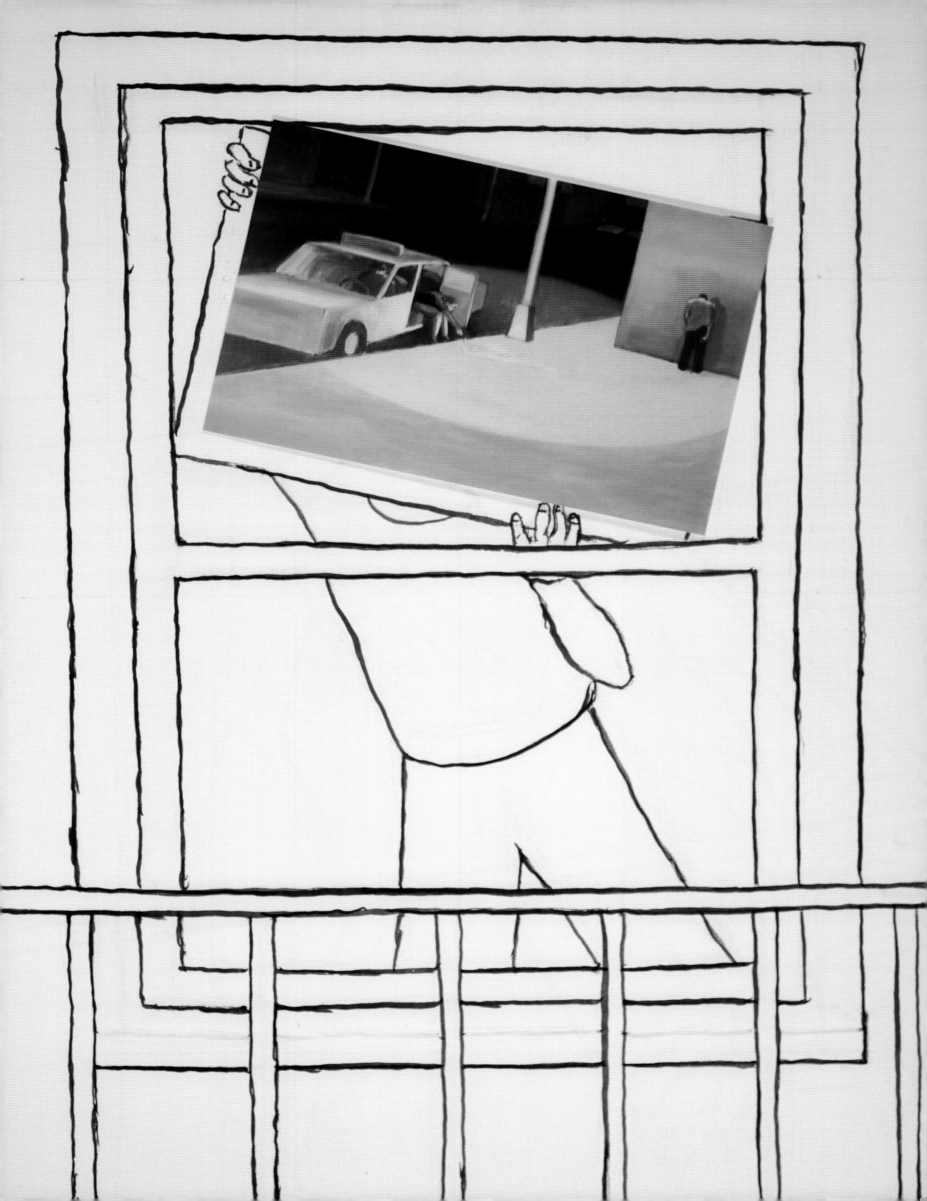

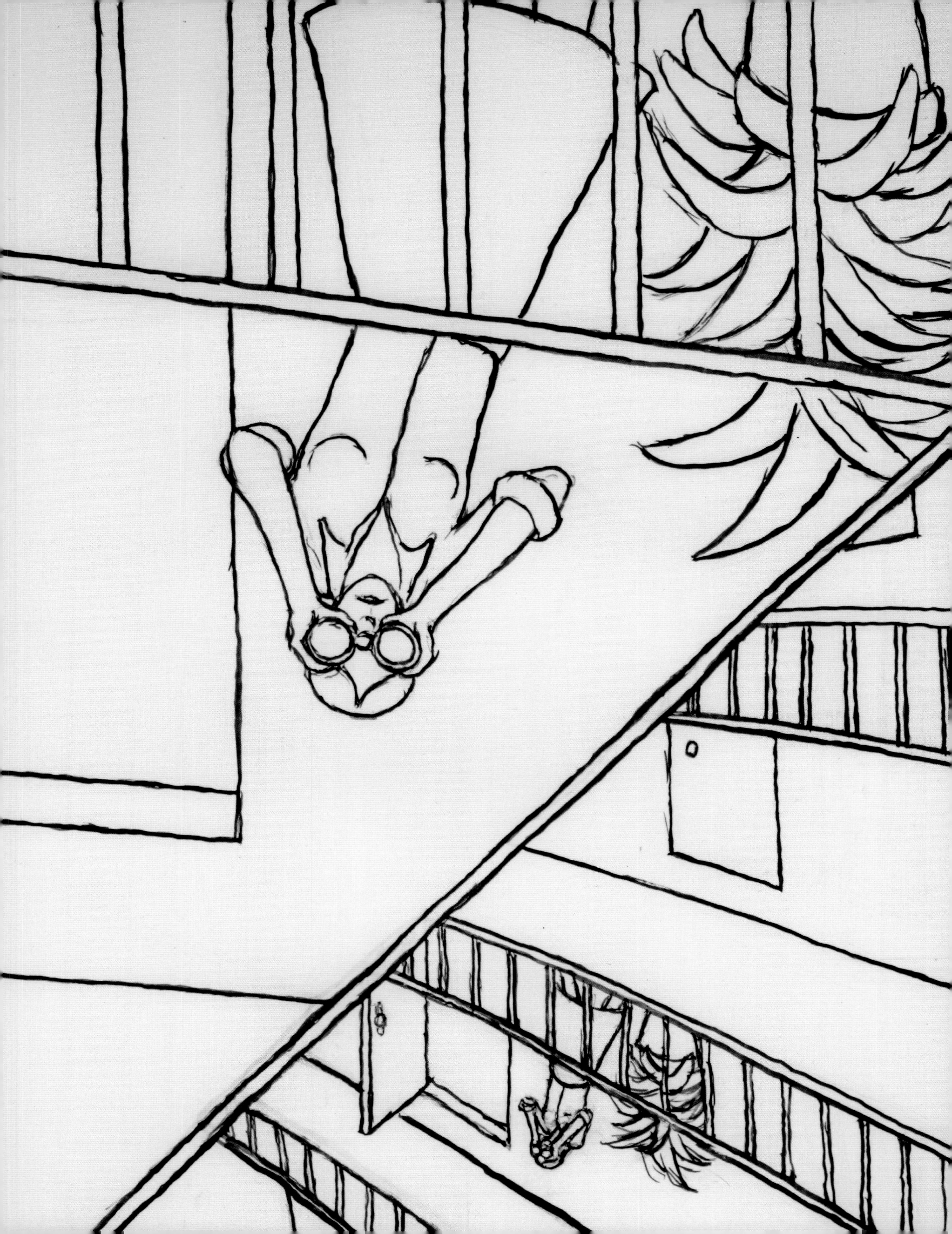

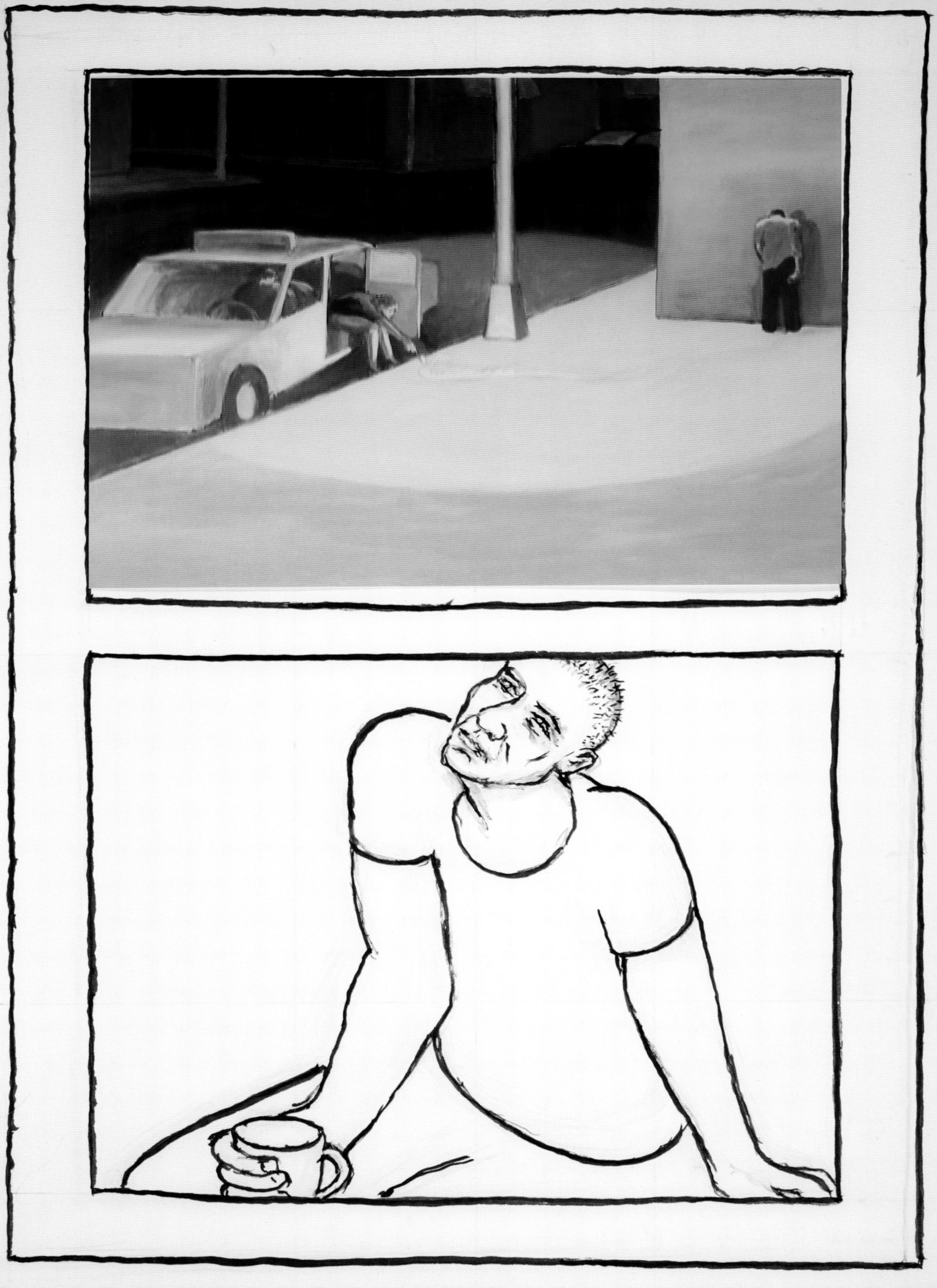

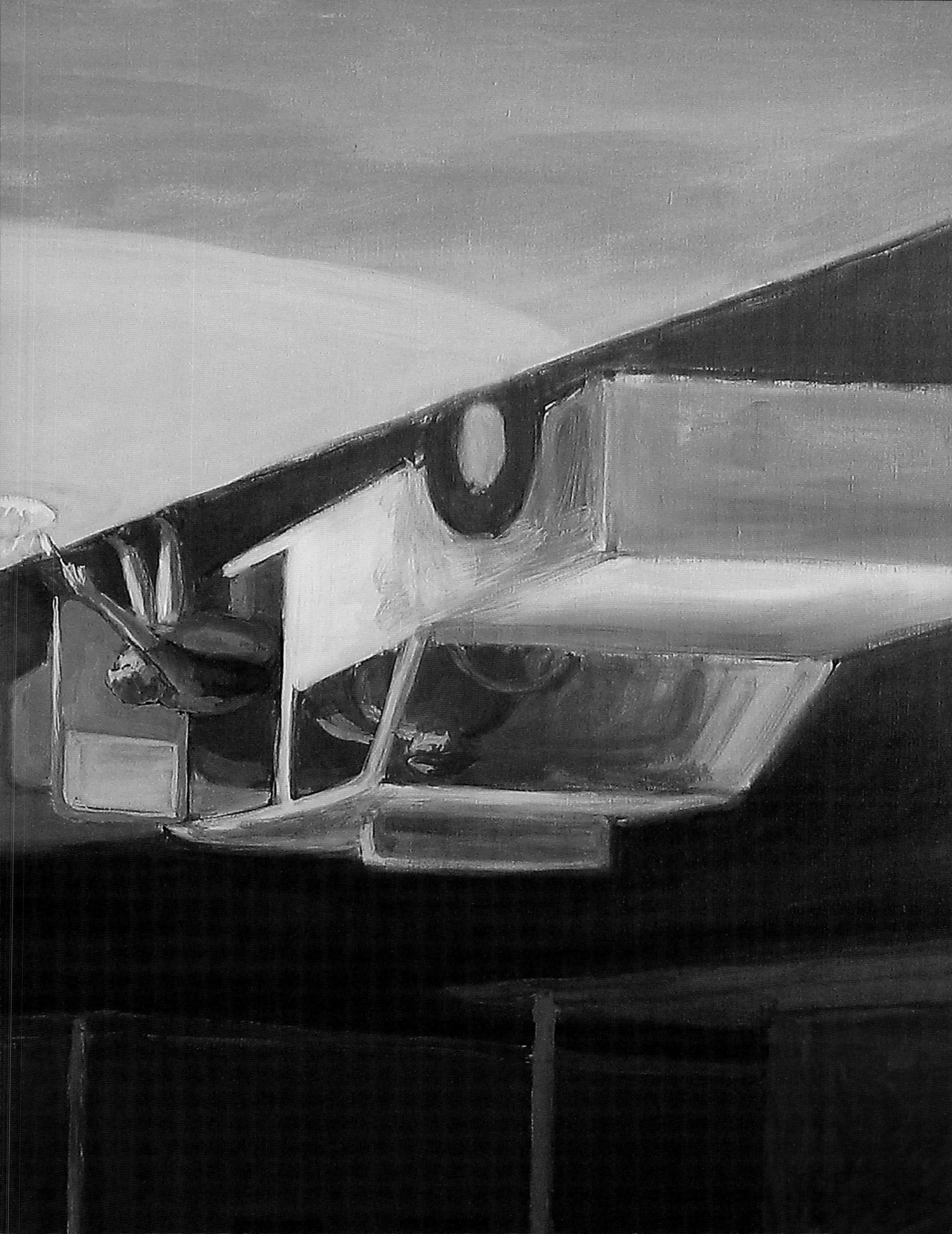

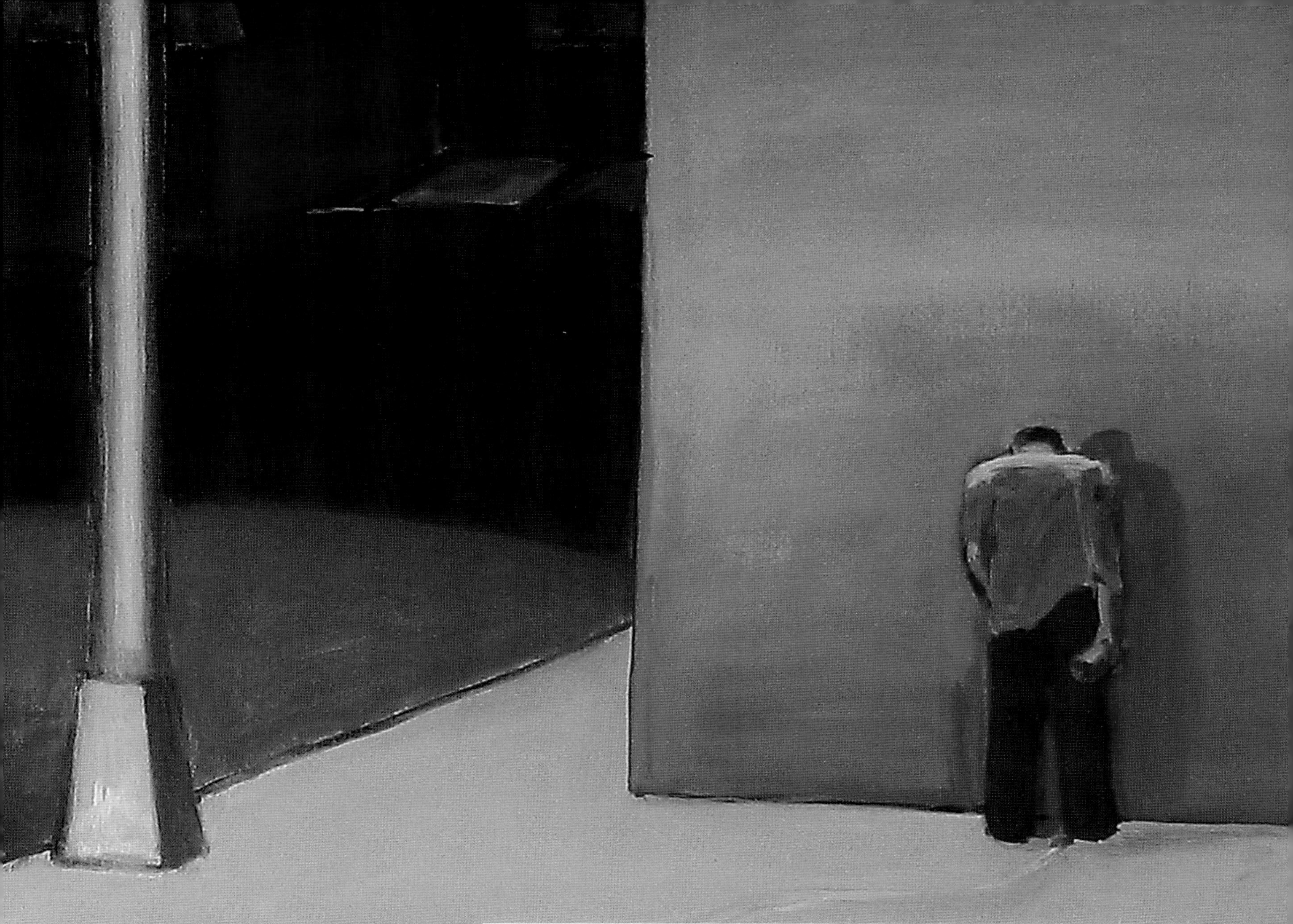

YUPPIE LOVE

Two yuppies arguing get into a cab and go down to Soho to a lawyer's party. In the fashionable loft they continue their argument. It's about investments. She wants to buy AT&T stock, and he wants to buy a summer house. The argument interests their fellow lawyers at the party. Sides begin to form as to the best investment. Among the guests is a judge. It is decided that the judge should make the final decision binding before the lawyer witnesses. Not wanting to antagonize a sitting judge the yuppie couple agree to these conditions. "It is my learned opinion that the summer house wins," announced the judge soberly. The yuppie wife clams up for the rest of the party. The winner celebrates with a lot of 120 proof vodka drinking. Finally, she drags her drunk husband away and hails a cab for the uptown trek. He has to piss so they stop the cab by a street light. Yuppie husband staggers to a wall and pisses a torrent of 120 proof vodka. The vodka stream snakes toward the curb making a puddle by the open back door of the waiting cab. Yuppie wife sees the puddle and a eureka smile brightens her face. Putting a cigarette in her mouth she strikes a match, takes a puff and drops the lit match into the puddle. The 120 proof vodka piss blossomed into an alcohol flame, which raced back to its source. The next day AT&T got a new shareholder.

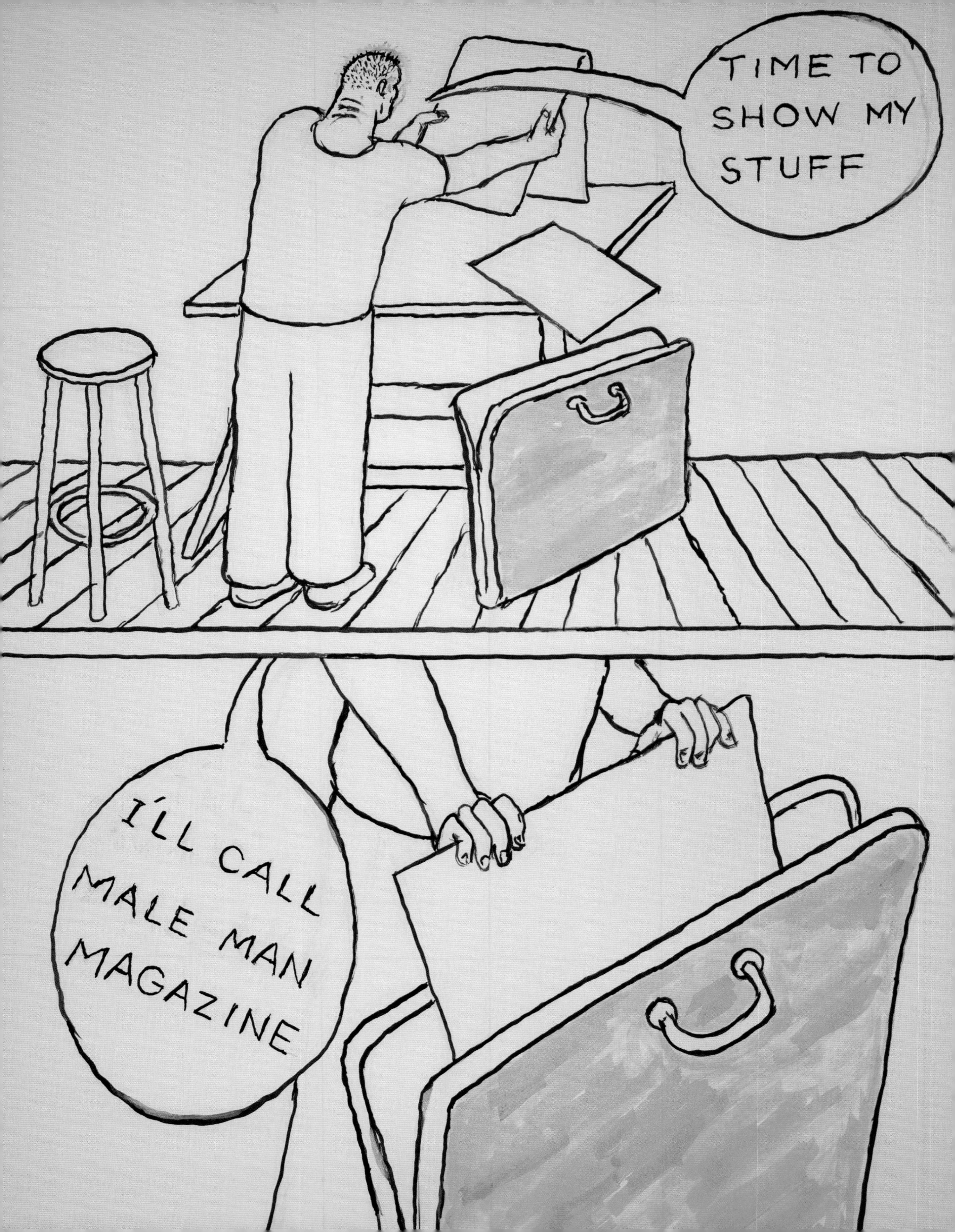
TIME TO SHOW MY STUFF
I'LL CALL MALE MAN MAGAZINE

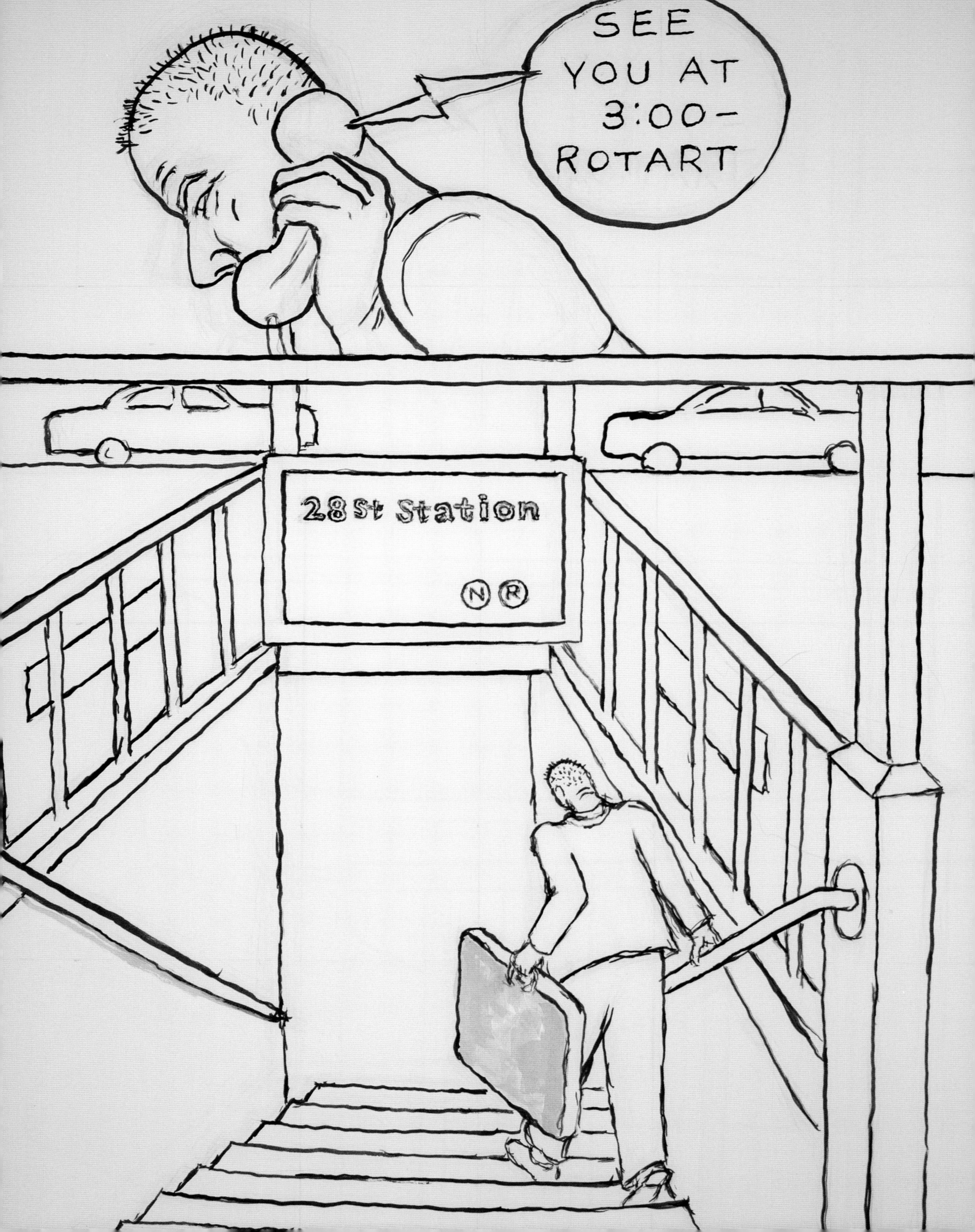
SEE YOU AT 3:00-ROTART
28St Station
N R

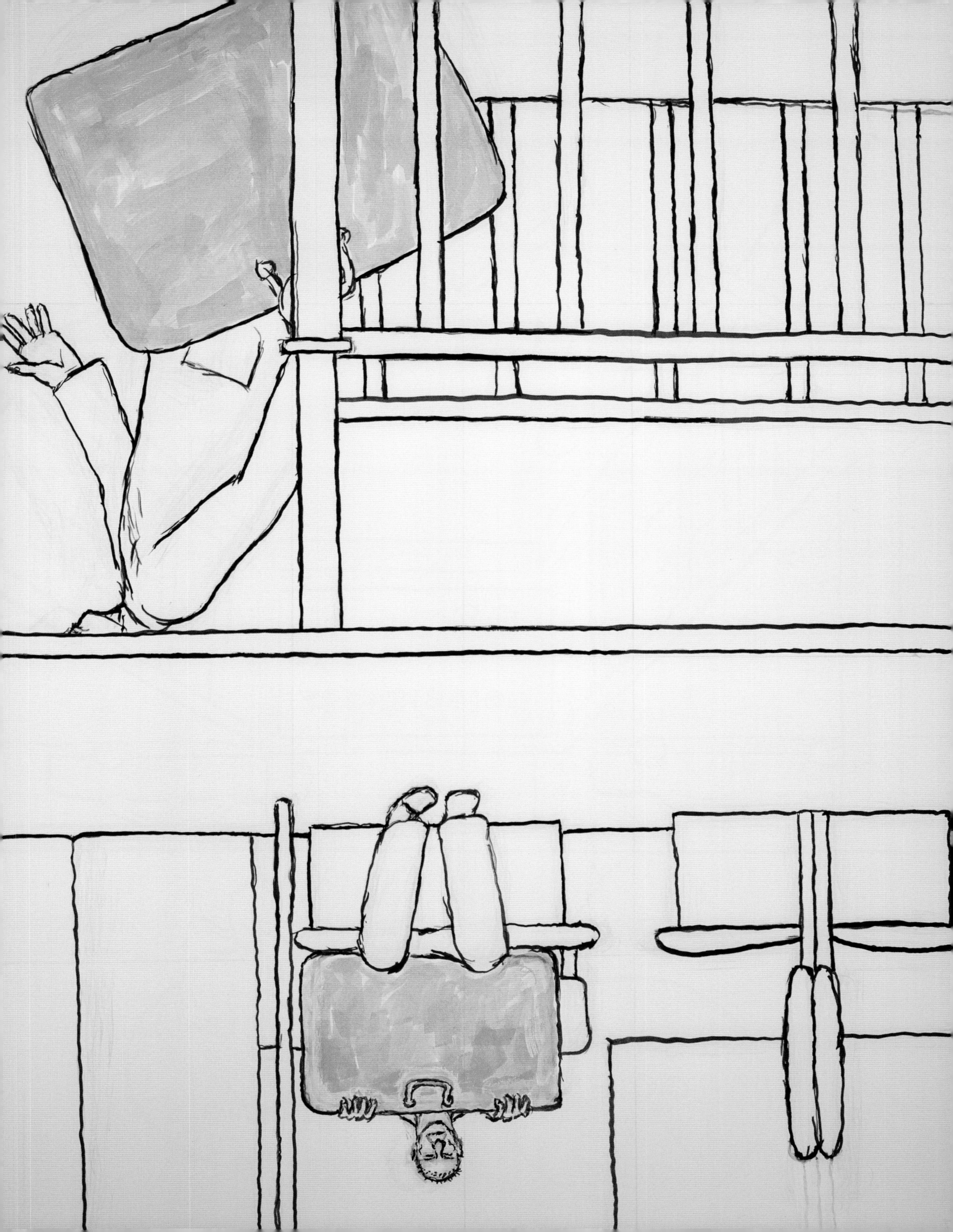

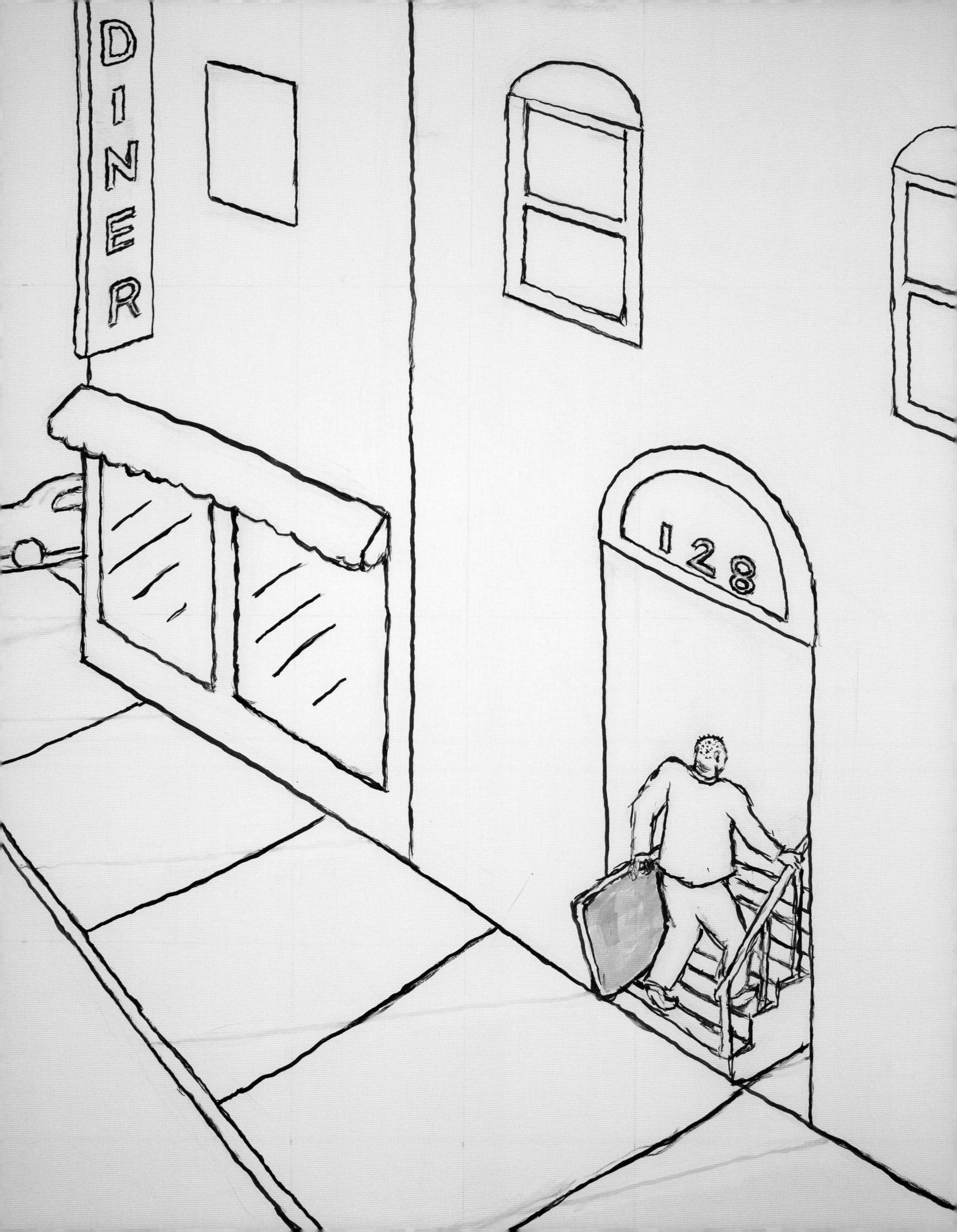
DINER
128

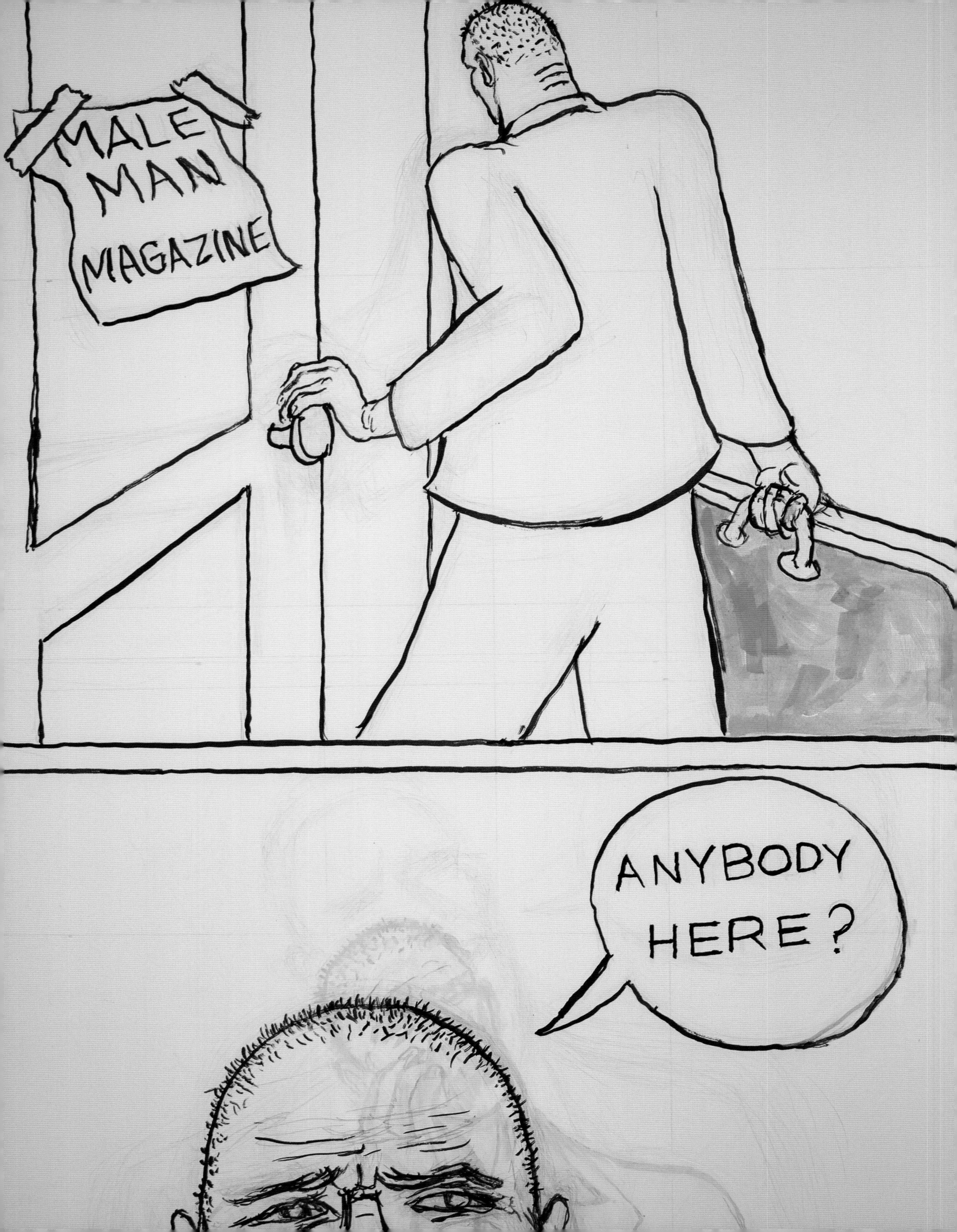
MALE MAN MAGAZINE
ANYBODY HERE?

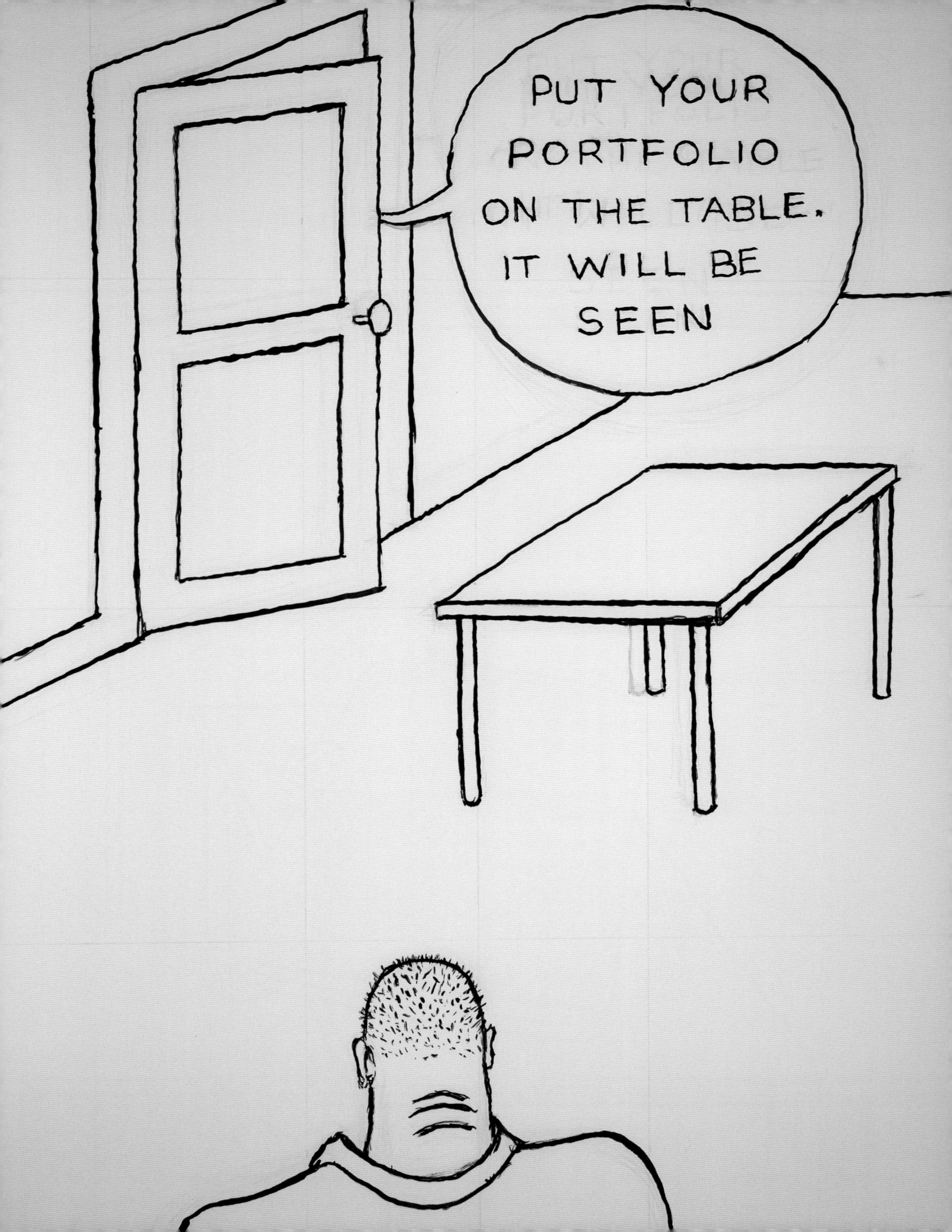
PUT YOUR PORTFOLIO ON THE TABLE. IT WILL BE SEEN

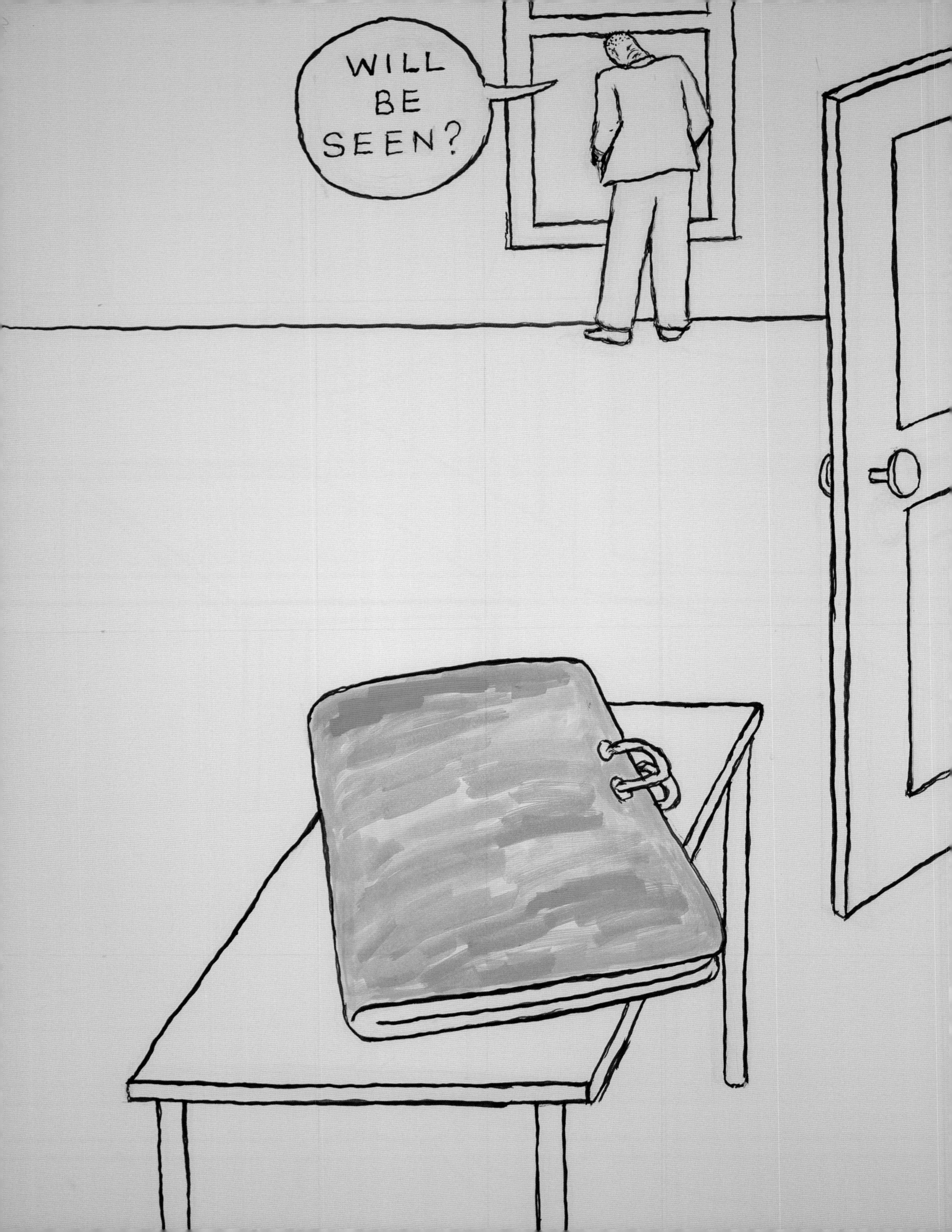
WILL BE SEEN?

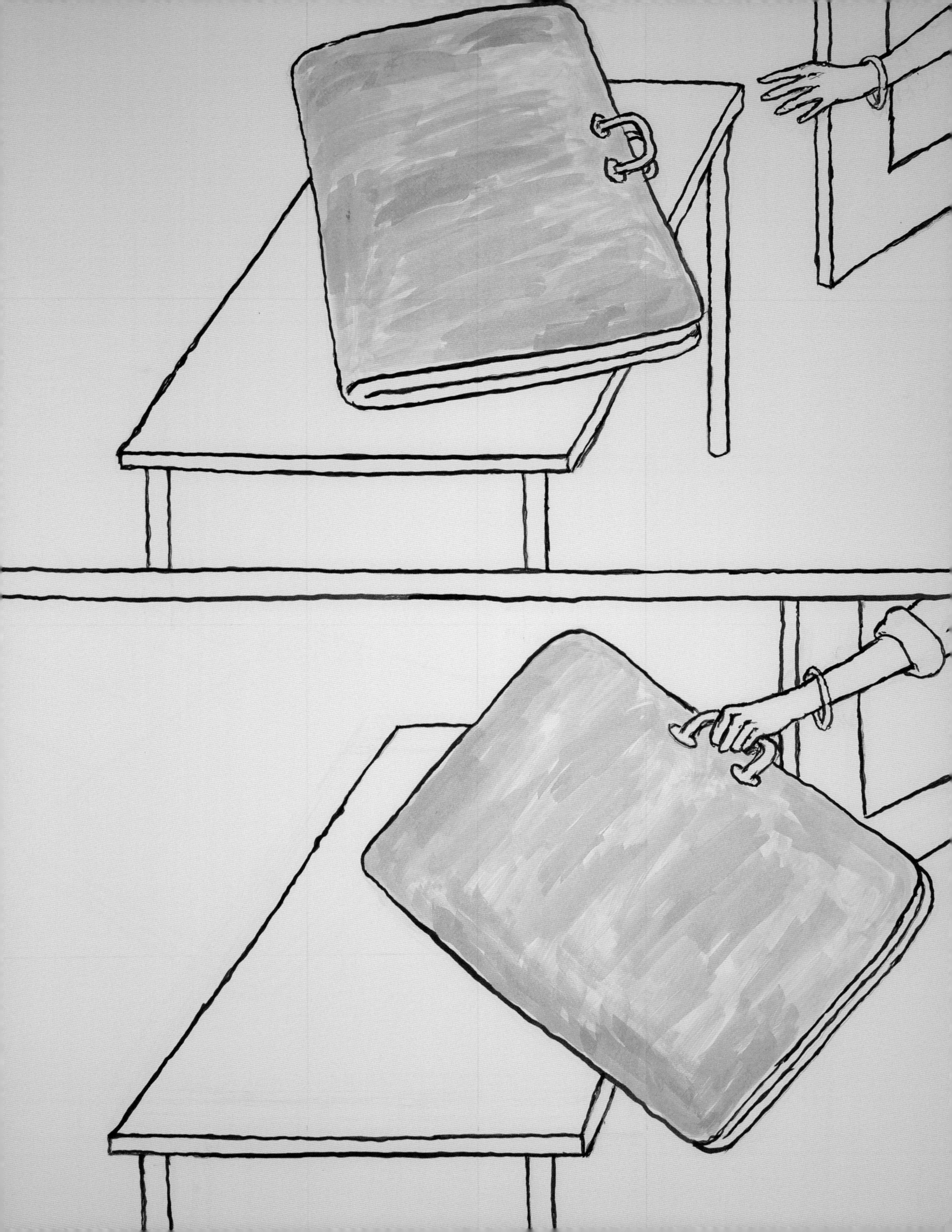

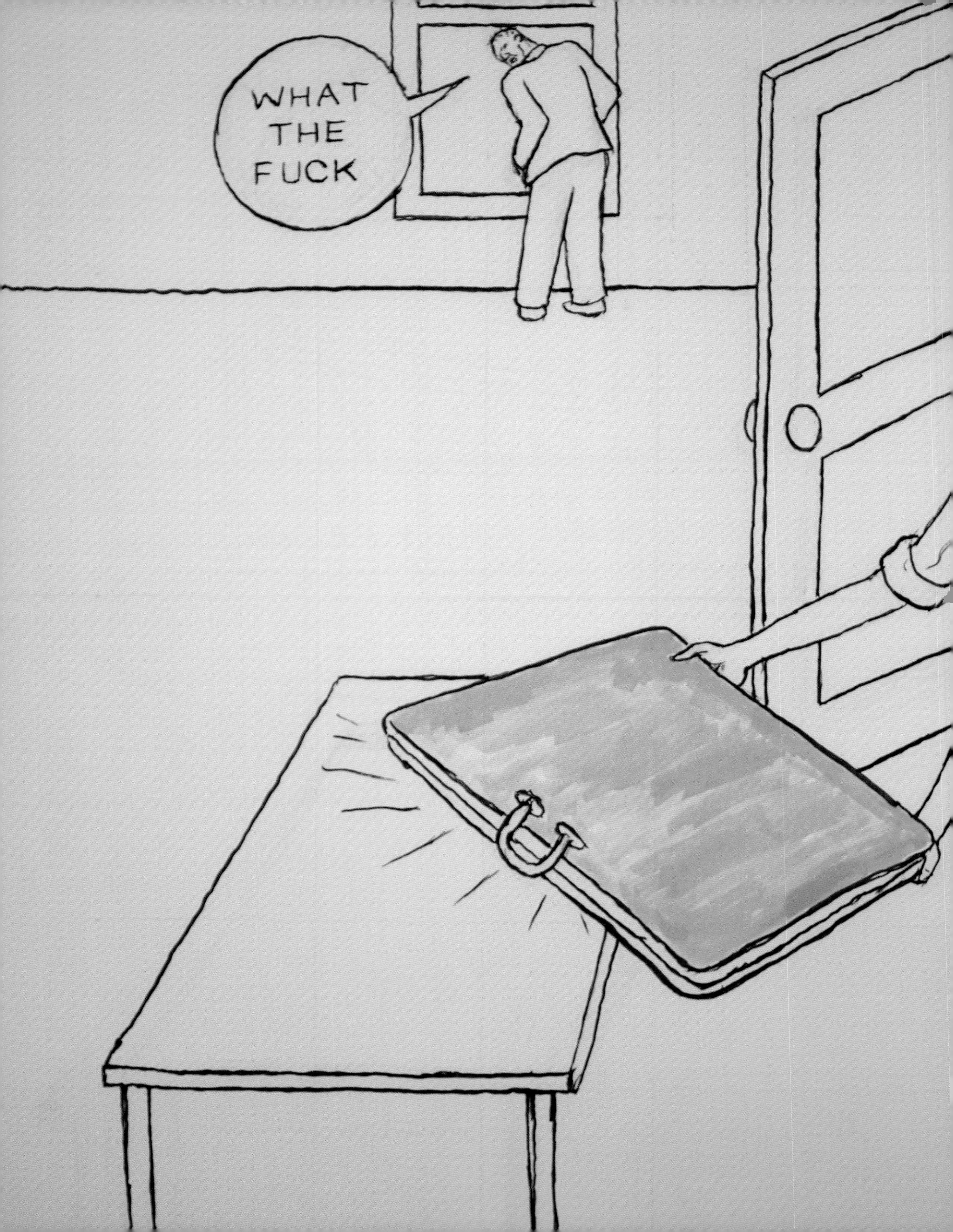
WHAT THE FUCK

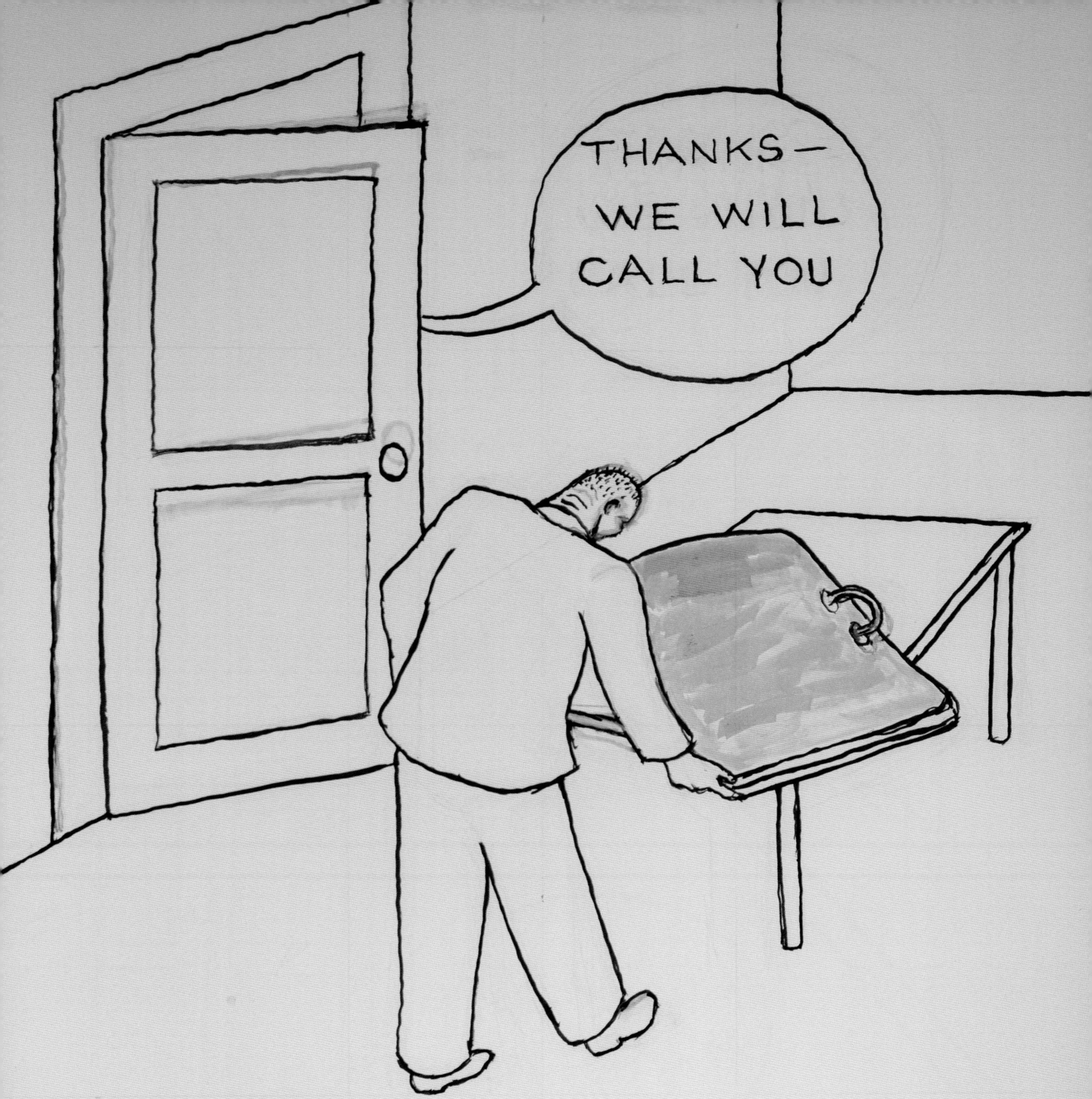
THANKS—
WE WILL
CALL YOU

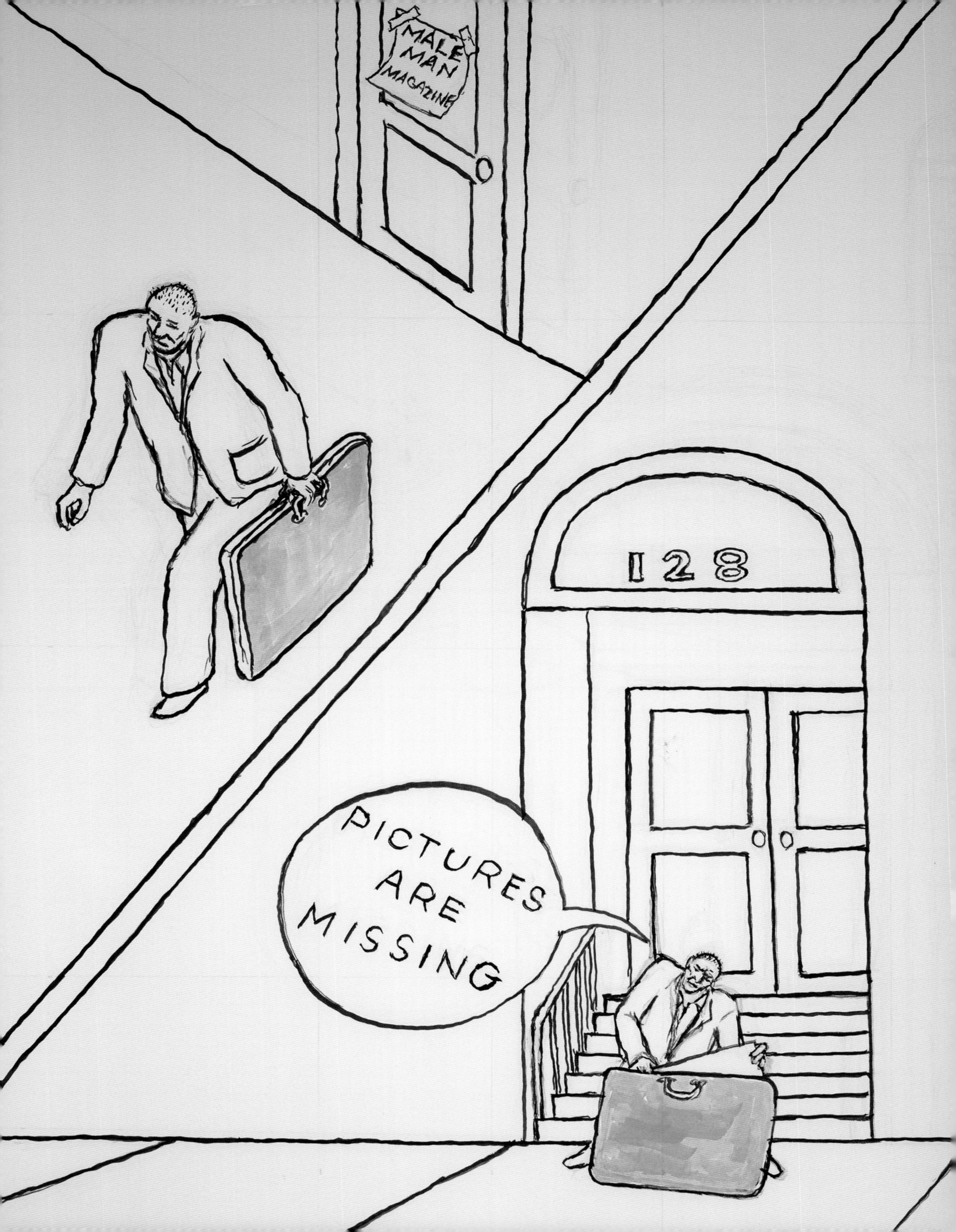
MALE MAN MAGAZINE
128
PICTURES ARE MISSING

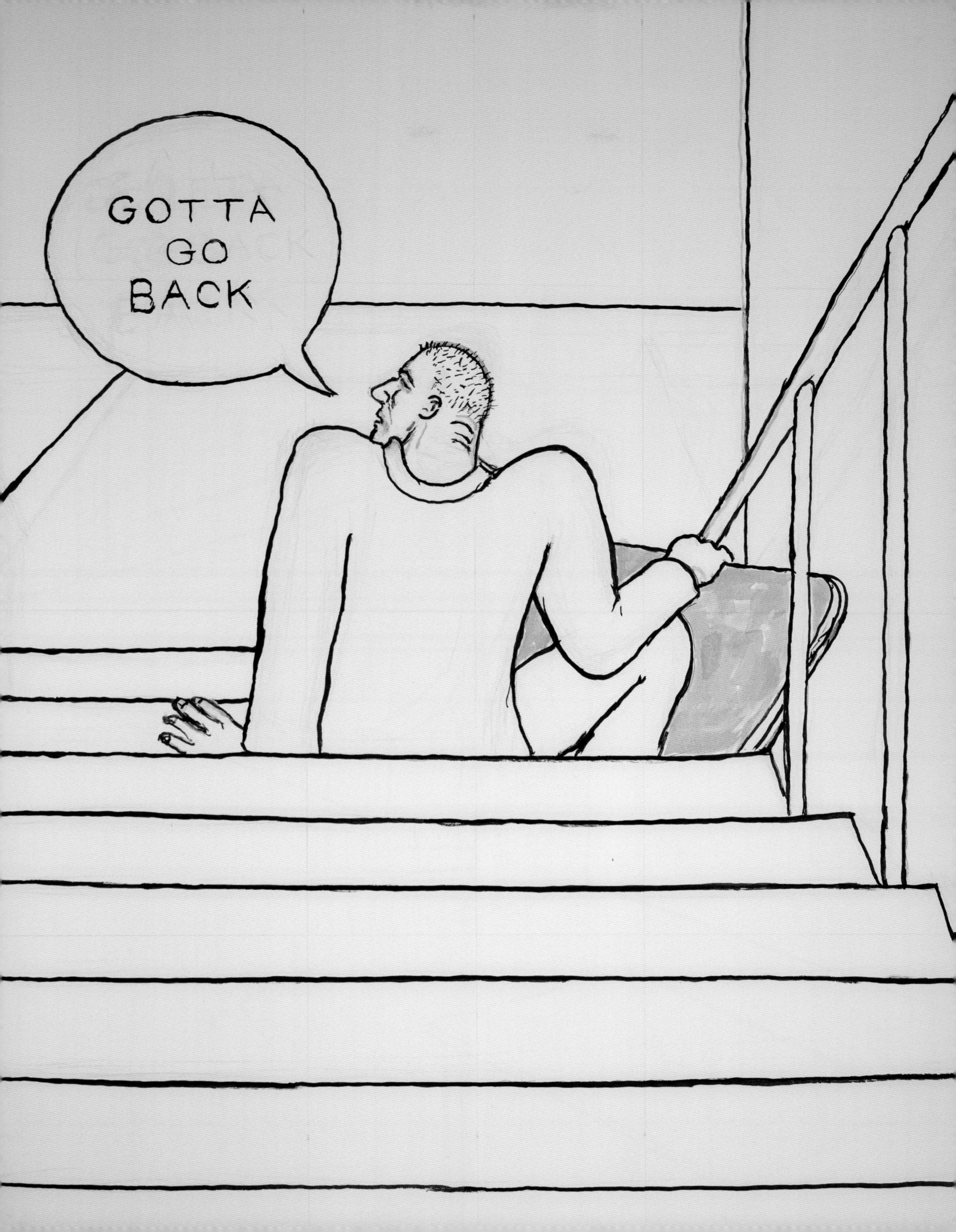
GOTTA GO BACK

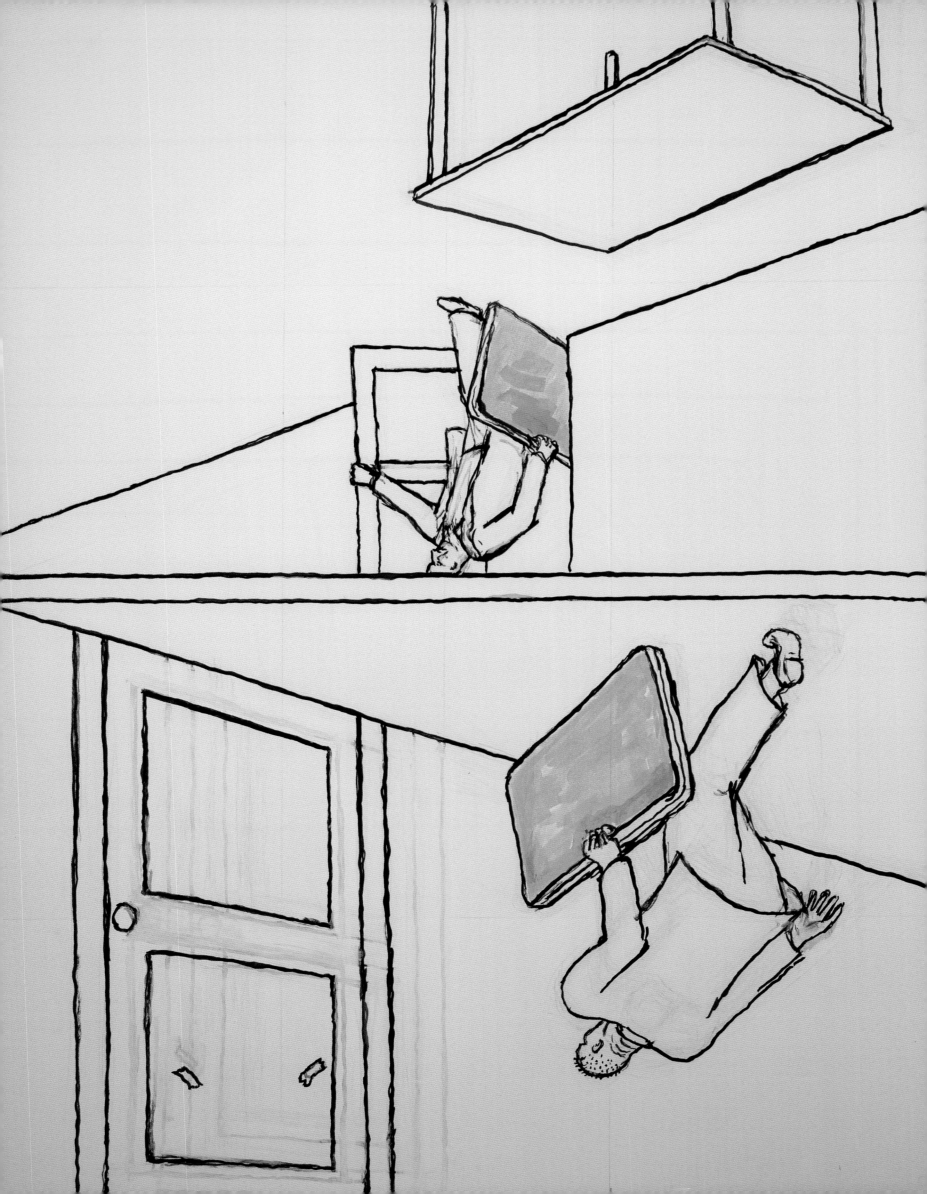

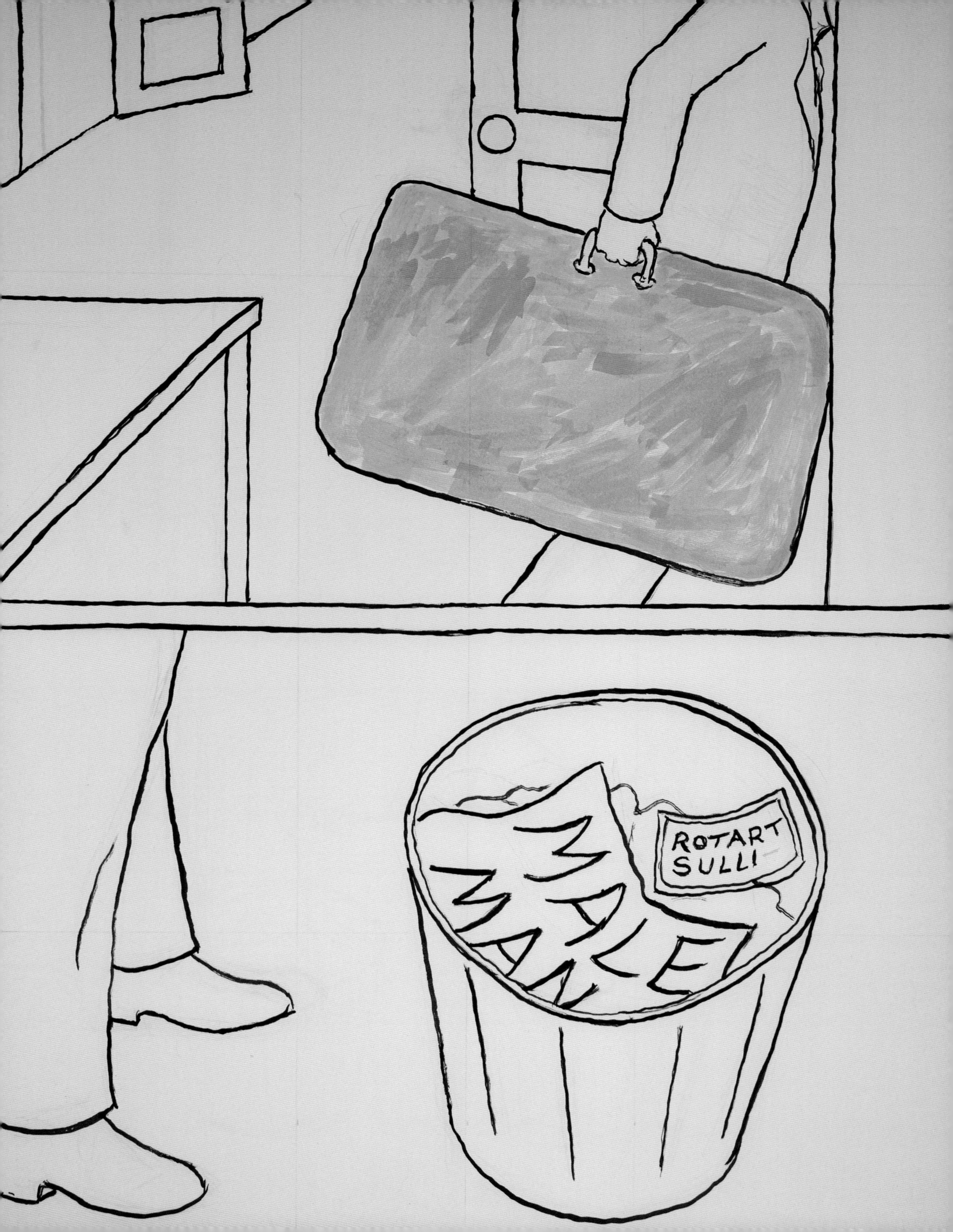
ROTART
SULLI

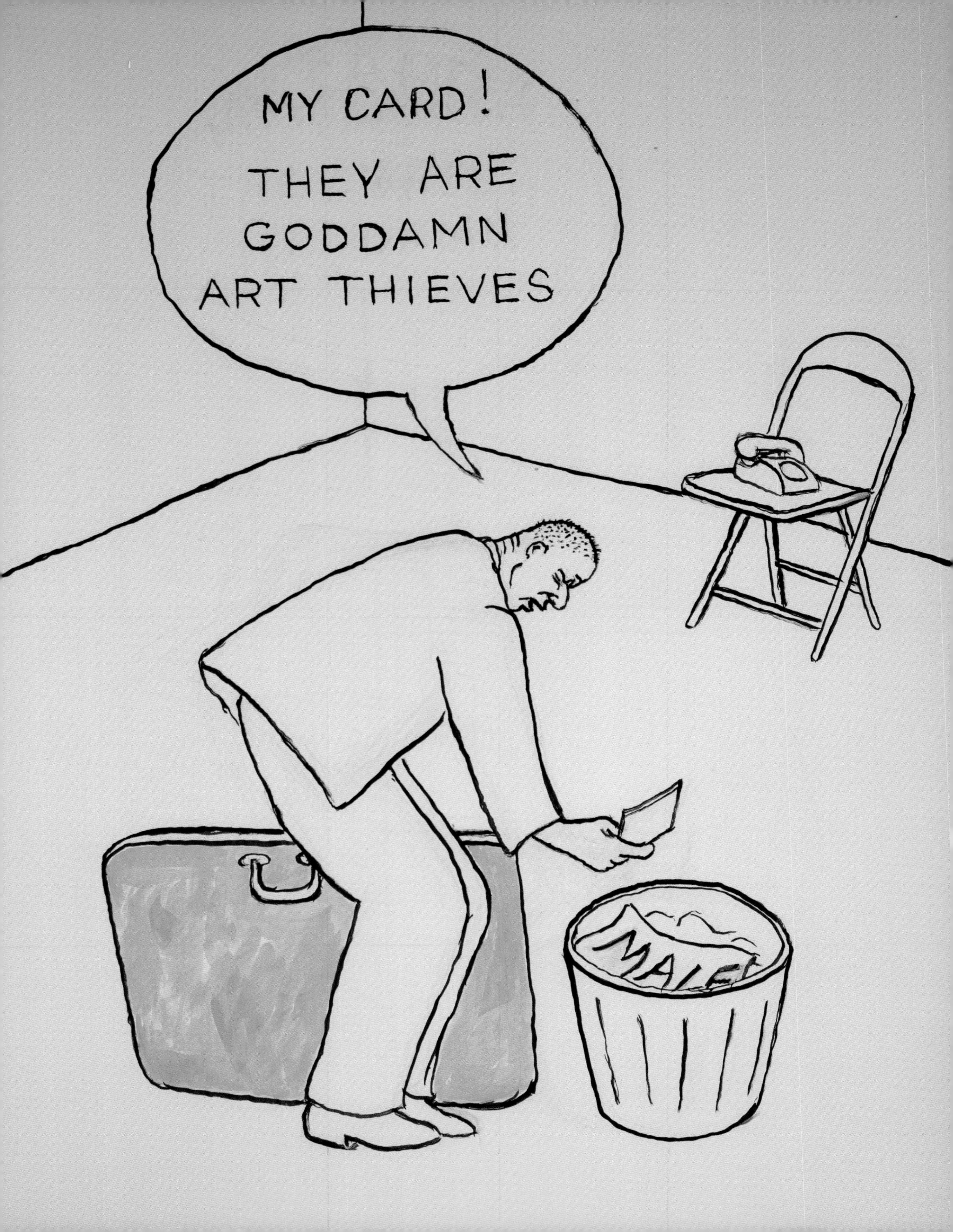
MY CARD! THEY ARE GODDAMN ART THIEVES

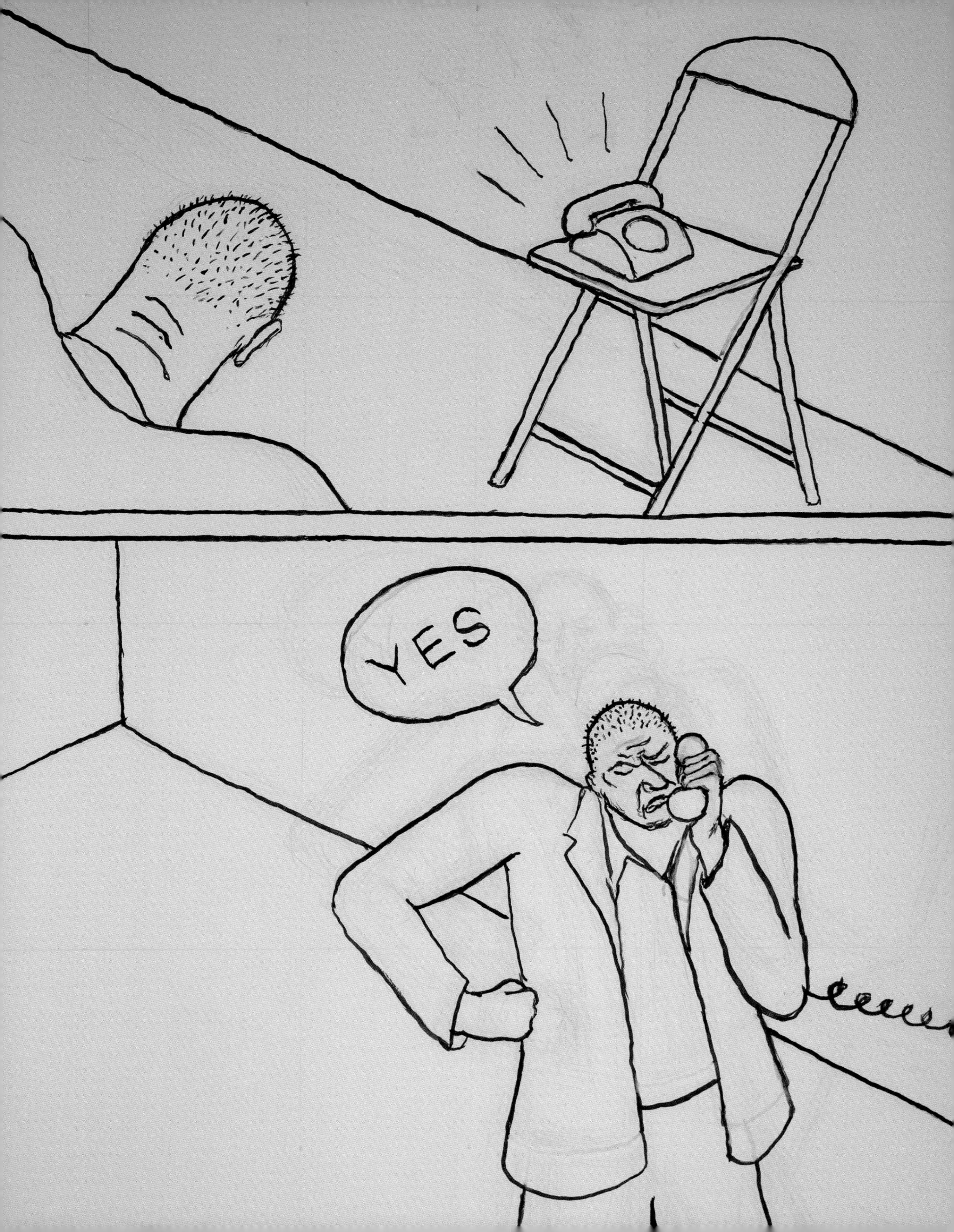
YES

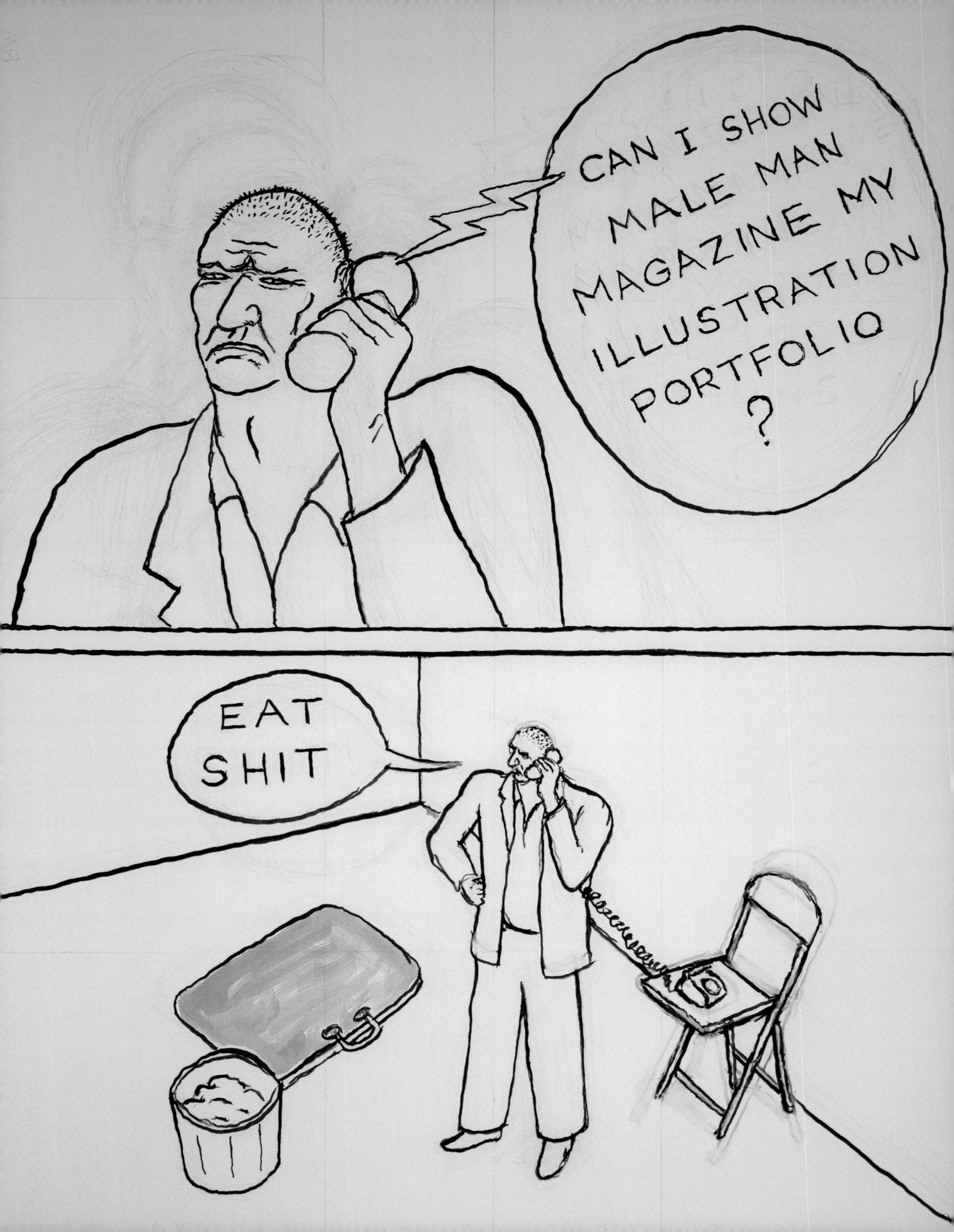
CAN I SHOW MALE MAN MAGAZINE MY ILLUSTRATION PORTFOLIO ?
EAT SHIT

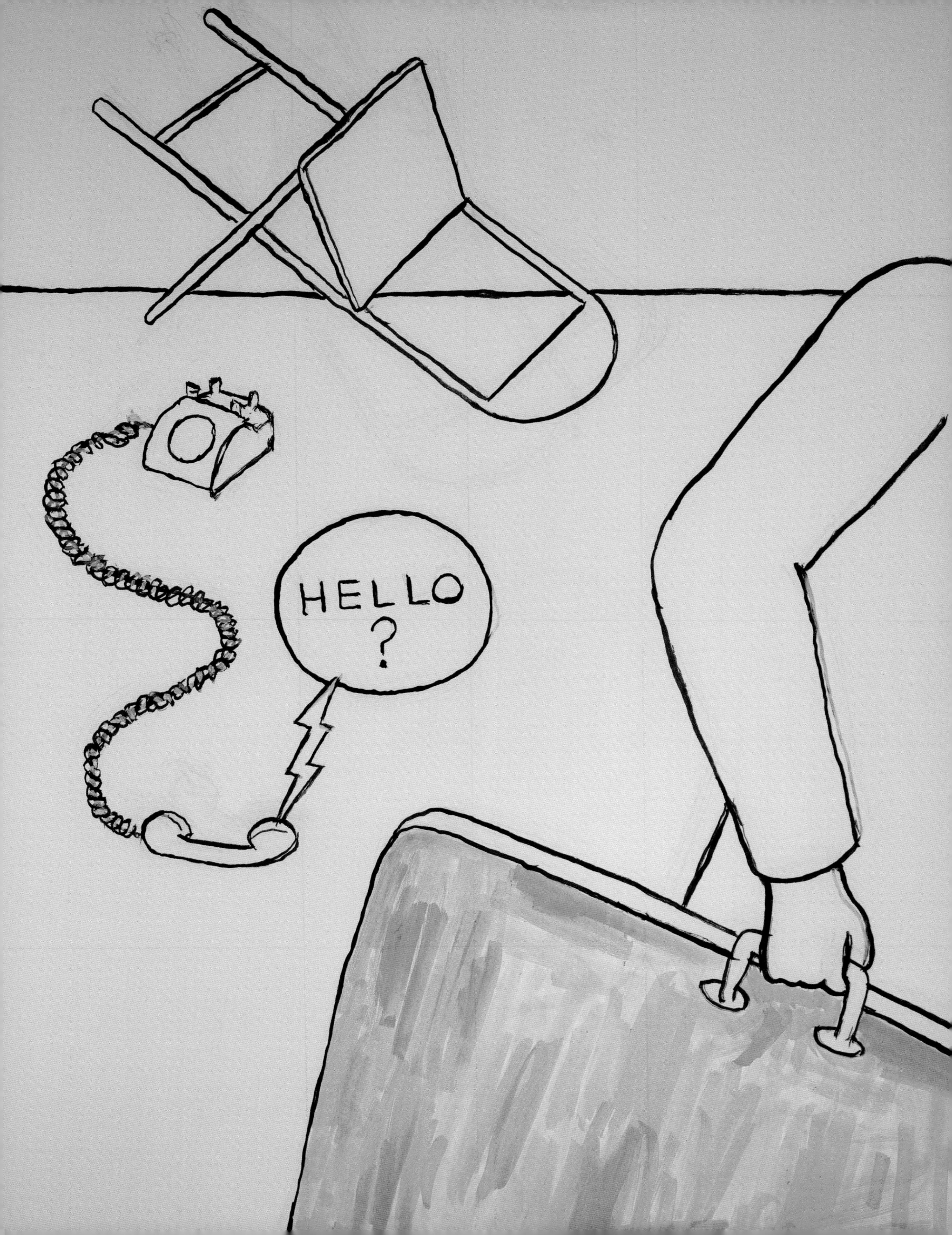
HELLO
?

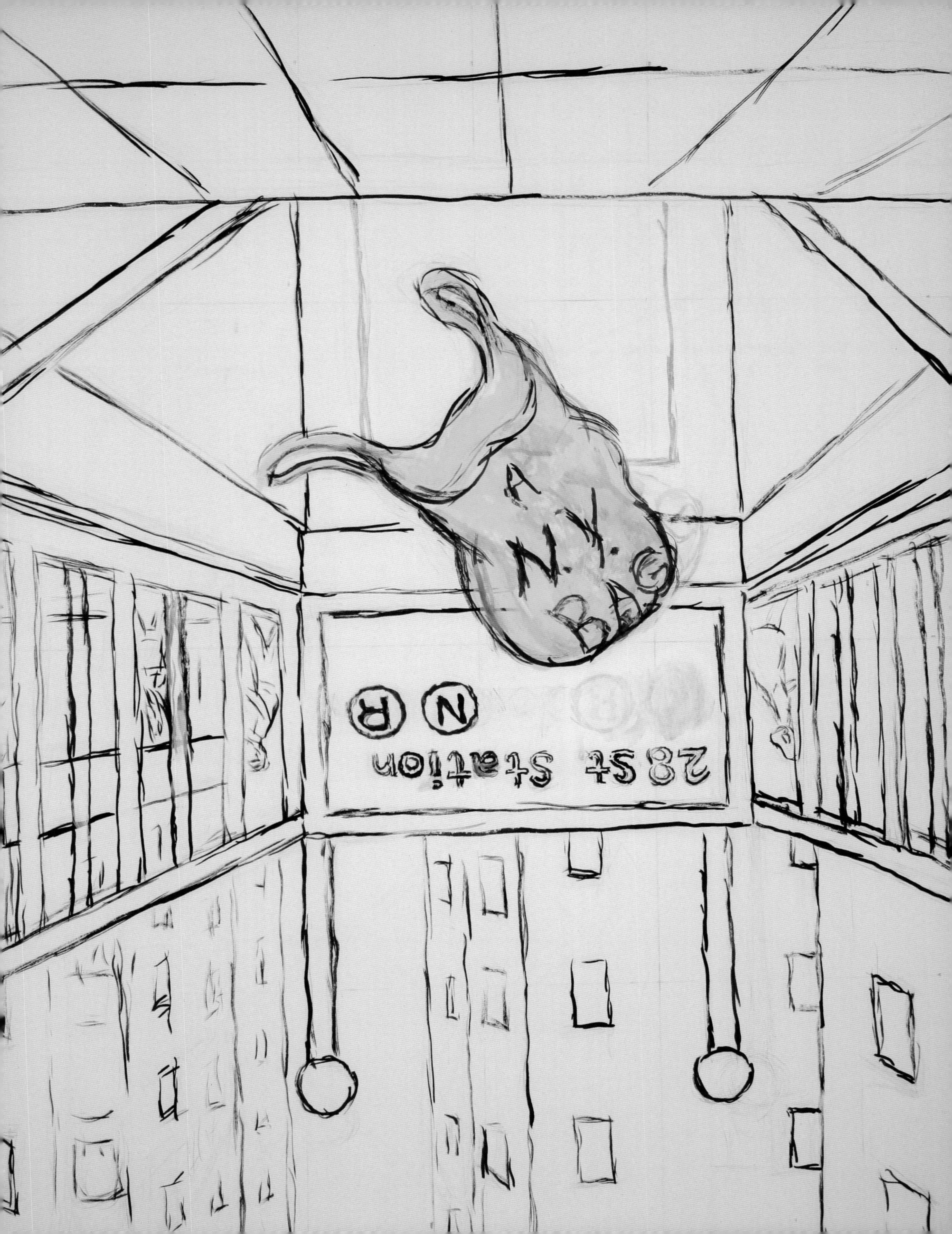
N
R
28St Station

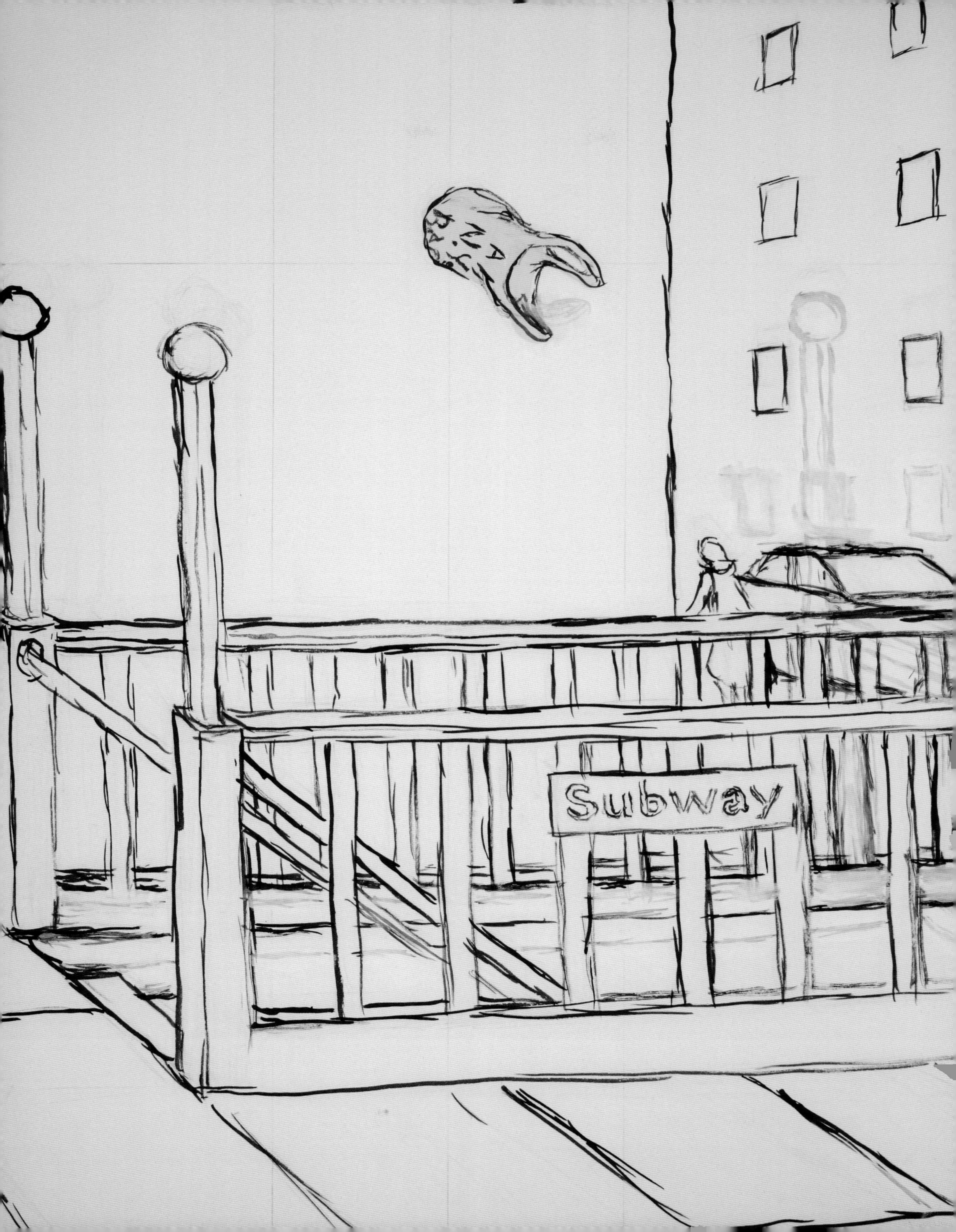
Subway

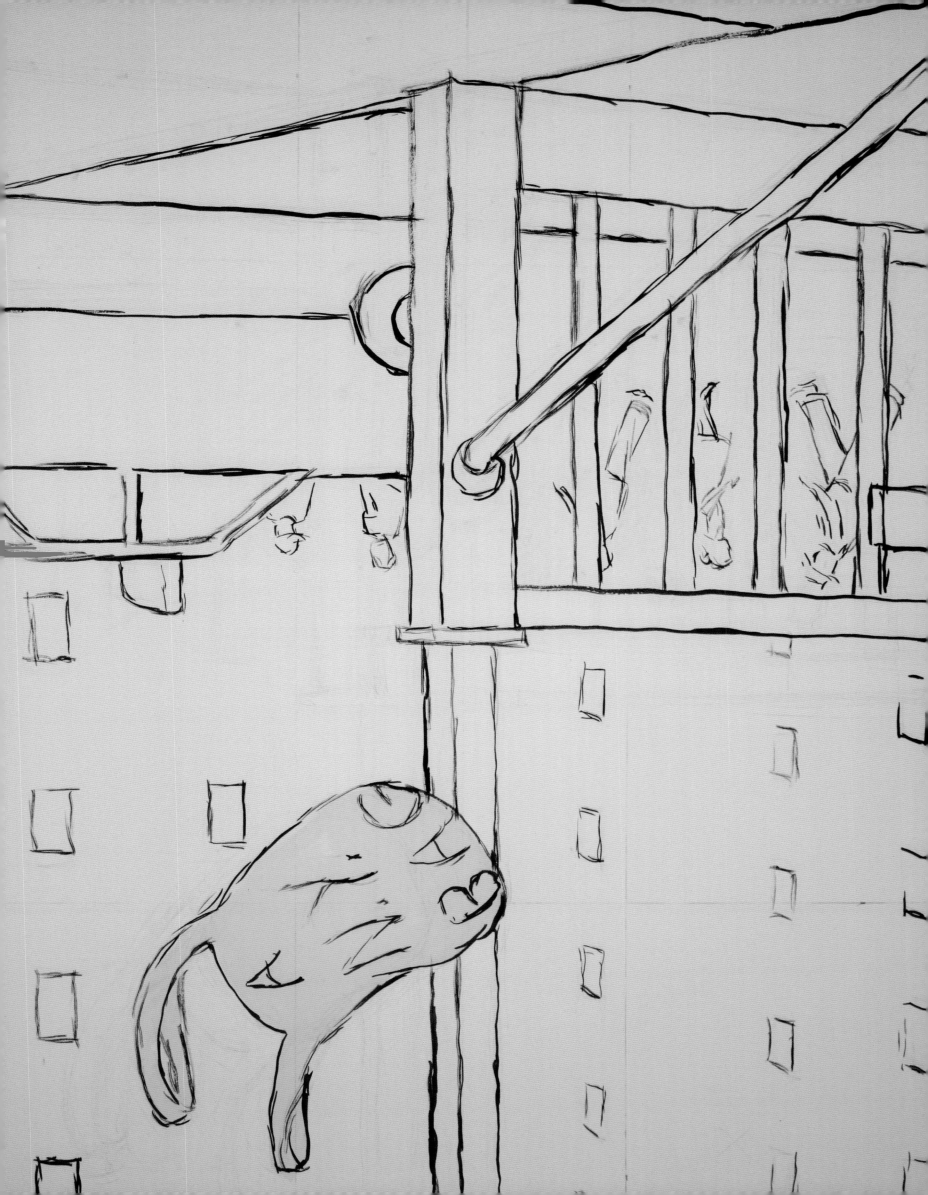

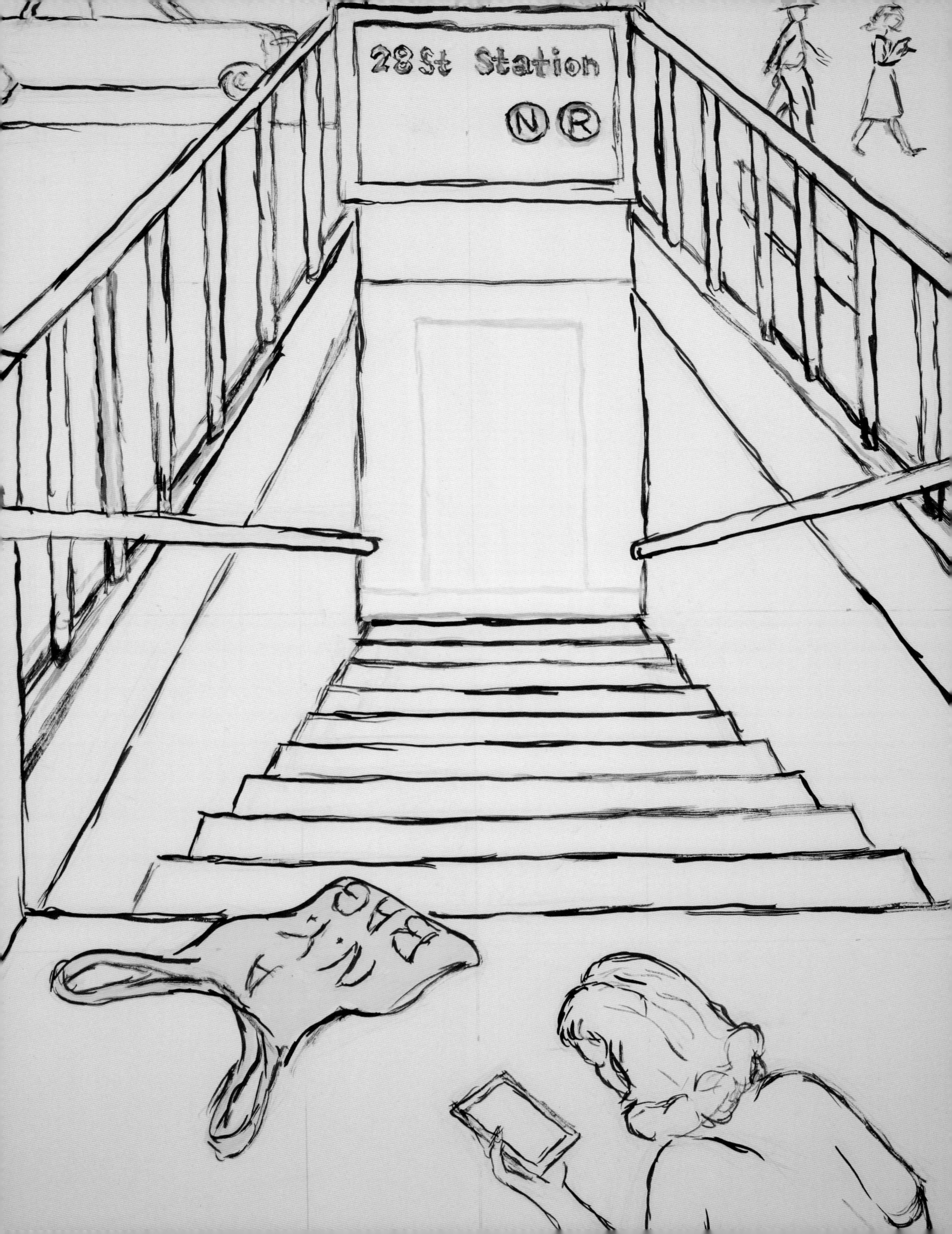
28St Station
N
R

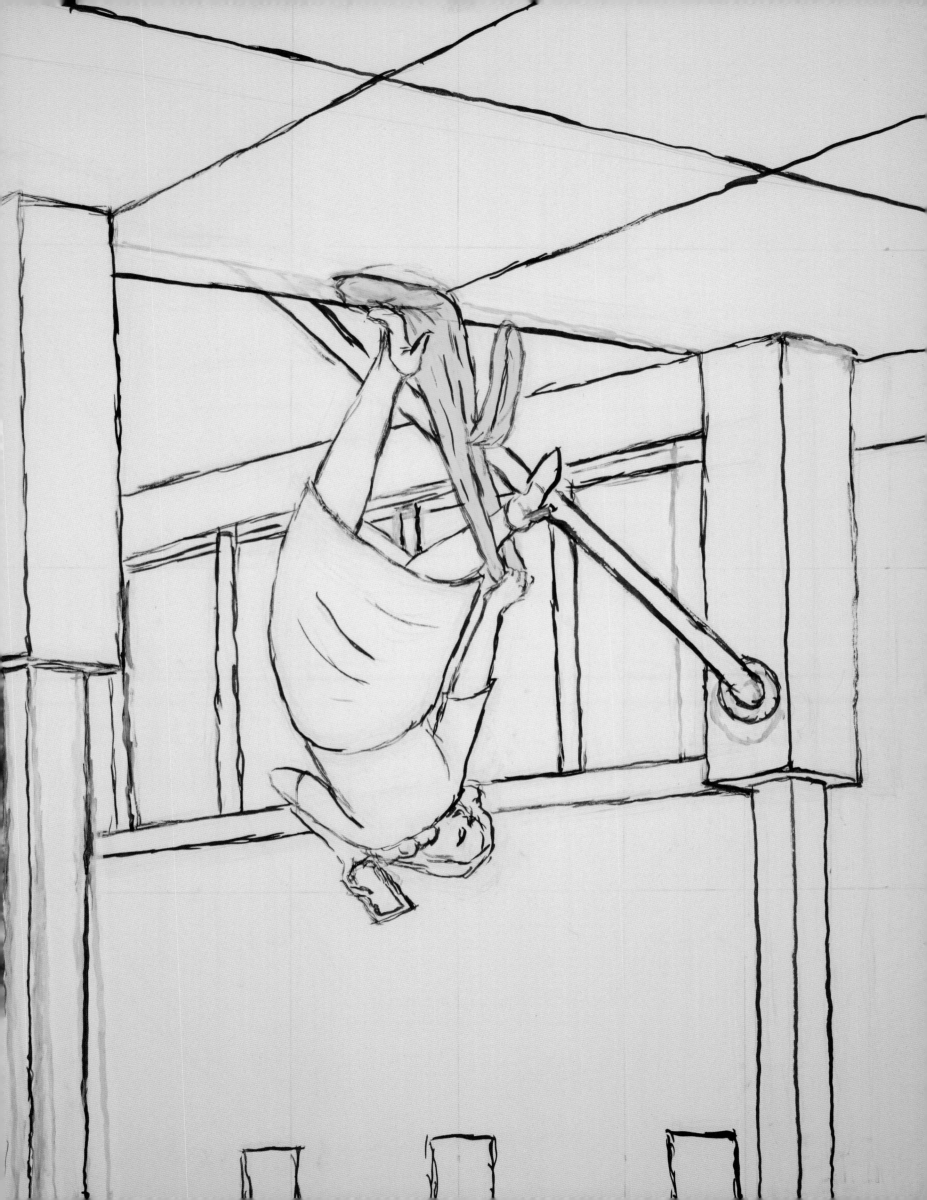

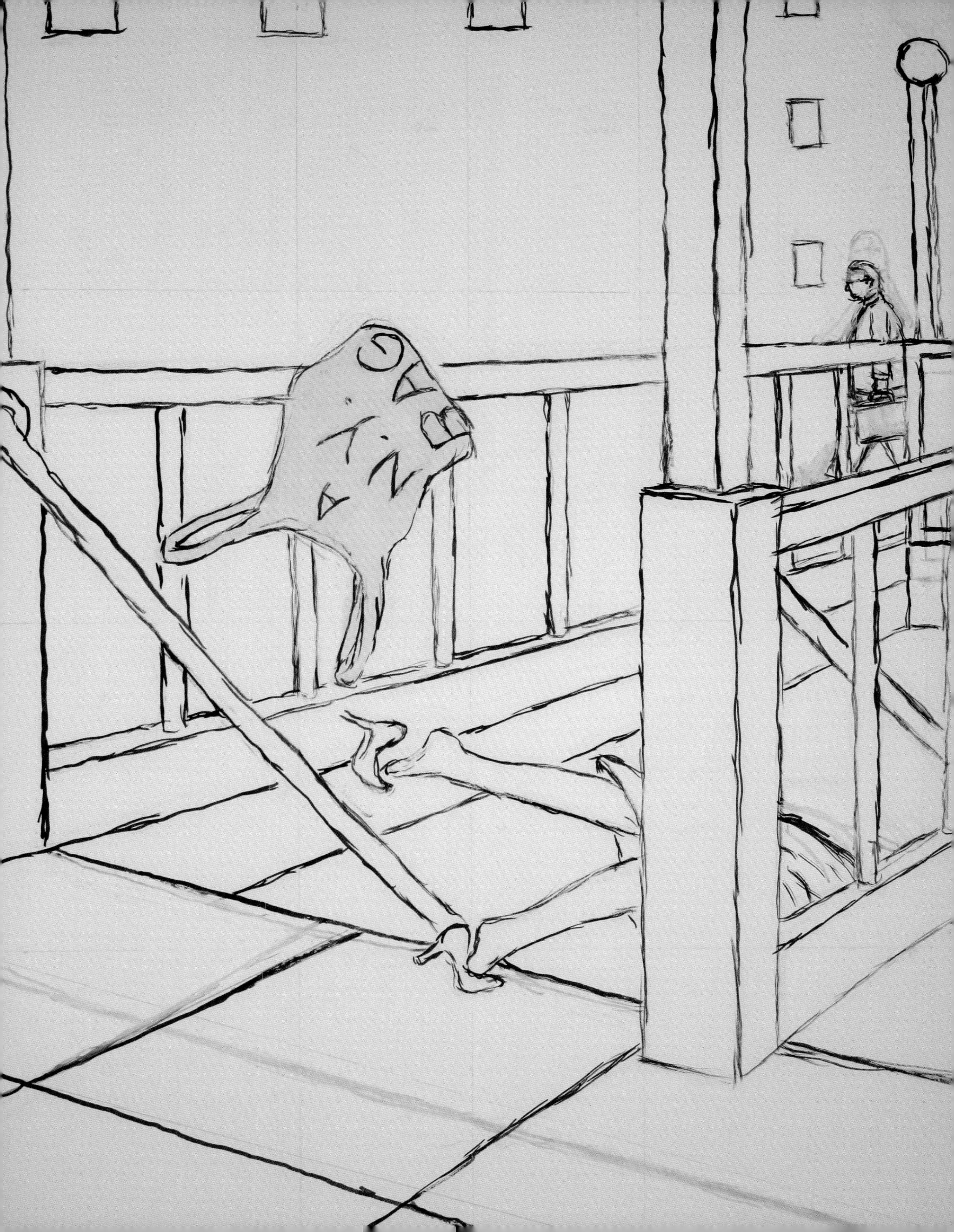

Jerry Moriarty was born on January 15, 1938 in Binghamton, New York. He attended Pratt Institute in 1956, and upon graduation became a painter and a freelance magazine illustrator. He started teaching at the School of Visual Arts in 1963. His earliest comics efforts were published in the first issue of *Raw* magazine in 1981. His autobiographical graphic novel *The Complete Jack Survives* was published in 2009, and his most recent narrative hybrid of comics and painting, *Whatsa Paintoonist?,* was published to much acclaim in 2017.

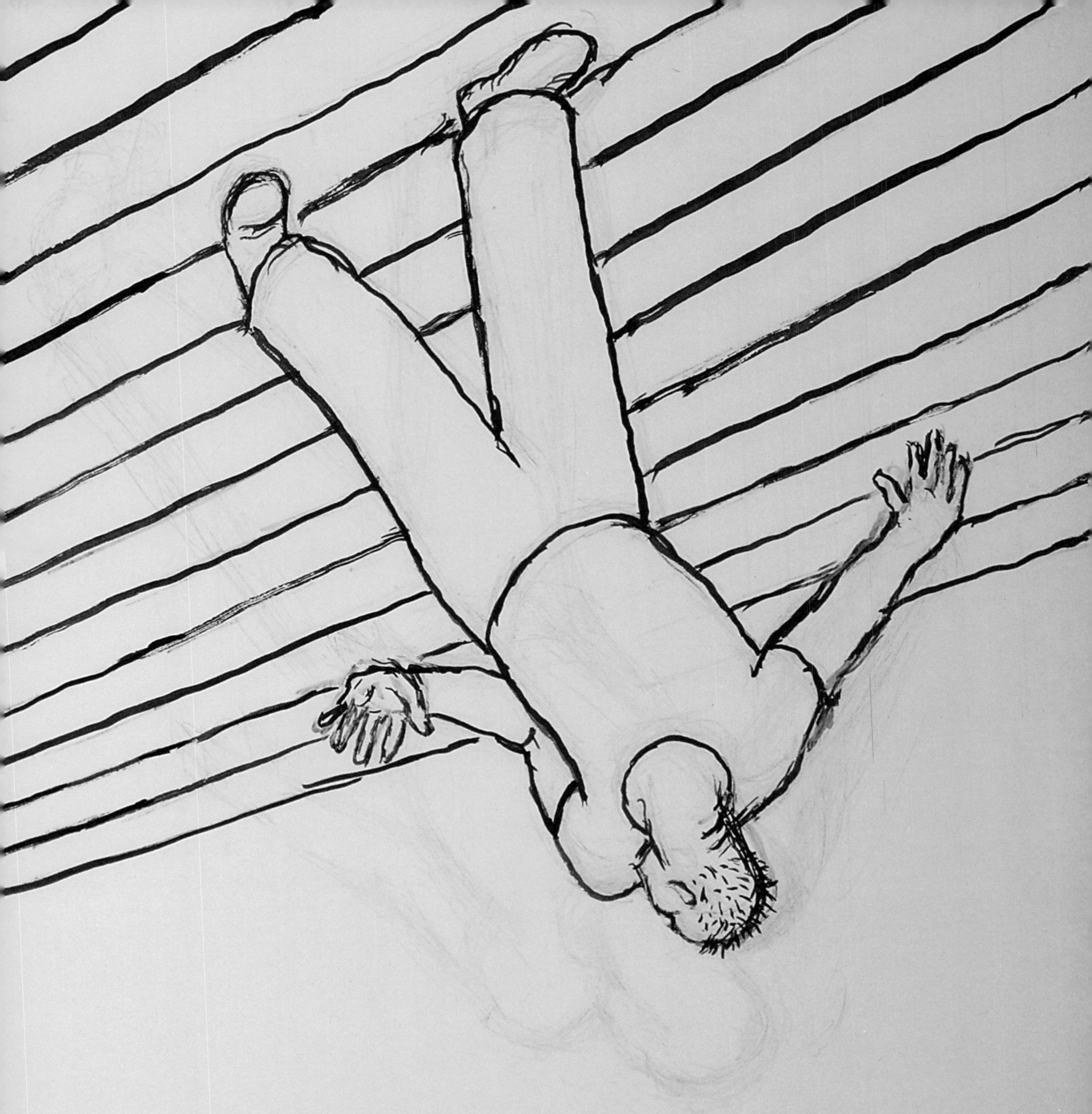